PRAISE FOR *HUNTING CHARLES MANSON*

"*Hunting Charles Manson* is the best true crime book you will ever read. No one could tell this story better—from its very beginnings to the riveting end—than Lis Wiehl: former prosecutor, legal commentator, and bestselling crime novelist. Fact is so much stranger than fiction, and Manson's dark and deadly life is proof of that. Lock your doors, keep the night lights on, and read this book."

—LINDA FAIRSTEIN, *New York Times* bestselling
crime novelist and former prosecutor

"Lis Wiehl is a pro who does her homework and knows what she's talking about. She's a storyteller extraordinaire and this one, though nonfiction, reads like a thriller. She gives voice and life to a troubling aspect of our history, one that is definitely worth remembering."

—STEVE BERRY, *New York Times* bestselling author

"You think you know everything about an infamous criminal case until brilliant writers and researchers like Lis Wiehl and Caitlin Rother come along to expose new layers and new insights. This is a must-read for true crime fans—and those who think they know everything about the Manson case."

—GREGG OLSEN, #1 *New York Times* bestselling author

"Lis Wiehl's real-life page-turner is jam-packed with new, fascinating, thoroughly researched, and relevant-today details about the making of a monster, the evolution of his dangerous charisma, and how he was finally brought to justice."

—KATE WHITE, *New York Times* bestselling author

MANSON

THE QUEST FOR JUSTICE IN THE
DAYS OF HELTER SKELTER

LIS WIEHL WITH CAITLIN ROTHER

NELSON
BOOKS
An Imprint of Thomas Nelson

Published in Nashville, Tennessee, by Nelson Books, an imprint of Thomas Nelson. Nelson Books and Thomas Nelson are registered trademarks of HarperCollins Christian Publishing, Inc.

Thomas Nelson titles may be purchased in bulk for educational, business, fund-raising, or sales promotional use. For information, please e-mail SpecialMarkets@ThomasNelson.com.

Any Internet addresses, phone numbers, or company or product information printed in this book are offered as a resource and are not intended in any way to be or to imply an endorsement by Thomas Nelson, nor does Thomas Nelson vouch for the existence, content, or services of these sites, phone numbers, companies, or products beyond the life of this book.

ISBN 978-0-7180-9211-5 (eBook)

Library of Congress Cataloging-in-Publication Data

Names: Wiehl, Lis W., author.
Title: Hunting Charles Manson : the quest for justice in the days of Helter skelter / Lis Wiehl.
Description: Nashville, Tennessee : Nelson Books, [2018]
Identifiers: LCCN 2017059418 | ISBN 9780718092085
Subjects: LCSH: Manson, Charles, 1934-2017. | Murderers--California--Los Angeles--Case studies. | Mass murder investigation--California--Los Angeles--Case studies. | Murder--California--Los Angeles--Case studies.
Classification: LCC HV6248.M2797 W54 2018 | DDC 364.152/30979493--dc23 LC record available at https://lccn.loc.gov/2017059418

Printed in the United States of America

18 19 20 21 22 LSC 10 9 8 7 6 5 4 3 2 1

To the victims of the Manson Family.
May they rest in peace.

CONTENTS

Author's Note ix
Prologue xi

CHAPTER 1   Charlie the Guru 1
CHAPTER 2   Indoctrination at Spahn Ranch 8
CHAPTER 3   The Gary Hinman Murder 13
CHAPTER 4   Lotsapoppa 22
CHAPTER 5   "Political Piggy" .27
CHAPTER 6   "Do whatever Tex says." 33
CHAPTER 7   The Sole Survivor 44
CHAPTER 8   The Bloody Aftermath 50
CHAPTER 9   "How could anybody be so cruel?" 58
CHAPTER 10 "Call the police!" 69
CHAPTER 11 Drug Burn or Robbery Gone Wrong? 75
CHAPTER 12 Raid at Spahn Ranch 84
CHAPTER 13 "I felt I could conquer the world." 93
CHAPTER 14 Doing Hard Time 100
CHAPTER 15 The First Family Members 106
CHAPTER 16 "Dennis Wilson: I Live With 17 Girls" 117
CHAPTER 17 Searching for a New Home 125
CHAPTER 18 "Somebody dropped the ball." 131
CHAPTER 19 Looking for Terry Melcher 137
CHAPTER 20 The Murder of Shorty Shea 144

CONTENTS

CHAPTER 21   Hiding Out in Death Valley 152
CHAPTER 22   Connecting the Dots 161
CHAPTER 23   The Dominoes Begin to Fall 169
CHAPTER 24   Forced to Cooperate 175
CHAPTER 25   The First Death Sentence 183
CHAPTER 26   "Mockery of justice" 191
CHAPTER 27   The Trial of the Century 198
CHAPTER 28   Ronald Hughes Disappears 207
CHAPTER 29   Folie à deux 216
CHAPTER 30   Death Penalty Overturned 225
CHAPTER 31   Manson Comes up for Parole 233
CHAPTER 32   Alternative Scenarios 242
CHAPTER 33   The Fight Against Parole 250
CHAPTER 34   Jason Freeman: "Charles Manson III" 260
CHAPTER 35   Manson's Legacy 269
CHAPTER 36   "I'm dying." 277

Epilogue 285
Acknowledgments 289
Sources and Methodology 291
Cast of Characters 305
Index 309
About the Author 319

AUTHOR'S NOTE

In taking on the quest for justice in the tragedy that was the summer of 1969, I thought about what made Charlie Manson do what he did.

Those killings changed American culture. People who didn't have home alarms quickly bought as fancy a system as they could afford. Mothers began walking their children to school. And parents and children alike had trouble falling asleep at night. Charlie Manson and his "children" robbed America of its innocence.

Nearly fifty years later, Charles "Tex" Watson, the man who carried out Manson's murderous plans, was asked by a parole board commissioner, "What made a God-fearing, churchgoing young man from Texas move to California and commit the worst killings this state has ever seen?" The commissioner's question was asked in a thunderous tone. He was met with silence from the prisoner and straight-on stares from family members of the victims. I could understand the silence. What answer could there be?

As the only reporter allowed in that parole hearing in California, I brought into the room fifteen years of national television crime reporting and, as a former federal prosecutor, hundreds of federal prosecutions. I am proud to be a third-generation federal prosecutor, after my father and grandfather before me. That same grandfather was also a judge, and my father had also served as an FBI agent. I have had a lifetime of law enforcement exposure and experience, and yet I was as bewildered as the parole commissioner by the crimes.

This mystery is part of the reason behind this reexamination of arguably the most notorious crime in American history. How could it have happened? I also wanted to explore the process by which justice was done. The Christian tradition, of which I am a part, has justice at its center, a consequence of the belief that God will ultimately put all things right. We should take seriously the process by which our governments work to see justice accomplished, and this book—as well as subsequent books in this series—attempts to do just that.

As a result of my legal experience, I knew when embarking on this quest what law enforcement agents on the scene in 1969 would have or should have been looking for, which made my discoveries of what they actually did all the more shocking. I knew what the lead prosecutor, Vincent Bugliosi, was attempting to do with his various motions and strategies, and how successful he was or was not. (Long after the Manson case, I got to know Bugliosi when he asked for assistance in writing a book about the Supreme Court.) And my television crime reporting experience was invaluable as I researched, wrote, and analyzed the defense's case and the various alternative theories about the crime.

Investigative journalist and true crime author Caitlin Rother brought thirty years of research and storytelling experience, as well as a breadth of knowledge about the criminal justice system, addiction, and mental illness. We agreed to approach the "known" sources—including the criminal case files—with fresh eyes. But we also set out with the goal of uncovering new details that would enhance readers' overall understanding of the case. I believe the book does just that, offering new and illuminating material that will not only surprise but possibly even astonish the reader.

In the end, I'm not sure we will ever be able to answer definitively the question of why. But I do believe these pages bring us closer than ever before. Read on.

PROLOGUE

"Today is a good day."

A grizzled old man with a long, bushy beard and a swastika tattoo on his forehead sat waiting in his prison blues for a special visitor one Saturday in late December 2013.

Charles Milles Manson probably received more mail than any other inmate in California, so he turned down or ignored many persistent invitations to correspond or visit with him here at Corcoran State Prison. But this particular visitor won him over somehow.

Afton Elaine Burton was just seventeen when she started to write him. On this Saturday morning seven years later, seventy-nine-year-old Manson was more than three times her age.

Still, they'd formed a bond. He'd always been good at drawing in young women, and it seemed his charms had endured.

Fenced in with curls of spear-tipped barbed wire, Corcoran had been Manson's home for the last thirty years of his most recent forty-five-year term. Surrounded by vast, dusty miles of nothingness and the occasional field of cotton, hay, tomatoes, or wheat, Corcoran is California's largest correctional facility. A second one down the road treats inmates for substance abuse. Other than the local inmates and corrections employees, however, few people want to live in the middle of nowhere, where the most touted downtown eateries include McDonald's, Taco Bell, Subway, and two pizza parlors.

But Burton didn't seem to mind. She had left her strict Baptist family back in Illinois to move here and had visited Manson regularly ever since. In turn, as he'd done many times for the underage girls and troubled women drawn to him over the years, he gave Burton a name in his own image: Star Manson.

When Star arrived for their five-hour visit at Corcoran's small Protective Housing Unit (PHU) that Saturday in 2013, the lanky young woman wore a short spring dress with ballet flats. Her dark brown hair was still growing out after she'd shaved it to show her support for Manson, just as his female codefendants had done during his first murder trial in 1970.

Some people said she even resembled a couple of Manson's earliest followers, Lynette "Squeaky" Fromme and Susan "Sadie" Atkins.

Decked out in his typical prisoner garb of jeans, a white T-shirt under a blue button-up collared shirt, and white tennis shoes, Manson greeted Star in the visiting room with a kiss on the lips. His thumbnails were long and yellow, and his swastika tattoo had long ago replaced the "X" he'd carved into his head during his first trial, when his followers spread his message that "I have X'd myself from your world."

The swastika, a symbol most often equated with Nazis and white supremacists, showed up after the sentencing. Partly for shock value, he said, it was also "for protection," inspired by his time with the Native Americans, to represent the sun god, the elements, happiness, peace, and prosperity—positive affiliations that pre-date the Nazis by several thousand years.

"Today is a good day, isn't it?" Manson said to a fellow inmate, whose female visitor had come with Star.

Manson's girl was well known to other PHU inmates because she'd sent them paper and writing utensils for Christmas. At Manson's prompting, she'd also put money into their commissary accounts and helped hook them up with women like the female visitor with her that day, who would write, talk to them on the phone, and even come visit.

But Star seemed like a good-hearted person who would have done it anyway. "I love all those guys—as long as they make Charlie happy," she told the other visitor softly.

When Star had first learned of Manson through one of her high school friends, it was not for his notoriety as one of the nation's most heinous murderers, but rather for his environmental activism and beliefs that the affluent white culture was destroying natural resources around the globe. In fact, like other Manson fans today, she didn't see him as a killer at all, because, as many point out, he wasn't physically present when his Family members carried out the Tate and LaBianca murders.

As he and Star grew closer, he began giving her more responsibility for his affairs on the outside, such as assuming partial control of ATWA, a nonprofit 501(c)(3) organization, originally formed in 1997. ATWA stands for Air Trees Water Animals or for All The Way Alive, and the acronym—along with its variation ATWAR, with the "R" for Revolution—has become a meme that thousands of Manson fans and followers cite in secret solidarity.

Created to carry out his wishes and to disseminate his "teachings," ATWA and its related websites celebrate Manson, perpetuating his claims that he was an innocent political prisoner who never killed anyone and providing global examples of environmental self-destruction.

During their weekend visit, Manson and Star held hands, talked, and laughed at the table nearest the vending machines full of snacks and sodas.

Although the couple wasn't joined in the eyes of the law, Star proudly took Manson's name and announced to the media that she thought of herself as his wife. At his request Star carved an "X" into her forehead at one point to protest one of his punitive stints in the Security Housing Unit (or SHU, pronounced "shoe"), which Manson called "the hole." She also wore a silver snake ring on her ring finger, just like he did.

Still, she wanted to make it official by getting a marriage license as a symbol of their unity now that California prisons no longer allow conjugal visits to consummate marital relationships.

But a long-term union of any sort between them was unlikely. At his age, he was not in great health, nor had he ever been one to follow rules or conventions. Over the years he'd spent many months in the hole for committing more than 113 rules violations ranging from possessing weapons to assaulting and threatening prison staff, spitting and cursing at female correctional officers, attempting to punch a nurse assistant, and possessing contraband items including cell phones and a hacksaw blade.

Star doted on him that Saturday. They rose from the lunch table in a theatrical fashion to stand side by side, about six inches apart, not quite touching. Raising their arms in tandem, they reached up and over their heads, swaying slowly and fluidly like trees in the wind.

Manson was surprisingly agile for his age. As they inched forward across the room, they danced toward the bathroom. They were in their own little world, as if they were at a Grateful Dead concert. The other female visitor tried not to meet Manson's gaze or watch this strange and quite intimate display.

Star bought an avocado from the vendor who sold fresh lunch foods and returned to their table, where she pitted and cut the fruit into slices, delivering them on a paper towel to her beau.

Manson might not have looked like more than a hobbit of a man, with his long beard braided or tied off into sections like a gang member, the sides of his head shaved, and the front tooth of his dentures knocked out to make them look, as he said, "more natural." But Charlie Manson was once quite handsome, with thick, shoulder-length brown hair, dark flashing eyes, a winning smile, and just enough musical talent as a singer and guitarist to impress the girls.

Starting in the Summer of Love in 1967, after he was paroled from federal prison, he became their pied piper, luring them one at a time into his flock. His Family.

Manson was a small man, but his girls talked a big game about his talents as a lover, bragging that he had sex as many as seven times a day, before and after every meal.

Initiating the new girls by wooing them with sex, flattery, and LSD-infused prophecies, he later humiliated, threatened, and hit them, thereby persuading, inspiring, or scaring them into doing whatever he asked. They had sex with men he wanted to recruit into the Family. They stole. They even killed for him.

For the rest of his days, he continued to captivate the public, not only across the United States, but all over the globe. In a digitally connected world, he had a much larger and potentially more dangerous base than ever before. Although his original Family members are now few in number, he had accumulated hundreds of thousands of fans and followers online, through social media and websites like ATWA.

Some of those who love and defend him even after his death in November 2017 are, like Star, antiestablishment souls who feel disillusioned, disenfranchised, and distrustful of the government and criminal justice system. They believe he was innocent and should have been freed. They contend that he was too old to hurt anyone again. As his cellmates and former Family members attest, Manson would have let a fly crawl all over his face rather than kill it. Animals, he proclaimed, have as much of a right to live on this planet as the rest of us.

Odd for a man who, prosecutors say, thought nothing of ordering nine of the nation's most gruesome murders in the summer of 1969, to say nothing of a couple dozen other slayings the Family has at times bragged about committing, either as collateral damage or in the name of revenge or retaliation.

Manson acknowledged all of this. He called himself a product of our media-fed culture and admitted that most people define him by the heinousness of those crimes. He knew that he was hated and feared by the mainstream, which still sees him as a black-and-white portrait of evil, a cult leader who mesmerized his followers and masterminded a scheme for them to kill rich white people in the most "witchy" way they could, to leave a mark—his mark—on society.

Most folks believe that Manson lived out his life right where he belonged, and that none of the four codefendants who remain behind bars should ever be paroled.

But to his dying day, Manson claimed that he never killed anyone or ordered anyone else to do so. As he told Diane Sawyer in one of his rare national TV interviews, "I never told anybody anything other than what they wanted to do."

CHAPTER 1

CHARLIE THE GURU

C harlie Manson began collecting impressionable young women, one at a time, as soon as he was paroled from federal prison in March 1967. He had served nearly a decade for driving stolen cars and prostitutes over state lines and stealing US Treasury checks.

Released from Terminal Island in Los Angeles, the thirty-two-year-old headed north to the Bay Area. There he picked up Mary Brunner, a young librarian who worked on campus at the University of California, Berkeley. Next, he recruited Lynette Fromme, a wild homeless teenager sitting on a curb in Venice. Then came Patricia Krenwinkel, a homely, insecure insurance clerk in Manhattan Beach. And Susan Atkins, a runaway-turned-topless dancer in the Haight-Ashbury neighborhood of San Francisco. Mary was twenty-three; the others were nineteen.

Charlie made each one of these young women feel special, telling her she was beautiful—or whatever else she needed to hear—while making love to her. In less than a year, he'd lured a small group of women, ranging in age from midteens to early twenties, into sharing his philosophy and his nomadic life up and down the Pacific coast as he tried to break into the music scene in Los Angeles. They, in turn, spread his word to others, until he had a loyal flock of followers.

In between weekly check-ins with his parole officer in San Francisco, Charlie and his growing harem traveled in a bus, playing music for food and a place to sleep. As he strummed his guitar and they sang along to the dozens of songs he'd written in prison, his dream of becoming a rock star became theirs too.

Charlie gradually collected some receptive young men as well, offering them a cocktail of sex with his girls, hallucinogenic drugs, and rock and roll. Unlike most of the girls, the men often came and went, so the number of women in the group was always much higher.

By spring 1968, Charlie had transferred his parole case to Los Angeles County as he pursued his musical career and looked for a home base for himself and the young people he called his "children." He found it in the spacious Spahn Movie Ranch, nestled between the rolling green Santa Susana Mountains and the Simi Hills.

Spanning a vast five hundred acres, with an entrance at 12000 Santa Susana Pass Road in Chatsworth in the San Fernando Valley, the ranch had a rural feel and an isolated location that offered Charlie and his people the freedom to do as they liked without outside interference.

The ranch's star-studded history added to its appeal. Silent movie star William S. Hart was the first to purchase the property, primarily for the stabling of horses used in movies. From there, it evolved into a film set.

After Hart died in 1946, George Spahn bought the place in 1948 and named it after himself, adding a children's pony riding ring and trail rides for adults.

Early on, directors shot scenes there for well-received Westerns such as *Duel in the Sun* in 1946, featuring Gregory Peck, Jennifer Jones, and Lillian Gish. Later, popular TV series such as *Bonanza* and *The Lone Ranger* were filmed there, as well as Western-themed commercials for products such as Marlboro cigarettes. But over time, the roster grew more obscure, and the big-name projects were replaced with cheesy low-budget Westerns and exploitation films.

By the time Charlie and a few of his people showed up in the spring of 1968, the film business had declined, but the ranch was still generating income by renting horses for trail rides up into the hills. Charlie made a deal with George, who was then eighty years old and nearly blind, to let him and his friends stay rent-free in exchange for maintaining the property, feeding and caring for the horses, and leading trail rides. Charlie played down the number of friends as his group, later known as the Manson Family, continued to grow and change.

Most of the ranch's daily activity took place in and around the set, known as Lee's Trading Post, a replica of an Old West settlement. Comprised of two rows of squat buildings facing each other, the compact village included the Longhorn Saloon and Rock City Café, a horse corral, blacksmith's shop, tack room, stables, jail, trailer, and large horse barn. A wooden boardwalk ran in between the buildings, parallel to a wide unpaved road topped by an inch of dust that got kicked up by passing cars or foot traffic. By the time Charlie arrived, the ramshackle structures were in severe decline, their weathered facades peeling paint and their signs faded, with letters missing.

George Spahn had left his wife and eleven children at his North Hollywood ranch to move here with Ruby Pearl, a former circus performer with long, stringy red hair known simply as "Pearl." As the forewoman, Pearl ran the place with a firm hand, dressed in cowboy boots, jeans, and a hat. "She didn't take no s*** from anybody," George's grandson later recalled.

George, who always wore sunglasses and a Stetson, lived in a run-down house in the village. It was more of a shack, really, with one bedroom, one bathroom, and a main room that served as the living room, kitchen, and dining area.

Initially, George enjoyed having Charlie's young hippies around, especially the girls, who spoke to him in soft voices and tended to him in his house. George listened to the radio and ate his meals in the main room, surrounded by newspapers soiled by the three yorkies that ran across the dining table and shared his half-eaten sandwiches. The room was so filthy the ceiling often appeared black, covered with flies.

Nevertheless, George's employees were attached to him and the ranch. Juan Flynn, a Vietnam veteran who arrived in 1968 to work as a ranch hand, "loved the place," he said. "It had the most beautiful trails . . . Then Charles Manson and his people came and trashed [it]."

———

Early on, Charlie projected an aura of peace and non-violence, drawing in young people with talk of a communal lifestyle based on making love, playing music, and escaping materialism. In practice, this meant sitting around the campfire smoking pot, exploring hallucinogens, singing Charlie's songs, discussing his counterculture philosophy, and spending time in nature.

When Charlie smiled at his people, they felt an explosion of bright energy and benevolent kindness. He seemed so wise, so all-knowing. These young people, many of whom sought a higher meaning in life, gladly accepted the new names he gave them as a way to shed their inhibitions and former selves. They saw Charlie as their guru, even a Christlike figure. He called himself "the Infinite Soul," or "the Soul" for short, so they did too.

This was the loving atmosphere seventeen-year-old Barbara Hoyt found when she arrived on April Fool's Day in 1969. Having run away from her home in Canoga Park, she was picked up near Chatsworth by two girls who were staying at Spahn. One of them was Deirdre Shaw, the daughter of actress Angela Lansbury. Deirdre lingered on the periphery of the Family before her parents whisked her away, but Barbara quickly believed she had found a safe haven at Spahn.

Barbara met Charlie her first night at the ranch, when the group sat on the floor, eating casserole and salad with shared spoons. Everyone took a few bites, then passed the bowl to the next person. After the meal, they passed around marijuana joints.

Barbara felt accepted. Loved. And part of something special. Her parents didn't understand her. She felt this group, this family of hippies, knew where she was coming from. Ranging in age from midteens to midtwenties, they all seemed so welcoming—good, hopeful folks.

Leslie Van Houten thought so too. When the nineteen-year-old former Monrovia High School homecoming princess joined the group in the late summer of 1968, she truly believed that Charlie was going to help foster positive social change. Touted as an antiestablishment guru, his whole gig was about peace, love, and music. What could be harmful about that?

For members of the Family, who numbered about twenty-five or so at any one time, a certain rhythm developed at Spahn as people drifted in and out of the group. At fourteen, Dianne Lake was the youngest, and other than Charlie, who turned thirty-three in 1968, Catherine "Gypsy" Share was the oldest when she joined the group at twenty-six.

Everyone got up around 7:00 a.m. to feed the horses and saddle them up for the first trail riders by eight o'clock. The rest of the day's work consisted of scrounging for food, cooking meals, taking care of the children, leading trail rides, tending to the horses, and shoveling manure. After the day's work, members had sex with whomever they (or Charlie) wanted. At night, they took in the beautiful hills that surrounded them and listened to Charlie make his music.

Many of them slept in sleeping bags on the floor of buildings in or near the village or in the trailers and cabins scattered around the property. Others camped in the hills behind the village, looking up at the moon. Charlie slept wherever he wanted, whenever he wanted, and with whomever he wanted.

———

Charlie's strong personality, bolstered by his confidence, persuasive philosophy, and charisma, commanded attention, loyalty, and obedience. Whatever he said, went; whatever he disapproved of was rejected, if not forbidden.

Members were told to let go of their need for worldly goods and to cast off all their inhibitions. They were asked to contribute whatever of value they could get—clothing, cash, or their parents' credit cards—which were used to buy gas and other items Charlie said they needed. If they had nothing to give, they were asked to procure items by borrowing or stealing from friends, family, or strangers.

Later on, Family members were barred from leaving Spahn without Charlie's permission, but at first, when the group was more nomadic, somewhat fragmented, and still in recruitment mode, such restrictions were more lax. Charles "Tex" Watson, for example, who joined the

Family in the spring of 1968, left for several months to sell drugs. Bobby Beausoleil, whom Charlie met playing music in Topanga Canyon in 1967, often went off to do his own thing. And Bruce Davis, a welder who also met Charlie in Topanga and was also older than most of the group, left for a period of months as well. All three were welcomed back by Charlie, who had few men on whom he felt he could rely.

Charlie himself loved to travel, so he often left on jaunts alone or with small groups, frequently without the permission or knowledge of his parole officers, and often bringing another young girl or two back with him. Others traveled in small subgroups by hitchhiking or borrowing old cars from one of the ranch employees to run an errand for Charlie or to go to a specific destination.

The rules governing life in the Family could change at a moment's notice, on Charlie's whim, but some remained constant: He allowed no clocks or watches on the ranch, and although there was a TV in one of the trailers, he did not want anyone reading newspapers. He also discouraged communication with relatives. He wanted his followers isolated, free of the materialistic, bureaucratic, and chemically hygienic ways of mainstream society, so he could reshape them. They even had to give up their birthdays.

Touting environmental causes, Charlie wore jeans or buckskin leather pants that the girls sewed for him, stitched together with leather cords. He also wore a leather thong around his neck. The girls wore whatever shoes they found lying around, but most of the time they went barefoot, not minding the manure that piled up everywhere.

———

Charlie designated subgroups to do different jobs. The women cared for the children, cooked, or went into town to get food. They hit up road stands, sneaked behind grocery stores that didn't lock their trash bins, scrounged for day-old bakery goods, or dived into dumpsters looking for discarded produce, meat, and packaged food that was off-color, in dented cans, or had recently expired freshness dates.

But most importantly, the underage girls and young women were expected to be submissive and to serve Charlie and the other men, which meant they could be asked at any time to have sex with someone whom Charlie wanted to please.

The few men in the Family were tasked with odd jobs around the ranch. They also fixed cars, procured drugs and more young women, and later, obtained knives, guns, and communication devices such as two-way radios and battlefield phones. Tex, who walked around the ranch with a gun and a knife in a scabbard, both tucked into his waistband, always seemed to know how to get drugs or cash in a pinch.

Charlie garnered sympathy and respect from these young people with tales of his upbringing, saying he was raised with no real family of his own and that he was a product of reform schools and prisons, not the blood relatives who had rejected and abandoned him. In so doing, this group of lost souls, many of whom had come from broken families, became his new Family.

Members of the communal group spread his philosophy by word of mouth, inviting those who seemed like-minded to come meet their "guru." Charlie had the girls administer LSD to men he wanted to recruit, then have sex with them in group sessions he orchestrated, hoping to produce children for his growing Family, the "chosen" ones. But he was especially partial to underage girls and runaways who seemed malleable or open to his wiles. He depended on Family member Paul Watkins to find "new love" on the Sunset Strip and bring girls back to Spahn for him.

Over time, those who stayed at the ranch, or lacked the emotional strength to leave, tended to be the most vulnerable to suggestion, or had the weakest personalities. The longer they stayed, the more entrenched in Charlie's philosophy—and the more inured to outside forces—they became. Those who didn't feel comfortable doing whatever immoral, illegal, or sexual acts that Charlie ordered were ousted or left of their own accord.

CHAPTER 2

INDOCTRINATION AT
SPAHN RANCH

Charlie was the absolute leader of the Family. After personally initiating new members—which for the girls meant having sex with him and discussing his teachings for an entire day—Charlie put them through indoctrination and programming. He called the entire group together for these sessions aimed at preaching his message to the new members and modifying or fortifying it for the others.

Sitting the young people in a circle around him, he had them open their mouths and placed a hit of LSD on their tongues. They were expected to sit and listen to him until he was finished, which sometimes took as long as seven or eight hours.

Some sessions were interactive. Telling them he had to strip them of their personalities, Charlie often singled out individuals to mock and humiliate, as he tried to break them down. On one occasion, he made twenty-one-year-old Patricia Krenwinkel, whom he'd renamed Katie, stand naked in front of the group while he called her ugly and pointed out what was wrong with her body.

Soon enough, members didn't need Manson to humiliate or program them; they did it to one another. "We became our own enemies," Leslie Van Houten said.

Charlie also ran the group through what he deemed fear-deprogramming exercises. He ordered the group to scream at a specific member, for example, which he claimed would expel their fears and direct them into that person.

He also claimed members could rid themselves of fear by sending it to Charlie. "Give it all to me," he would say. "Just let it go and be free."

Some sessions led his followers to believe he had special powers as Charlie tossed drugged cats into the air to prove they could stop reacting with fear. He also picked up birds that he claimed were dead, blew on them, and they magically flew away. "I believed that he had some kind of alternative source of power," Katie said. "I believed that he could blow life into dead birds, that he could control the weather."

Occasionally, Charlie put on a white robe to lead a session. With his long chestnut hair and his skin tanned from riding the horse trails and working outside, his followers thought he looked like Jesus, his face shining with light, even more so after he gave them the acid. He even carried out elaborate crucifixion reenactments so his drug-addled followers believed he actually *was* Jesus Christ.

Charlie also tested members' love and loyalty. "Do you trust me?" he asked, expecting them to respond in the affirmative. "Do you love me enough? Will you die for me? Will you be my finger on a hand? Will you be me?"

Other nights, he'd simply have the group sit around the campfire while he played his guitar and they sang along in a Family jam. With Charlie, you never knew what to expect.

———

As spring turned to summer in 1969, a darkness steeped in paranoia seemed to settle over Spahn Ranch. Leaving the Family was now no longer an option as Charlie became increasingly preoccupied with a twisted perception of death and its relationship with fear.

As he explained it to Paul Watkins: Fear was equivalent to awareness. Heightened awareness led to a greater capacity for love. Fear was thus desirable, because more fear led to more love. With enough fear, you reached a state of total awareness, which Charlie called "Now." Death, therefore, was beautiful, because people feared death so much.

"A revolution is coming," Charlie announced. The Family needed to prepare for it. The blacks, he said, were going to rise up and fight back against the white establishment: "Blackie," as he called the black people, was going to put an end to a society ruled by "Whitey," the rich whites who were destroying the planet.

He called the revolution "Helter Skelter," after the Beatles' song on the White Album, which he played over and over. Although the term referred to a British amusement park ride, for Charlie it signified the apocalypse. Armageddon. The end of mainstream culture as they knew it.

With the help of some local bikers he'd recruited to help provide security at the ranch, he began to amass a cache of guns, ammunition, and other weaponry they would take with them to the desert later, where they would wait it out.

Only the chosen people—the Family, the ones with no fear—would survive, he said, by living underground in a bottomless pit in the aptly named Death Valley. After realizing they couldn't rule on their own, Charlie said, the blacks would join under him as their leader.

On Barbara Hoyt's first day at Spahn, she was immediately informed of the coming apocalypse. She saw the dune buggies being armed with gun mounts, the clothes made out of buckskin, and the map of the desert where they were going to hide until it was over.

"Everything the Family did," she observed, "was for Helter Skelter. All the talk was Helter Skelter."

Charlie was now testing Family members daily to ensure their conformity with his way of thinking. Purposely bumping into them on the boardwalk, he made faces and expected them to mirror him.

"Baa like sheep," he instructed a group on the walkway one day. When they all did as they were told, it seemed to dawn on him just how much control he had over them. According to Leslie, "something moved inside of him" that day. She felt intense pressure to "be one with him." The idea was to "surrender yourself." We were told that "we were all one, that bodies are shells, that our spirits live forever, that there is no death."

As Charlie told Paul, "in order to love someone you must be willing to die for them and must be willing to kill them too. You must be willing to have them kill you. You must be willing to experience anything for them."

To this end, Charlie had the Family practice killing imaginary people as the once-peaceful haven turned into more of a hippie boot camp. He ordered the men to patrol the ranch with guns at all hours, keeping watch on rooftops for cops and outsiders. He also had Tex teach classes on how to shove a knife into a person and rip through the tissue to cause as much damage as possible.

Meanwhile, Charlie grew more violent with the girls, even during "lovemaking." When they did or said something he didn't like, he beat them and threatened them with knives. Or he grabbed them by the hair and forced them to have sex with multiple partners, including Charlie. "You can make love with six or seven people at the same time, if you get tuned in," he said.

Charlie brought his point home in late July. Gathering about twenty Family members and four guests in a structure known as the bunkhouse, he told a sixteen-year-old girl to lie on the floor in the middle of the room. As he began to kiss and touch her, she tried to push him away, but he persisted. She bit him on the shoulder. He hit her in the face. Then she gave up fighting. Charlie told Bobby to take over and do his thing with her, then he instructed the others to join in and "make love" with one another in one of the biggest orgies he'd ever orchestrated.

———

All the programming sessions and talk of revolution began to wear down some Family members. Leslie became so exhausted she wanted to leave. When she told Charlie she wanted to get away, he drove her to the edge of a cliff in a dune buggy. "If you want to leave, you may as well jump, because you'll get caught in the revolution and you're going to die anyway," he said.

But she felt powerless to leave. Tired or not, she was loyal to him. She loved him and believed in his philosophy. She would even kill for him.

Katie, too, grew weary of the mind games and tried to leave.

Later, she realized that slowly, bit by bit, she'd been giving up little pieces of herself, until she'd thrown away every part that was good. She'd gradually accepted what she'd never thought she could. As Charlie constantly redefined what he wanted from her, she, in turn, was forced to keep moving the line for what she would do or accept. She justified all of this by telling herself that he would finally love her the way she wanted him to.

Until she finally gave up trying to be someone he would love. Until she felt no self-worth at all. "I became a monster," she said.

Meanwhile, reprisals increased for expressing disagreement with Charlie. He insulted Katie's cooking, saying it was so bad he had to feed it to George's dogs; then he stood her in front of the group and called her too stupid to do anything right. Eventually, Katie had enough and sneaked off to Redondo Beach with one of the bikers.

But Charlie came and got her. He said he had a special purpose for her: he wanted her to grow her hair even longer so she could make him a blanket out of it. The clear implication, Katie said, was "that I was his, and that was it." He also threatened the biker, so Katie returned to the ranch.

Katie and Leslie weren't alone. Charlie now wouldn't let anyone leave the ranch by themselves for any reason. Members could only go in groups of five or six, and always with a purpose and destination. If no cars were available, which was often the case, they had to hitchhike.

Beaten down and wracked with paralysis and fear, most saw no way to escape. Someone was always watching or listening, and even the men feared Charlie's disapproval or violent retribution.

Then in late July, Charlie turned up the pressure, telling them to go out and find money or anything of value that they could steal or sell to pay for their big move to the desert. They were told to do whatever it took, even knowing that Los Angeles sheriff's deputies, police officers, and firefighters were visiting the ranch on patrols with increasing frequency, asking questions, searching buildings for runaways, and running the license plates on cars.

CHAPTER 3

THE GARY HINMAN MURDER

Charlie had heard that Gary Hinman, a musician friend of the Family who lived in Topanga Canyon, had come into an inheritance, and he wanted a piece of it.

Set in the beautiful chaparral-covered hills of the Santa Monica Mountains near Malibu, Topanga was a spiritual mecca for Buddhists like Gary, a practicing member of the orthodox Nichiren Shoshu branch. Many artists and musicians were drawn to this bohemian enclave as well.

A classical pianist, Gary taught music lessons at UCLA, where he was working on a PhD in sociology. And as the only professional musician in the Nichiren's Bagpipe Corps, he was helping them plan a parade in Santa Monica for Sunday, July 27. He even had his own set of bagpipes.

Before settling on Spahn Ranch as his home base, Charlie had spent quite a bit of time in Topanga. In fact, he was playing there in a band called the Milky Way when he met Bobby Beausoleil, then a gifted nineteen-year-old guitar player and artist.

Unlike others who were lured in by the promise of sex with Charlie's girls, Bobby didn't need any help hooking up. A pretty boy who was popular with the ladies even though he couldn't grow a beard, the girls called him Cupid.

But after hopping a freight train for LA from his hometown of Santa Barbara when he was twelve, Bobby became a ward of the state. Finding his way to the underworld occult scene in the Haight, baby-faced Bobby played psychedelic experimental rock numbers with his band, the Orkustra, and half-naked female dancers in the nearby Glide Memorial Church. Occult film director Kenneth Anger was so inspired by Bobby's performance that he asked Bobby to play the lead role in his film *Lucifer Rising*.

From there, Bobby found his way down to Topanga, where he played music with Charlie and was drawn to the songwriter's creative energy. With no strong role models or a family of his own, Bobby liked being part of Charlie's communal group. By the summer of 1969, Bobby, now twenty-one, still felt the need to win Charlie's acceptance, but he also wanted to impress the tough bikers hanging around the ranch.

On Friday night, July 25, Bobby asked Mary Brunner if she wanted to come with him and Sadie to Gary's house. Mary agreed. Gary had let Bobby and Mary stay at his house previously, just as he'd allowed other friends in need to do.

The plan that night was to persuade Gary to join the Family and hand over his inheritance. "The offer-you-can't-refuse type thing," Bruce Davis explained later.

———

It was almost midnight when Bruce drove Bobby, Mary, and Sadie to Topanga in a yellow 1953 Ford four-door sedan and dropped them at the 900 block of Topanga Canyon Road. Bruce left them down the street a bit from Gary's house, which was on the side of a hill about fifty feet above street level, so Gary wouldn't see them pull up, then he returned to the ranch.

The group had agreed that Mary and Sadie would get Gary to invite them in, saying that Bobby was dealing with car trouble. Then Sadie would signal from the living room—light a match or cigarette in the front window—if it was safe for Bobby to come inside.

Mary didn't see the gun, which Bobby had in a holster, until they were out of the car. Bobby had never used a gun before. It belonged to Bruce, who had purchased it just a couple of weeks earlier. Bobby asked Mary to put the holster in her purse, then tucked the pistol away.

Bobby also had a knife that he kept in a leather sheath hooked to his belt. The knife had an eagle's head on the handle, with an inscription in Spanish engraved on one side of the blade and a desert cactus scene on the other.

Because they'd both stayed at Gary's place before, Mary knew that Gary didn't have much money, and she figured Bobby was aware of that too. He'd said that if Gary didn't come through for them they might have to rough him up a little, but she still couldn't see Bobby using the gun. Not when they were all friends. The prospect of hurting Gary was just not on Mary's radar.

The twenty-five-year-old strawberry-blond librarian was more educated than the rest of Charlie's flock. The oldest of three daughters of a sporting goods store owner from Wisconsin, Mary had earned a bachelor's degree in European history, then aborted a master's program in library science to take a job on the Berkeley campus. But within a few months she'd left all that to join Charlie on the road.

Before meeting up with Charlie, Sadie had been involved, like Bobby, with an occult group in the Haight. A topless dancing vampire, she wore high heels, dark lipstick, and wild painted eyebrows in the "Witches Sabbath Revue," a ritualistic nightclub act staged by Anton Szandor LaVey, founder of the Church of Satan. LaVey's shows featured naked women engaging in candle-lit ceremonies with skulls and five-pointed stars as vampire men emerged from the shadows in black hooded robes.

Notwithstanding their unusual and disparate pasts, Mary, Bobby, and Sadie had no history of violence. Tied together by their love and loyalty to Charlie and the Family, they had gone to Gary's on what was supposed to be a simple mission to collect some cash.

———

Gary let Sadie and Mary into his house, then sat with them in the kitchen until Sadie felt it was safe to send Bobby the signal. After Bobby joined them, the group talked around the card table for a while before Bobby broached the subject.

"We really need money," Bobby said. "Do you have any we can have?"

"No," Gary said, "I don't have it."

"We're not kidding," Bobby said, pulling out the gun. "We really do need some money."

"Put the gun away," Gary said. "Don't be ridiculous."

Gary pushed Bobby, then tried to get the gun away from him. The rectangular kitchen, narrow and short, fed into a hallway and the living room, so there wasn't much room for Mary to escape the line of fire in case the gun went off. When it fired during the struggle, the bullet missed everyone, harmlessly striking a cabinet drawer.

The two men crashed into the table, breaking its metal legs and causing it to collapse, then Bobby pistol-whipped Gary until he cut bleeding gashes into Gary's scalp, which seemed to take the fight out of him.

As Gary sat in a chair next to the fridge, Mary got a wet towel and tended to his head wound, while he pleaded with them to go.

"Please, we'll forget it, call it scratch," he said. "Just leave. Get out of here."

No one paid any attention.

They straightened the table legs to stand it upright again, then Bobby gave Sadie the gun and told her to guard Gary while he rummaged through the living room for cash or anything of value.

Gary's checkbook showed that he had less than a hundred bucks in his account, and he said his father had his stocks and bonds certificates, so they couldn't sell those either. All Bobby could find were the pink slips for a couple of cars, which he had Gary sign over.

Out of options, Bobby called the ranch from the living room.

"Gary ain't cooperating," Bobby said.

Meanwhile, Gary tried to talk Sadie into handing over the gun in the kitchen. "Cut this out," he said, standing up.

Sadie backed away, but Gary kept coming toward her. When she couldn't back up any farther he reached out and took the gun from her.

"He's got the gun!" Sadie shouted.

Bobby rushed back in and the three of them ended up on the floor wrestling for the gun until Bobby got it back again.

It wasn't long before they heard footsteps on the stairs outside and Charlie and Bruce stormed through the front door. Charlie was carrying one of his favorite weapons, a pirate's sword with a curved blade nearly two feet long, which he liked to throw at hay stacks at Spahn.

Within an instant they had pushed into the living room, where a quick, hot mess of fists and scuffling broke out, as Gary futilely fought to regain control of his house.

"Call the police," he yelled toward the door.

Mary retreated into the kitchen as Bruce took his gun back and held it on Gary.

"Give me the money, Gary," Charlie said.

"I don't know what you're talking about," Gary replied. "I don't have any money."

Charlie swiped Gary's face and the side of his head with the sword, practically slicing his ear in two.

This wasn't what Bruce had signed up for. At the sight of blood, he grabbed Gary's keys and left, heading back to the ranch in the used Fiat that Gary had bought recently.

Charlie joined Mary in the kitchen, the sword dangling from his right hand, and showed her a cut on the fleshy part of his left index finger that was dripping blood. He asked her to bandage him up while Sadie did the same for Gary in the living room.

Charlie said he'd probably cut Gary's ear off, but Mary didn't see the wound until later, after it had clotted up. Gary also had a deep gash running down his cheek.

Once Charlie was patched up, he returned to the living room to talk to Gary for a few minutes, then drove the Ford sedan back to the ranch.

Even after all this mayhem, Gary managed to doze off in the far right corner of the living room, where he normally slept, next to a Buddhist shrine comprised of tin foil and tiny Oriental characters.

His three captors took turns sleeping—Bobby in a chair and the girls on the floor—so they could make sure Gary didn't leave the house or call the police.

At one point Gary attempted to escape through what was called the tree room—where a tree was literally growing through the house, just off the front porch—but the door was locked and his captors managed to stop him. After that, he stayed in his corner.

Gary had enough food to last through Saturday. On Sunday, Sadie hitchhiked to a local store for some eggs, milk, and a few other groceries.

While she was gone Gary asked Mary to sew up his ear. She tried to join the two pieces back together, using a needle, some dental floss, and an ice cube. When Sadie returned, she realized she'd forgotten to buy gauze and adhesive tape for Gary's injuries, so she had to make another trip. It was a fifteen-minute ride each way.

The trio tried to persuade Gary to come back to the ranch with them, saying they were all about to head out to the desert, but he declined.

Over the course of the weekend, several of Gary's friends called or came to the door, but the girls managed to get rid of them. Disguising her voice with a heavy British accent, Sadie told one male caller that Gary had gone for a walk. She told another that Gary had gone back to Colorado because his parents had been in a car accident. Mary also made excuses to a caller who said he'd phoned earlier, claiming that Gary had said he could stay there.

Afraid that Gary would go to the police if they left him, Bobby called Spahn Ranch again for direction on Sunday afternoon.

"You know what to do," Manson said.

After the call, Bobby told Mary and Sadie that they had to kill Gary.

"It's going to be tonight," he said.

"We better not," Mary said. "We can think of something else."

When Bobby didn't answer her, she focused on cooking dinner. Gary was sitting up by that point, so the four of them ate together in the living room.

While Mary was doing the dishes and Sadie was in the bathroom, they heard a noise in the living room. As they both rushed in, they saw Bobby standing with a knife over Gary, who was on the floor, bleeding from the chest.

"Don't do any more," Gary said.

Bobby told Gary to chant, as he'd been doing throughout the weekend.

"Nam-myoho-renge-kyo," Gary chanted, a Buddhist mantra that signifies faith in the energy of life and the unlimited potential to overcome difficulties and end suffering. Then, apparently in shock, Gary abruptly stopped chanting, got up, and walked into the bathroom.

Without exchanging a word, Sadie and Mary stood up in unison and started cleaning the house. They wiped the place of their fingerprints, mopped up the blood, picked up the soiled bandages, and put them into garbage bags to take with them when they left.

Emerging from the bathroom, Gary retreated to his corner and chanted some more. Then he stopped and lay still with his eyes open. He finally shut his eyes and seemed to lose consciousness.

"Gather the stuff together," Bobby said, directing them to stage a fight scene by breaking the table legs again and turning over one of the kitchen chairs.

He called the ranch to see if anyone could pick them up, but no car was available.

While Susan and Mary waited for Bobby in the tree room, he wrote "POLITICAL PIGGY" on the living room wall with Gary's blood. He also drew a cat's paw print, hoping to cast suspicion on the Black Panthers. Then, he locked the front door and joined the girls outside.

"It's all over," he said, which Mary took to mean that he'd gone back and stabbed Gary one more time. "Let's go."

They were about to head out when they heard a loud raspy noise coming from the living room. It was a death rattle, the sound a body makes as it gasps its last breaths, fighting the saliva and mucous accumulated in the throat and upper chest.

With the front door locked, Bobby had to climb back inside through the kitchen window, then come around to let the girls in again.

By now the rasping was loud enough that Bobby was worried a neighbor might hear it, so he grabbed a pillow and held it over Gary's face.

Gary was still breathing when Bobby asked Mary to take over. When he called her into the kitchen a few minutes later, Mary handed the pillow duty over to Sadie.

Once Gary finally stopped moving, Sadie let the others know, and

Mary came back in. Making sure that Gary was dead, she reached into his pocket and retrieved his wallet. She took his last twenty dollars, then they locked the front door again and left through the tree room.

Mary didn't want to hitchhike back to the ranch.

"We ought to take the Volkswagen," she said.

They didn't have the keys to Gary's aging VW microbus, which was dark red with white trim and had a thunderbird painted on the side, but they were able to hotwire it using Mary's penknife.

Driving to a restaurant, they dumped the bloody rags and the garbage bags in a Dumpster. Then they went inside for a cup of coffee and a piece of cake before heading back to the ranch in the minibus, which held Gary's bagpipes.

Mary felt numb that Sunday afternoon. She really didn't understand why they'd had to kill their friend.

—

Once they got back to Spahn Ranch, Mary heard the sheriff's deputies raiding the place again that night, in the wee hours of July 28, so she slept in the hills. It seemed as though the cops had been there almost every day the past couple of months.

Charlie didn't say anything to her about Gary until the next day. "How do you feel?" he asked.

"I'm okay," she said.

Bobby took off in Gary's Fiat for a couple of days. He said he was going to get rid of it, but when he showed up again he was still driving it.

He said he'd gone back to Gary's house and his body was right where they'd left him. He also said he'd had second thoughts about the paw print, so he'd tried to erase it.

—

When Gary hadn't appeared at the parade on Sunday, several of his friends became concerned and called his house, where a woman with an

English accent explained his absence. But when he still hadn't turned up by Thursday, three of them headed over there.

They didn't need to enter to know something was terribly wrong. As they watched the black flies swarming in and out of an open window, they almost keeled over from the foul smell of a body that had been decomposing in the summer heat for four days. They immediately called the cops.

CHAPTER 4

LOTSAPOPPA

Compelled by Charlie's demands for cash to fund the Family's move to the desert, Tex came up with a plan: Why not set up a drug burn and steal from dealers, who would never report the theft to police?

Tex asked his girlfriend, Rosina Kroner, with whom he'd lived during his months away from the ranch, to help him. He told her he wanted to get some drugs for a dealer client and resell them for a profit, but in reality he intended to take the client's money and run out the back door, burning Rosina *and* the client. Trusting her boyfriend, Rosina reached out to a friend named Del, who had a specific dealer in mind.

Bernard Crowe was a big black man, five feet eleven inches tall and weighing more than three hundred pounds, hence his nicknames: Lotsapoppa, or Poppa for short. Although he was only twenty-seven, he liked to say that friends came to him for advice, like their Poppa, although he wasn't so good at taking his own counsel.

His buddy Del had arranged a buy with a female dealer in Hollywood he didn't know named Rosina, promising that Crowe would get some weed to sell out of the deal. While Del and another buddy went into the woman's apartment around 11:00 p.m., Crowe sat in his car in a nearby lot, next to the Magic Castle on Franklin Boulevard.

Crowe was a little surprised when his friends came out with the woman *and* a man.

"This is Poppa," Del said, as he introduced Crowe to the couple and got into the back seat with them. "Poppa, this is Tex, Rosina's old man."

Tex and Crowe said hello and shook hands, then Crowe turned on the radio, which sparked a conversation about their musical tastes as they drove to El Monte to get the drugs.

When they pulled up to the dealer's duplex, Crowe was surprised again. "Give me the money and I'll be back in fifteen or twenty minutes," Tex said.

Crowe looked at Del, Del looked at Crowe, and Crowe smiled.

"It wasn't supposed to be like that," Crowe told Tex, explaining that he thought Tex would buy the drugs, bring them out to the car, then collect Crowe's money. "You didn't say we had to [give the money] to you and leave you."

"What do you want to do?" Del asked Crowe.

"Well, it's up to you," Crowe replied. "You know these people and I don't."

As Del hesitated, Rosina jumped in to vouch for Tex.

"I know him. I mean we've been together for six months," she said, adding that they were planning to get married and live on a ranch.

Crowe grudgingly agreed to go along with Tex's plan, but he laid the money end of it at Del's feet. "It's your responsibility, Del," Crowe said as he handed his friend $2,400.

Del took the cash and gave it to Tex, who was supposed to buy a large quantity of marijuana and bring it back to the car.

As Tex was walking toward the building, Crowe got a bad feeling. Having only just met Tex and Rosina, he hopped out and ran up to the duplex to see for himself that the tall man had gone inside with the money.

But he was too late. Tex was nowhere to be seen. Crowe climbed back into the car and tried to be patient. "It probably will be okay," he said.

From their vantage point out front they couldn't see that Tex had run out the back, where TJ, a fellow Family member, was waiting in a car to drive him to the ranch.

Over the next half hour, tensions rose among the crew waiting in the car. What was taking Tex so long? Everyone but Rosina got out to see if they could hear anyone talking or arguing inside, or find a window shade open to confirm that the deal was going down. They looked in the bushes, too, in case Tex was hiding out. But there was no sign of him.

They waited one more hour before giving up and heading back to Rosina's around 1:00 a.m. Crowe was not happy, and he felt bad for Rosina. She seemed to have trusted this man, Tex, and he'd burned her too.

"I can call out to the ranch and see if I can shake him up," she said, clearly upset.

Back at her apartment, she dialed a number and asked to talk to Charlie.

"Do you know what Tex has done?" she asked him. "He ripped off twenty-four hundred dollars from these people, and these people mean business."

After talking to Charlie for about five minutes, Rosina handed the phone to Crowe. Charlie didn't introduce himself, but he said he'd had nothing to do with the events of that night. And although Tex was standing right next to him, Charlie told Crowe that Tex had run off someplace and that he didn't know where.

When Crowe recounted the scene in court later, he said he'd simply stated, "All I want is the weed or the money," then handed the phone back to Rosina.

But Charlie and Tex claimed that Lotsapoppa had threatened to come to the ranch with his crew and kill everyone there if he didn't get his weed or his money. The threat prompted Charlie and TJ to immediately jump in the car and head over to Rosina's apartment.

Charlie believed that he had to take care of his people—to protect the Family *and* clean up Tex's mess—just as he'd done six days earlier when he'd gone over to Gary Hinman's house to try to straighten out that situation.

After Crowe hung up with Charlie, he left Rosina's to pick up his friend Steve, who had been waiting for him to finish up his business. Crowe hadn't expected any trouble that night, so he was curious to get Steve's take on the deal.

Steve told him to just let it go. "Shine it on, man," he said.

In fact, Steve tried to discourage Crowe from going back to Rosina's at all, saying that was just looking for more trouble. But Crowe wanted to see if he could learn more about Rosina and Tex, and suss out what had happened.

As they walked into the second-story apartment about forty-five minutes later, Crowe saw two men there with Rosina and Del. The one with shoulder-length brown hair, sitting on the bed, seemed to be in charge. The other one stood nearby, like a soldier or bodyguard.

The main man introduced himself as Charlie Manson and got up to shake Crowe's hand. Then they both sat down—Charlie on the bed, Crowe in a chair next to him—to talk it out.

"It doesn't sound like Tex would do something like that," Charlie said. "That is my brother, you know."

Charlie did most of the talking, and even complimented Steve on his shirt, a rust-colored suede top with fringes. Then he stood up. "Of course, I came ready," Charlie said.

Taking a step or two away from Crowe, he reached behind his back, pulled a .22-caliber Buntline revolver from his belt—the same gun Tex would use in a violent set of murders a week later—and squeezed the trigger. It held nine bullets, but it didn't fire.

Click.

He tried again, but the gun still didn't go off.

Click.

"Why do you pull a gun on me?" asked Crowe, who was not carrying that night.

Click.

As Crowe leaned forward to get up and disarm his assailant, Charlie fired again.

"This one is loaded," he said.

Charlie was right. This time the gun went off. The bullet hit Crowe in the gut, hurtling him into the chair.

When Crowe tried to get up, he fell to the floor. He wanted to go after Charlie but his intuition kicked in.

Play possum, he told himself. So he lay still and held his breath.

It worked.

"Give me your shirt," Charlie told Steve.

Steve handed it over. "Sure, brother," he said.

"Awareness through fear is where it's at," said Charlie, who got down on the floor and kissed Del's foot. "Now we're even."

As Charlie walked toward the door, he said, "If you people know what is good for you, you won't say anything." Then he and his man walked out, leaving Crowe for dead.

Crowe's buddies rushed over to see if he really had stopped breathing. When he opened his eyes he saw that Steve was bare-chested.

"Shush," Crowe said softly, "let him get down the steps first. Call the ambulance and you all go ahead and get out of here."

The police and the ambulance arrived at 4:00 a.m. and rushed him to General Hospital, where his heart stopped twice on the operating table.

"They sent telegrams to my family, telling them they didn't think I'd make it," Crowe told reporters later.

The doctors didn't remove the bullet for fear of paralyzing him, because it was lodged right next to his lower spine. They also thought it might move on its own.

After eighteen days in the hospital, spent mostly in critical condition and collapsing when he tried to move around, Crowe went into hiding. But like Charlie, he was no snitch and he wouldn't tell the cops or the media who had shot him.

"I always say it takes more courage to die than it does to live," he said.

Charlie grew more paranoid after the shooting, especially after hearing a news report that the body of a Black Panther was found near UCLA that same night. Thinking it was Crowe, Charlie was convinced that the black people who showed up at Spahn Ranch asking to ride the horses were Crowe's people—Black Panther spies—watching them. He was also worried that Crowe's associates would carry out his threat to kill everyone at Spahn Ranch.

Charlie increased security even more after the shooting, making sure that the bikers and Family members were armed and stationed around the property, night and day.

CHAPTER 5

"POLITICAL PIGGY"

The same night that Tex was doing his drug burn in Hollywood, Los Angeles County Sheriff's Department (LASD) Homicide Sergeant Paul Whiteley and his partner, Deputy Charles Guenther, were dispatched to Gary Hinman's house in Topanga Canyon.

Arriving around 10:00 p.m., Whiteley shined the flashlight up ahead as he and his partner entered through the unlocked door to the tree room, off the patio. As flies buzzed around them in the hallway, he pushed aside a white sheet that hung across the doorway to the living room. Scanning the room with the light beam, he settled on a figure in the corner, covered with a green blanket.

Peeling it off, they found a man lying on his back, with his head against the north wall, under a Buddhist shrine. His white shirt had two tears down the front, the top button of his jeans was undone, and he was still wearing his wristwatch. A set of chanting beads lay on the floor, about six inches from his hand, where he'd let go of them as he took his last breaths.

Whiteley pulled out the wallet protruding from the victim's pants pocket, and examined his driver's license to confirm his identity: thirty-four-year-old Gary Hinman.

In what looked like the victim's blood, his killer had written "POLITICAL PIGGY" on the wall above Hinman's head. A simulated paw print was also drawn in blood to the left of the words.

In a green filing cabinet, Guenther found a pink slip to the Nash Rambler parked out front. With no carburetor, the car proved to be inoperable. The detective also found paperwork for two used cars, a Fiat and a Volkswagen minibus, which Hinman had purchased "as is" in March. Failing to locate either vehicle on or near the property, they put out an APB flagging them as stolen from a homicide victim, which, in those days, took a couple of days to distribute.

In the kitchen, they took note of the window, left ajar, above the table, whose legs were broken. A trumpet case, some Scottish plaid material, and a checkbook lay on the floor underneath.

Just below the sink, they found a bullet hole through a cabinet drawer. Although they couldn't locate the bullet, a ballistics expert located a 9-millimeter slug in the exterior wall behind the sink a month or so later. Ballistics tests determined that it came from an Astra, Browning, Luger, Radom, Star, or Walther semi-automatic pistol.

The detectives also found a trail of blood on the north wall that flowed up from the table, to the cupboard, and onto the fridge. Inside the cupboard they found a homemade scale with some curious white powder on it. But the powder tested negative for narcotics, which conflicted with the stories circulated later by Bobby and other Manson Family members that Gary was a drug dealer.

The doorjamb leading into the tree room was fractured and dented as if someone had kicked in the door and forced his way through. The question was, who? And why fatally stab a simple-living music teacher, then leave his watch but steal his two beat-up used cars?

———

Gary Hinman's colleagues and family were just as confused as the sheriff's investigators about why anyone would kill the friendly Buddhist.

The phrase "pig" or "piggy" was typically used by hippies to ridicule cops or a member of the establishment. "POLITICAL PIGGY" seemed to be a variation on that, but Gary was neither kind of piggy, nor was he involved in politics.

"It didn't make sense," said his friend Darren Crabstreet.

Crabstreet had met Gary at the Buddhist Shakubuku in North Hollywood about eighteen months before his death, when he said Gary had been "in a bad way" with "drugs and other problems."

Describing Gary as shy with a warm smile, Crabstreet recalled talking with him about his marijuana use. He told Gary that he could reach a higher level of consciousness without smoking pot, and as far as he knew, Gary had quit after that.

Although Gary came from a well-off family who lived in Fort Collins, Colorado, his cousin Kay Hinman Martley said he had no money of his own by the time he was murdered, because he'd spent it all to go on a pilgrimage with his Buddhist group to pay homage to the Dai-Gohonzon in Japan.

Gary's mother was rocked to the core by the news of her favorite child's murder. She died a year later of a brain aneurism or stroke.

"His death took her so hard," said Martley, who was three years older than Gary and grew up playing with him. "The whole family has always said that's what killed her, the trauma . . . It was like it took part of her body with her. She just idolized Gary . . . They're buried next to each other, which, again, shows you."

———

On August 6, ten days after the Hinman murder, Bobby was driving Gary's Fiat on Highway 101 just past San Luis Obispo, when it broke down, unable to make it up the Cuesta Grade.

With no money, no options, and several days of little or no sleep, Bobby crawled into a sleeping bag in the back seat and fell asleep. He woke up at 10:50 a.m. to see a California Highway Patrol (CHP) officer at the window.

"What's the problem?" the officer asked.

Bobby replied that his car had broken down. He was going to try to fix it and head on his way.

Asked for his driver's license and registration, Bobby wasn't able to produce any identification, but said his name was Jason Lee Daniels. As Bobby was flipping through his wallet, a Union Oil credit card in a woman's name caught the officer's eye. Bobby said it belonged to a friend.

When the patrolman also noted that the car's pink slip was in someone else's name—Gary Allan Hinman—Bobby claimed he'd bought the vehicle from a black man about two weeks earlier for two hundred dollars, another attempt to deflect blame onto the Black Panthers.

The final straw came when a check on the Fiat turned up the APB from the LASD. The officer promptly arrested Bobby on suspicion of auto theft and called the LASD.

At the jail, Bobby admitted to the booking deputy that his real name was Robert Kenneth Beausoleil. He also gave his address as Spahn Ranch in Chatsworth.

———

Deputy Guenther and Sergeant Whiteley hit the road for San Luis Obispo as soon as they got the call, arriving around eight o'clock that night. First thing, they headed to Jim's Body Shop to search the Fiat, which had been towed and secured in the garage.

The detectives opened the rear door, lifted the rubber floor mat, and removed the wooden cover over the spare tire. Lifting out the tire, they found a knife in a leather sheath tucked underneath, with what they described as "Spanish hieroglyphics" on the blade.

At the jail, Guenther took note of Bobby's real name and address, and collected the pink slip as evidence.

Under questioning, Bobby admitted to being at Hinman's house with two women, but refused to identify them. He said they would come forward on their own volition to clear him, because he was innocent.

The detectives said they would be happy to find the women if that would absolve him, but Bobby wouldn't budge.

"I would want to talk to an attorney before I give you the names of the girls," he said, which promptly ended their conversation.

Arresting Bobby for the murder of Gary Hinman, the detectives brought him back to Los Angeles, where he was formally charged with murder with malice aforethought on August 7.

Bobby called the ranch collect from the LA County jail that night, saying he was being held without bail on suspicion of murdering Gary.

Charlie was on a road trip to Big Sur at the time, but Bobby's call sent ripples through the Family. They discussed ways to free him, ranging from breaking him out of jail to casting blame for the murder on someone else, like the Black Panthers.

Sadie was already doing her part to deflect by telling alternative versions of the events at Gary's house that gave her a larger role in the killing. In one story *she* was the one who stabbed Gary, because he was attacking her. In another, Bobby stabbed Gary, but so did she. Other versions had drug dealers at Gary's house, whom he had burned by not paying them, or who had given him bad dope, or vice versa.

"She had stories, you know," Mary testified later. "Sadie's imagination runs sometimes."

Sadie also claimed that she, not Bobby, had written the words in blood on the wall, and that Leslie had been there with them. Leslie, who had lived with Bobby for a while and was still very tight with him, was upset by the news of his arrest.

Mary tried to take Bobby some clothes to wear to his arraignment the next day, but the jail deputies wouldn't let her see him.

———

The next morning, Friday, August 8, Charlie returned to the ranch in a white bakery van with Stephanie Schram, a seventeen-year-old he'd picked up hitchhiking near Big Sur a few days earlier. Stephanie, who had been living with her sister in San Diego, was on a road trip with a male friend whom she ditched immediately after meeting Charlie.

Mary talked briefly with Stephanie, then used the white van to drive to San Fernando, where she and Sandy Good were arrested for using stolen credit cards. They both ended up at the women's county jail, the Sybil Brand Institute, charged with forgery.

Later that evening, Charlie took Tex aside to talk to him about his plan to start a killing spree that night, one that would send a tremor throughout the country.

Then he carefully selected three girls whom he knew would not challenge his directives to go along with Tex: Katie, Sadie, and a new girl named Linda Kasabian.

Linda had only been with the Family for about a month. Gypsy had brought the long-haired sandy blonde and her baby girl Tonya to the ranch on July 4 after suggesting that Linda join the "love, beauty and peace" at the commune.

Serving as a proud surrogate for Charlie, Tex had sex with Linda that first night, before she'd even met the group's leader. Later describing himself as Charlie's "right-hand man," Tex said he helped to introduce Linda to the Family's "truth" that night, even though he knew Charlie typically performed the new girls' sexual initiations.

Linda, who had just turned twenty, had already been married twice, but said she'd never had such a "total experience" making love with anyone else. She felt "possessed" during their lovemaking, and couldn't unclench her hands afterward. Twenty-three-year-old Tex was moved, too, feeling "a more complete sensation of oneness" with her than he'd felt with any other girl before.

Asked, as usual, if she had any money to contribute to the Family, Linda told Tex about a five-thousand-dollar inheritance that a friend had planned to use to send her and some others on a sailing trip to South America.

When Tex tried to convince her to steal the money, Linda initially resisted. "Hey, I can't do that, he's my brother," she said.

But he kept on her about it until she gave in. "There is no wrong," he said, explaining that it wasn't her friend's money; it was *everybody's* money, there for them to take. So they did, and turned it over to the Family.

After that first "caper"—as some group members called such crimes— Tex and Linda grew very close. And after making such a sizable monetary contribution to the Family, she quickly became a trusted member.

CHAPTER 6

"DO WHATEVER TEX SAYS."

Around 9:00 p.m. that Friday night, Charlie pulled Linda off the front porch and tracked down Katie in the kids' trailer, then told them and Sadie to each grab a Buck knife and some dark clothing.

As they were getting ready to go, Tex snorted some speed that he kept hidden in a Gerber baby food jar under the porch. Sadie had some too.

Tex's drug use had been escalating since he'd joined the Family more than a year earlier. Along with the LSD and cocaine he'd been using, he'd taken up chewing wild belladonna root, a natural hallucinogenic that grew on the ranch. He'd also been sniffing speed every day for the past month to help fuel the long hours that he and Bruce were putting in to retrofit the dune buggies with VW engines so they could travel the desert's sandy terrain more quickly and easily.

Although only Tex and Sadie were high that night, all four of the twentysomethings felt the lingering effects of their consistent and long-term use of hallucinogens, which perpetuated a sense of non-reality.

They were all wearing the same black outfits they'd worn in recent months during "creepy crawlers," when they crept into rich people's homes at night to move things around and scare them. Upset the balance of the mainstream and the establishment. Maybe steal some clothes, credit cards, traveler's checks, or audio taping equipment, which helped keep the Family fed and clothed. Another of Charlie's directives, the exercises also helped eliminate their fears and inhibitions.

But this night was different. According to Tex, Charlie took him aside and told him to take the girls to kill people on Cielo Drive, a narrow road that wound through the secluded, woodsy neighborhood of Benedict Canyon on the west side of Los Angeles.

"Go up to the house where Terry Melcher used to live. Kill them, cut them up, pull out their eyes and hang them on the mirrors," Charlie said, his dark, hypnotic eyes flashing. "As gruesome as you can."

Charlie had met Melcher, a music producer and the son of actress Doris Day, in the summer of 1968 when Charlie, Tex, and some of the girls were living at the luxurious beach home of Beach Boys drummer Dennis Wilson in the Pacific Palisades.

Charlie, strumming his guitar in the back seat of Dennis's car, had accompanied the drummer as he drove Melcher back to his house on Cielo Drive from the Palisades one night. Charlie felt that Melcher had promised to record and produce an album of his music, and he was angry that Melcher had reneged on the deal.

Charlie made sure to equip Tex with the right tools for the grisly job: his favorite gun, the long-barreled .22-caliber Buntline that he'd used to shoot Lotsapoppa in Hollywood a week earlier; a Buck knife; some rope; and a pair of bolt cutters to cut the phone wires.

Gather all the people in one room, Charlie told Tex, then kill them. Make sure to leave no witnesses behind. Then, after hitting the first house, go to every house on the street to kill those people too. Bring back as much money as you can find, and don't come back with less than six hundred dollars.

Like the other Family members, Tex was willing to do whatever he needed to do to win Charlie's approval. He also knew he owed Charlie for cleaning up his mess with Lotsapoppa.

———

Waiting with Linda outside the Rock City Café for further instructions, Sadie tucked her black capri pants into her boots and told Danny DeCarlo, a member of the Straight Satans biker club who had been staying at the ranch for the past few months, that they were going out on a caper.

Charlie told the girls to pile into the same yellow Ford sedan that Bruce had used to drive the other group to Gary Hinman's a couple of weeks earlier.

"I want you to go somewhere. Get in the car. Do whatever Tex says," he said. Then, sticking his head in the window, he gave them one last directive: "Leave a sign. You girls know what I mean, something witchy. Let them know you were there."

Ranch hand Juan Flynn came up to the car just before they drove away. "Where are you going?" he asked.

"We're going to go kill some mother-f***ing pigs," replied Sadie, who thrived on being outrageous.

———

Tex got lost as they were driving to Benedict Canyon, listening to Charlie's voice in his head.

Kill them. Cut them up. Hang them up on the mirrors.

Charlie had preached that they had to kill themselves to be free. A difficult concept to accept, it's partly why he gave them new names—to kill off their egos so they could lose themselves and be one with the group. So it wouldn't be hard to kill others. After all, he said, love was nothingness. Love was death. Death was love.

It all made sense when you were on acid, and Charlie only gave them "awareness drugs," not downers. He didn't even like his people drinking alcohol.

Charlie had talked to Tex during his morning chores for some time—an exercise Charlie called "computing"—to reinforce his philosophy and ensure that Tex was capable of the duties he and the others would need to carry out in the future. Now that it was time to do the real thing, Tex was ready.

Knowing, perhaps, that the drugs would help make the violent acts seem unreal, Tex later claimed he'd consciously loaded himself up on speed to face up to the task that night, to numb his morals and inhibitions, and to silence the scriptures that he'd been taught in the Methodist church growing up.

———

Tex pulled up to the driveway at 10050 Cielo Drive and stopped near a telephone pole. Like Charlie, he had been to the house when Melcher had lived there, so Tex already knew the layout.

Charlie knew Melcher had relocated to Malibu, and he rightly assumed that other rich and beautiful people had moved into the house. For the Family's purposes, it didn't really matter who they were.

Climbing on the hood of the Ford, Tex shimmied up the tall, thick wooden pole.

Cut the wires.

Tex snipped several of the thick black cords, unsure if they were electricity wires or phone lines, then moved the car down the street. As the cords fell, they got hung up on the wooden fence below.

The fence, which was six feet high and twelve feet wide, had a chainlink electric security gate across the driveway that allowed cars to go in and out with the press of a button on either side. Because Tex didn't know if the fence was armed with an alarm, he led the group up the brush-covered slope at the end of it, where they were able to hop over to the other side.

They moved in the dark like animals. Bodies without minds. Creeping toward the house like predators.

To them, Charlie was who he said he was: Jesus Christ, God, their father, and the Devil himself. He was in their minds. He could see what they were doing and read their thoughts. He was there with them, he *was* them, and they were him. They were all one. He'd also taught them that they were invisible to the outside world. No one could see them. But they still needed to take precautions.

Don't leave any witnesses.

Headlights started toward them as they walked up the driveway, past the lawn that spanned the length of the house to their left. The upscale bungalow had a stone façade that was broken up by a series of white-framed windows, and was topped by a dark shingle roof, like a French country house.

A stone walkway led from the driveway to the front door of the main house. It also connected to other short throughways that ran along the façade, back to the pool and patio area off the master bedroom, and on to the red wooden guesthouse at the rear of the property. A separate dirt path started at the driveway a distance from the main house and snaked its way across the lawn, past the pool and patio, in a more direct route to the guesthouse.

"Lie down and be still," Tex told the girls, who ducked down and hid while he stepped out of the bushes. Tex strode toward the white Rambler Ambassador and approached the driver's side window with a knife in one hand and a gun in the other.

"Halt!" he said.

The driver, a tall redheaded teenager with glasses, looked up at Tex with fear in his eyes. "Please don't hurt me," he said. "I won't say anything."

Tex responded quickly. Without feeling. Like a machine programmed to kill. As the boy raised his left arm defensively, Tex slashed at the kid's palm with the knife, slicing through the band of his wristwatch. Then, without a second thought, he shot the kid four times point blank.

Tex told Linda to go back down to the front gate to keep watch in case anyone came, then he led the others toward the house.

"C'mon," Tex said.

Cutting the window screen next to the front door, Tex opened the window and crawled into the house to let Sadie and Katie in through the front door, where two blue steamer trunks were sitting in the entryway.

From there, they went into the living room, where a blond man was sleeping on the couch with an American flag draped over him. Tex kicked him in the head.

"What time is it? Who are you?" the man asked, confused. "What do you want?"

"I'm the devil, and I'm here to do the devil's business," Tex said.

Tex tied the man's hands behind his back with the rope, then told Sadie to bind his wrists with a towel. When the man tried to object, Tex cut him off.

"Don't move or you're dead," he said.

Sadie and Katie, told to go through the house and bring any other occupants into the living room, brought in a young brunette who had been reading in her bedroom.

Next, Sadie went to the master bedroom, where she collected a beautiful, very pregnant blonde in a bikini top and panties sleep-set and a short, handsome brown-haired man, wearing a dress shirt and vertically striped black and white pants.

Tex told the occupants to lie face down on the floor, but the short man refused. "I know karate," he said.

At five feet six inches and only 122 pounds, he was dwarfed by Tex, who was six feet one inch tall and had an athletic build after playing on the football, basketball, and track teams in high school.

Tex wrapped the length of rope around the short man's neck, threw one end over the wooden beam above, then started wrapping the other end around the pregnant woman's neck so they would strangle themselves if they struggled.

"Can't you see she's pregnant?" the short man replied, taking a step toward Tex. "Let her sit down."

Tex responded by shooting the man in the chest. He fell to the floor, where Tex smacked him in the face with the butt of his gun.

"Where's your money?" Tex barked at the group.

"In a wallet on the desk," the blond man said.

Katie rifled through the desk, but there was no money in it.

"I only have seventy-two dollars," the brunette said. "I just went to the bank yesterday."

Hearing the short man groaning, Tex stabbed him, which sent the women into hysterics.

"What are you going to do with us?" they asked.

"You're all going to die," Tex said.

The blond man jumped up from the couch and started toward the front door, erupting into a tangle of arms and legs as he kicked at Sadie, pulled her hair, and fought to get free of the towel binding his wrists.

"Kill him!" Tex shouted.

Sadie stabbed at his legs, but somehow he got loose and went after her hard.

"Tex! Help me!" Sadie yelled. "Do something!"

Tex smashed the butt of his gun into the top of the man's skull so hard that the wooden grip broke into several pieces and went flying.

Tex didn't know that the blond man had taken MDA that night, a new party drug that seemed to make him almost superhuman. His girlfriend had taken some too.

Like a wild bull, the blond man kept up the fight, pulling his assailants toward the front door and out onto the porch. In the struggle to wrestle him into submission, Sadie lost her knife.

Tex felt like an animal, making "happiness noises," as he later described it, while he stabbed the big man on the front porch again and again until finally the man began to succumb.

"Help me, oh God, help me!" he pleaded.

Just then Tex heard a woman's voice erupt in the yard. "Make it stop!" she cried out.

Looking up, he saw Linda, who had left her post at the gate and was now standing on the path, watching the scene in total disbelief.

"It's too late!" Sadie retorted.

Meanwhile, the brunette had broken away and run out the back door of the master bedroom into the pool area, and was now running across the lawn.

"Someone is getting away!" Sadie yelled.

When Tex looked over he saw Katie in a wild state, a knife in her raised hand, chasing the brunette until she fell on the lawn, where Katie proceeded to hold her down and repeatedly plunge the knife into the length of her five-feet-five-inch frame.

"Stop! I'm already dead," the woman said.

Hearing her voice as a call to action, Tex ran over and stabbed her some more.

39

By then, the powerful blond man had crawled from the front porch onto the lawn, where he was bleeding profusely. Tex went back and stabbed him again, too, just for good measure, then told Katie to check the guesthouse to ensure they left no witnesses alive.

The victims had made sounds as Tex stabbed and shot them, but to him the sounds had no meaning. Their faces were unreal. They didn't look like people, but like psychedelic cartoons.

Everyone had been running around the house—at him, away from him, screaming and pleading. He was jumping around too. But it wasn't really happening. It was another reality. It was perfection.

I'm an animal. It's the end of the world, he thought. *I'm the living death.*

Inside, Tex found Sadie with the pregnant woman, who was screaming, crying, and begging them for her life.

"Please don't kill me," she pleaded. "I don't want to die. I just want to have my baby."

Sadie bragged later that she stared the woman dead in the eye and, without a hint of remorse in her voice, said, "Look, bitch. I have no mercy for you. I don't care if you're going to have a baby. You had better be ready. You are going to die."

Kill her!

Sadie and Tex both claimed later that they stabbed the pregnant woman. Sadie also testified that she thought about cutting out the baby, but couldn't bring herself to do anything except hold the woman down while Tex stabbed her. Either way, the outcome was the same: the woman and her unborn son died as she lay in a pool of her own blood, calling out for her mother.

Completing the last task to fulfill Charlie's vision, Sadie took a towel, dipped it in the pregnant woman's blood, and wrote "PIG" on the white front door, reminiscent of the message Bobby had left at Gary Hinman's house.

Their job finished, the trio headed back down the driveway toward the gate, which Tex opened with the touch of his bloody finger on the button.

Linda was waiting for them in the car with a change of clean clothes. They drove down the street, looking for somewhere to wash off the sticky red blood and dump their sopping wet pants and shirts.

Stopping near a house, they found a hose and were rinsing off when an older man came out. Tex told him they were out on a late-night stroll and had gotten thirsty. "We're just getting a drink of water," he said. "Sorry we disturbed you."

But the man didn't believe him. "Is that your car down there?" he asked.

"No," Tex said. "We're walking."

Tex had no idea that the man was a sheriff's reserve police officer. As the group trotted back to the car, the officer's wife yelled from the house that he should get their license plate number. Although the officer tried to reach inside the car and take their keys, Tex was able to close the window, start up the car, and drive off before the officer could stop them.

The officer did manage to get the plate number, but he didn't bother to report the incident to police.

———

Cruising along Mulholland Drive, Tex swerved all over the road.

"Pull over," one of the girls said.

They stopped, threw their wet clothes into a canyon, and continued on.

While Linda was wiping the Buck knives clean of fingerprints and tossing them out the window, Sadie announced that she'd accidentally left hers at the house. Tex threw the Buntline out the window and into some bushes.

Once they reached the San Fernando Valley, they stopped at a gas station, where Tex told the girls to go finish washing off the blood.

As he stood in the men's room, Tex looked in the mirror, trying to figure out who he was. He didn't see himself. He saw an animal looking back at him. He couldn't remember the order of the victims he'd killed that night, only that he'd stabbed or shot every single one of them.

When he returned to the car, he was happy to let one of the girls drive back to the ranch.

———

It was the middle of the night when they arrived at Spahn. But Charlie was still up and waiting for them, wondering why they were back so soon.

Tex explained what they'd just done, gruesome and gory just like Charlie had ordered, and waited for his approval.

"Do you have any remorse for your actions?" Charlie asked each of them.

None of them wanted to disappoint him, so they gave the answer they knew he wanted: "No," they said.

Truthfully, Katie felt dead inside. Empty. She'd conditioned herself over the past eighteen months to try to feel nothing as she followed Charlie's orders and subverted her own will. Yet she felt dirty, hopeless, and miserable nonetheless.

"Charlie, they were so young," said Katie, who, like Sadie, was twenty-one, at least five years younger than all their victims that night.

When Tex had told her to go to the guesthouse, Katie knew that she was supposed to kill anyone she found inside, but she didn't have the energy to even try. She was simply spent. So she just waited outside until things quieted down, and by the time she returned to the main house it was time to go.

Thinking that Charlie seemed satisfied with their night's work, Tex went to bed without saying another word about it. He slept late and got up as if nothing had happened, as if it were all a dream.

———

Later that day, biker Danny DeCarlo sensed that something was up. People knew something they weren't telling him.

"What did you do last night?" DeCarlo asked Clem, fishing for clues.

Clem was an eighteen-year-old Family member who always had a smile on his face. He didn't seem very bright, had done a short stint at the Camarillo state mental hospital after an arrest for indecent exposure, and regularly did so many drugs—from mescaline to angel dust, LSD, and heroin—the others called him Scramblehead. But Charlie liked and trusted him, because he was loyal and did what he was told.

Clem gave DeCarlo a half-smile as he looked over DeCarlo's shoulder. Turning around, the biker saw Charlie standing behind him, looking at the kid with an expression that said, "keep your mouth shut."

"We took care of business," Charlie said, then walked away.

Pressed for details, Clem would only say cryptically that, "We got five piggies."

With no idea what Clem was talking about, DeCarlo shrugged it off.

CHAPTER 7

THE SOLE SURVIVOR

Nineteen-year-old William Garretson was living rent-free in the guesthouse at 10050 Cielo Drive that summer. All this small-town boy from Martins Ferry, Ohio, had to do was keep the place clean and take care of owner Rudi Altobelli's three dogs—two poodles and a Weimaraner—while he was away in Europe. For that, Altobelli, a music and film talent manager whose clients included Henry Fonda and Katharine Hepburn, paid Garretson thirty-five dollars a month.

LA was in the middle of a heat wave on Friday, August 8, but it was a little cooler there on Cielo, high on the hill, where Garretson could look across the canyon at night and see a cascade of lights flickering all the way down to Sunset Boulevard.

Altobelli had met Garretson in Hollywood, likely cruising the Sunset Strip, a happening street of bars, night clubs, restaurants, and office buildings that housed business managers for some of the biggest names in the music industry. Celebrities and regular folks were also known to pick up hookers or casual sex partners there.

The previous caretaker of the Cielo property was a longtime friend of Altobelli's, but she'd let his bird die and trashed the place with parties every night, so Garretson was a welcome change—even if he had been arrested on two misdemeanors: possession of marijuana and contributing to the delinquency of a minor. Garretson had moved in the day Altobelli flew to Rome with Sharon Tate, his tenant and friend, on March 24.

Around 8:00 p.m., once the hot temperatures had dipped a bit, Garretson decided to hitchhike down to Sunset. After walking the Strip for a while, he stopped at the drug store to buy a TV dinner, some Coke, and cigarettes, then hitched a couple of rides back to the house around ten o'clock.

He watched a little TV, snacking on chips and soda while his dinner was cooking, and was about to eat around 11:45 p.m. when Christopher, the Weimaraner, started barking at the sound of a car pulling up.

It was Garretson's new friend Steve Parent. The two had met a couple of weeks earlier when Garretson was hitchhiking on Sunset, and Parent gave him a ride home. Parent, who worked at a stereo store, knocked on the door that night with a clock radio in hand.

"You live here by yourself?" Parent asked.

"Yeah," Garretson replied. "You want a beer?"

At eighteen, Parent wasn't old enough to buy beer any more than Garretson was, so he happily accepted the offer of a Budweiser. But Garretson, who was still recovering from some overenthusiastic partying, didn't join him.

The night before, Garretson had asked one of the gardeners to buy him some beer in return for letting the gardener use the guesthouse to make out with a girlfriend for a couple of hours. The gardener agreed and gratefully threw in a couple of marijuana joints and a pill—Dexedrine or some other pharmaceutical, Garretson wasn't really sure. Nonetheless, he'd drunk four of the beers, smoked both joints, and taken the pill before promptly throwing up.

That morning, he'd felt unwell and stayed close to home all day, cleaning the guesthouse and nursing his hangover.

After parking in the driveway, Parent followed one of the walkways to get to the guesthouse. On his way, he must have observed the blond and brunette ladies through the long picture window in the living room of the main house because he asked about them.

"Who are they?" he asked Garretson.

"Mrs. Polanski and Abigail Folger," the caretaker replied.

Pressed for more details, Garretson gave him some backstory. Movie director Roman Polanski, whose film *Rosemary's Baby* had been nominated for two Academy Awards that year, had been leasing the main house since March with his wife, an up-and-coming actress whose stage name was Sharon Tate.

The other couple staying at the house were Roman's friend Wojciech "Voytek" Frykowski, who had grown up in the same small town in Poland, and Voytek's girlfriend, Abigail "Gibby" Folger.

Even before the Polanskis moved in, Altobelli had leased the house to other well-connected figures in the music and movie industries, including record producer Terry Melcher, who had worked with the Byrds and collaborated with Bobby Darin, Randy Newman, and the Beach Boys.

Melcher had lived there with his girlfriend Candice Bergen, the actress and fashion model, until the first week of January 1969, when he moved to a house his mother owned on Pacific Coast Highway in Malibu. With four months left on his lease, Melcher sublet the house to Sharon and Roman, who moved in February 15.

There had been lots of visitors and some big parties at the main house that year, clearly one of *the* places to be and be seen in Tinseltown. It didn't surprise Garretson when he saw people from the Hollywood crowd using marijuana, LSD, cocaine, and mescaline there. He'd already tried LSD himself.

In March, before the Polanskis left the house for Europe, the couple had thrown a catered bon voyage party for more than a hundred guests, many of whom showed up high on their drug of choice. Sharon's former fiancé, Jay Sebring, who was known as the "Hairdresser to the Stars" and was still a close friend, came with one of his girlfriends, Sharmagne.

Asked by the Polanskis to housesit that summer, Voytek and Gibby later threw another big party themselves with ten cases of champagne, a band, and three parking attendants who lined the street with cars that spilled onto Bella Drive, a nearby cross street.

Celebrity guests also came over regularly for casual visits and swims in the pool, which was shaped like the sole of a shoe and was situated in between the main house and guesthouse. They included John Phillips, the lead singer of the Mamas & the Papas, and Bruce Lee, who was teaching kung fu to Sharon and Jay. Voytek liked to shoot home movies poolside, especially when naked girls were frolicking in the water.

Despite the fast lives and open relationships of many of their friends, Sharon and Roman had decided to get married in 1968, and didn't wait long to start a family. Now eight and a half months pregnant, the twenty-six-year-old actress had returned from Europe to get the house ready for the baby.

The Polanskis had asked Gibby and Voytek to stay on until Roman returned on August 12, in time for the birth.

Sharon had been entertaining friends by the pool that Friday afternoon. There was talk of a party that night, but she decided she was too tired and preferred to spend a mellow night at home with Jay, Gibby, and Voytek after having dinner at the El Coyote Café, a restaurant on nearby Beverly Boulevard.

———

As Parent drank his beer, he showed Garretson how the clock radio worked, and asked if his friend wanted to buy it. Garretson didn't have an electric clock, but he still said no thanks.

For some reason the Weimaraner seemed unusually agitated that night. He would not stop barking.

"What's the matter with Christopher?" Parent asked.

"I don't know," Garretson replied, explaining that the dog often barked when a stranger showed up on the property. It was odd, though, because Parent had been there for a while.

Around midnight, Parent used the phone to call a friend, who invited him to meet up in West Hollywood. So Parent finished his beer and said goodbye to Garretson at the door about fifteen minutes later.

As far as Garretson knew, his redheaded friend followed the dirt path back to the driveway, climbed into his 1965 white Rambler Ambassador, drove out the gate, and headed for Santa Monica Boulevard.

After Parent left, Garretson ate his TV dinner on the couch, then wrote some letters, listening to records of the Doors and the Mamas & the Papas on the stereo.

At some point, Christopher started barking again. Garretson thought he heard a woman's scream but dismissed it until he looked over at the door and saw that the handle was off-kilter. He remembered locking it after Parent left, so it should have been in a horizontal position. But instead, it was in a vertical, or down, position, as if someone had tried to get in.

Then Garretson heard another scream.

He got up and looked out the little window in his walk-in closet to see if anyone was moving around outside. The outside lights of the main house were on, so he was able to see a man straddling another man on the lawn and two girls running toward the guesthouse. Toward him.

What the . . . ? he thought, backing away with fright. Then he heard a woman's voice outside in the yard.

"Stop! I'm already dead."

How can you be dead and still talking?

Freaked out, Garretson quickly went to the back door and, seeing that it wasn't bolted, pushed the latch across.

Garretson wondered what time it was. The sky was still pitch black, but with no clock, he picked up the phone to call the number for "time" and find out. Hearing no dial tone, he went into the other room, found a different phone, and plugged it into another outlet. Still nothing. The phone was dead, which did nothing to alleviate his anxiety.

He'd been scared other nights too. Back in March, he'd heard someone trampling around outside, which prompted the poodles to scamper about. But nothing like this.

Still freaked out, he stayed up until the sun started coming up. Only then was he able to drift off to sleep on the puffy brown couch, facing the front door.

———

Neighbors up and down Cielo Drive and across the canyon told police later that they'd heard strange noises throughout the night. Sound carried in the canyon, but it wasn't always easy to identify the source.

Mr. and Mrs. Seymour Kott, who lived next door, about one hundred yards north of the Polanskis, were used to hearing sounds coming from their neighbors' house: guests chattering, music playing, and "even the tinkle of cocktail glasses."

The Kotts said goodbye to their dinner guests around midnight and were in their bedroom when they heard four gunshots fired in quick succession. Seymour told the police that his wife heard the shots between 12:30 and 1:00 a.m., but he told a reporter three weeks later that she heard the shots "no earlier" than 2:00 or 2:30 a.m.

Down the hill and south of the Polanskis' house, a counselor supervising a sleep-out at the Westlake School for Girls heard a man yelling in distress for about ten seconds, sometime after 12:40 a.m.

"Oh, God, no. Stop. Stop. Oh, God, no, don't," the man screamed.

Also hearing dogs barking, the counselor got into his car and drove around the neighborhood to Beverly Glen and back, but didn't see anything out of the ordinary so he didn't call the police.

A fourteen-year-old boy who lived directly across the canyon from the Polanskis and could see the front of their house from his bedroom was up late when he heard several people arguing for a full minute around 4:00 a.m. The argument frightened him enough to close the window and note the time as he crawled into bed.

Two security guards with Bel Air Patrol independently reported to their on-duty supervisor that they'd heard sounds like shots fired that night. One initially thought what he heard at 3:30 a.m. was a car backfiring, but then he decided that the blasts were too sharp and short to have come from a car. The other guard reported that he'd distinctly heard several gunshots, with two- to five-second pauses in between, around 4:00 a.m. Their supervisor promptly relayed this information to the West LA Division of the Los Angeles Police Department (LAPD).

"I hope we don't have a murder," said the LAPD officer who answered the phone. "We just had a 'woman screaming' call in that area."

CHAPTER 8

THE BLOODY AFTERMATH

Winnie Chapman, who had been the Polanskis' cook, party caterer, and housekeeper for the past sixteen months, got dropped off a little late for work on Saturday morning, August 9.

As she approached the gate she could see the downed black wires on the fence and wondered if the phone would be out, making a mental note to check the line inside.

Starting up the driveway toward the house, she noticed a white Ambassador that was parked askew, but paid it no mind because the Polanskis often had visitors who stayed the night.

She picked up the newspaper on her way, then headed into the garage to turn off the outside lights. A string of outdoor holiday lights were always on, a decorative contribution from the previous tenant, Candice Bergen, but someone had left on the overhead light as well.

Chapman then walked to the service entrance on the west side of the house, grabbed the key from the rafter above the service door to unlock it, and replaced the key in its hiding place.

When she tried the phone in the kitchen it was dead, as she'd feared. So she proceeded into the dining room, where she was taken aback to notice that two trunks were sitting in the front entry hall—with blood on them. They hadn't been there when she'd left the house the day before. The front door, which she'd just scrubbed clean of finger marks and paw prints, was also wide open.

Standing in the foyer, she couldn't believe what she was seeing: the walls were covered with swatches of red, and as she looked out the door to the lawn, there was a lifeless, bloody figure of a man lying on the grass.

As she ventured onto the porch in shock, she glanced down at her feet to see numerous reddish pools and a yellow towel, marked with dried blood.

Hysterical and frightened now, she ran along the stone path to the driveway as fast as she could, past more spots of blood, and headed for the front gate. Passing the white car from a different angle this time, she could see that a young man was slumped over in the driver's seat.

She couldn't get out of there quickly enough.

"There's bodies and blood all over the place!" she yelled as she scrambled to the Kotts' house next door, and rang the doorbell.

Her heart was beating so hard she couldn't wait any longer for them to answer the bell, so she took off for the next house. This time someone came to the door.

A teenager who lived there called the police department to report what the highly emotional woman communicated to his parents on their doorstep. He made several calls in fact, because it took some time for the officers to respond. A diligent Boy Scout looking toward a law enforcement career, he clocked the time of his first call at 8:33 a.m. However, a snafu with LAPD's records logged only one call, reporting a possible homicide, at 9:14 a.m.

"You better get a police car over here right away," he told the dispatcher. "There's a man lying on the front lawn and blood all over the place. It looks like a bad one."

——

After the first three officers from the LAPD arrived, they quickly scanned the scene, first taking in the bodies on the lawn. Moving inside, they discovered the bodies inside the main house, noting that all the inside lights were off except for a desk lamp in the living room and one in the hall that led to some of the bedrooms.

The officers listened for sounds but heard only an eerie silence broken by the buzzing of flies hovering over the deceased. Their ears perked up, however, when they heard a dog barking at the rear of the property.

"Shhh, be quiet," a man's voice said.

As the three officers headed cautiously toward the guesthouse, they mentally prepared to find the shooter waiting for them inside the one-story red building.

When they burst in around 9:30 a.m., they saw a bare-chested teenager on the couch in the front room. He may have been unarmed, but he was, after all, the only person on the entire property who was still alive.

———

William Garretson was startled awake by Christopher barking again. Moments later, three police officers stormed through the front door, guns drawn and pointed at him.

"Freeze!" they yelled.

Now barking like crazy, Christopher charged straight for the officer who was holding a rifle on Garretson. The dog bit him on the leg, then jumped up and snapped his jaws around the tip of the barrel.

As that officer wrestled with the Weimaraner, the other two grabbed the teenager off the couch and pulled him outside to the patio, where they pushed him down and snapped handcuffs on him.

"What's wrong?" he asked, genuinely confused.

"Shut up!" they said.

"What's the matter?"

"We'll show you."

They took him out to the lawn, where they pushed him to the ground again, ripping a hole in the knee of his pant leg. Dragging him toward the closest body, they showed him a barefoot woman in a bloody nightgown, lying on her back. Garretson quickly averted his eyes.

Next, they took him sixty feet north to the limp body of a blond man lying on his right side in blood-stained clothes on the grass. Garretson would never forget the image of that man's eyes, still wide open.

The bodies were so mutilated and bloody that they were almost un-recognizable. Garretson initially thought the dead woman was the maid, Winnie Chapman, an African American in her midfifties. So that's what he told the officers.

A few minutes later, when he saw the maid talking to an officer across the yard, he realized his mistake. He later learned that the victim was actually Abigail Folger, who was twenty-five and white.

The officers took Garretson back to the guesthouse for questioning, then promptly arrested him. On their way past the white Ambassador in the driveway he saw a body slumped in the driver's seat. But Garretson couldn't see his face, so he couldn't identify him either.

Garretson was frightened. And even more confused.

How come I wasn't murdered? he wondered.

More than that, he was highly agitated and anxious because he'd been arrested for murder. He was informed that two other bodies were inside the main house, a man and a woman, for a total of five victims.

Within minutes of obtaining authorization to arrest Garretson, the officers walked him to the patrol car. On their way out the gate, an officer pressed the button to open it, even though he saw that it was covered with blood. This, of course, obliterated any chance of lifting a fingerprint, although Winnie Chapman had likely pressed that button already.

When the police realized that among the victims was Sharon Tate, a beautiful Hollywood ingénue and the pregnant wife of a famous director, the department responded quickly, with plenty of manpower. Within a few hours, the Cielo Drive property was swarming with law enforcement personnel.

By the afternoon, they numbered about forty, from detectives to super-visors and evidence techs, collecting blood samples and lifting finger-prints. There were so many investigators—officers from the LAPD's West LA and Robbery-Homicide Divisions, the Beverly Hills Police Department, and even the county coroner-medical examiner himself—that the LAPD's first investigative report didn't even try to list the order of their arrival.

Given the high-profile nature of the Tate murders, one of the homicide lieutenants assembled a team of veteran investigators, with Sergeants Michael J. McGann and Jess Buckles taking the lead, and three other detective sergeants assisting.

Reporters and photographers, who routinely listened to police scanners, showed up quickly, setting up camp outside the gate and crowding the long driveway with their bodies and equipment. Because the police had sealed off the perimeter, this was as close to the action as they could get.

Early police reports were purposely vague, but sensational: "It looked like a battlefield up there," a sergeant told the *New York Daily News*.

One neighbor caused confusion by telling the press that Terry Melcher, the previous tenant, still "owned" the place. But once it got out that the house was actually leased by Roman and Sharon Tate Polanski, word of the murders spread faster and wider than a California wildfire, first by word of mouth, then by broadcast news, followed by newspapers and magazines.

After a series of unsuccessful attempts by family members and associates to reach the victims by phone, Sharon's mother called the wife of William Tennant, Roman's business agent, to see if her husband could find out what was going on. She had Tennant paged at his tennis club.

Arriving at the crime scene in his tennis outfit around noon, Tennant pushed through the throng of media to talk to detectives. Going from body to body, he was able to confirm several of the victims' identities—Sharon, Gibby, and Voytek. And although he wasn't positive, he thought the man with the towel over his face was Jay Sebring.

He didn't recognize the kid in the white Ambassador, who remained John Doe 85 for most of the day, because no one had a chance to run his license plate and registration through the Department of Motor Vehicles to get a name and address.

Afterward, Tennant threw up from the horrors he knew he could never unsee.

———

While LAPD Sergeant McGann was observing the first autopsies at the county morgue in the Hall of Justice basement, his partner, Sergeant

Buckles, got a call from two sheriff's detectives working the murder of musician Gary Hinman in Topanga Canyon.

Sergeant Whiteley and Deputy Guenther said they thought their case might be related to the Tate slayings because the killers had written messages about pigs in the victims' blood at both scenes. They had a suspect in custody, a young guy who lived at the Spahn Movie Ranch with a group of hippies led by a Jesus Christ wannabe named Charlie.

But Buckles dismissed any connection, saying he was sure the Tate murders were "part of a big dope transaction."

When McGann asked Buckles what the call was about, the detective didn't even think enough of it to tell his partner. "It was nothing," Buckles said.

Looking back years later, McGann said, "That was a screw-up, a major screw-up. Let me tell you, we would have solved that case in a month if I'd known about this."

———

It was immediately obvious to investigators that the savagery was far too extreme to be the work of a lone assailant with a knife and a gun.

During the autopsies, the pathologists determined that the victims' massive deep cuts likely were made by a bayonet with a six-inch blade, a decidedly unusual murder weapon. Additionally, a large number of stab wounds typically indicated a crime of passion by someone who knew the victim. But there was nothing typical about this human slaughter.

Whoever had cut the overhead wires didn't seem to know what he was doing. One turned out to be a telephone cord; the other had once connected the button at the gate to a buzzer inside the house, but it was no longer in use.

After Sergeant McGann arrived around 1:30 p.m., he quickly made his first tour of the scene and all five victims. This was by far the worst and most grotesque crime scene he'd witnessed in all his years working homicides.

Peering first into the white Ambassador, he noted that the teenager in the driver's seat had been shot in the face, chest, and left arm. His right forearm was on the arm rest. A vertical cut on his left palm, which went between his small and ring fingers, looked like a defensive wound. It was the only visible cut on his body.

The ignition switch and emergency brake were both in the off position; the shift lever was in second gear. The boy's wristwatch, found on the back seat with its band severed, was apparently sliced off during his altercation with the killers.

Voytek Frykowski was lying on his right side on the lawn nearby, his left arm outstretched and perpendicular to his body. His hair was matted with blood, as were his purple shirt, leather vest, and multicolored pants. He had almost too many stab wounds to count, primarily on the exposed left side of his body. He died clenching a fistful of grass.

Abigail Folger's body was also lying on the lawn, south of the stone bungalow, between it and the guesthouse. Her face was marred with blood from several slashes to the left side of her face and chin. Her blood-soaked nightgown was ratty with tears from stab wounds that started at her breasts and ran down her body.

As McGann headed through the front door, past the blood spatters and the word "PIG" scrawled in blood, he crossed through the foyer into the living room. There, he found the very pregnant Sharon Tate lying in a fetal position on her left side in front of the sofa, facing the fireplace. Her pink and white bikini was drenched with blood from the stab wounds around her breasts and upper abdomen. She'd also been stabbed in the back of the right leg.

Jay Sebring, shot in the chest and also stabbed, was lying on his right side in the living room, about four feet from Sharon, in front of a chair. He had a sizable abrasion on the left side of his face, with bruising and swelling around that eye and across the bridge of his nose. A light-colored towel, also drenched in blood, had been placed over his head and face like a hood.

Curiously, Sharon's entire body was smeared with dried blood. Based on the blood pools that the officer from the Scientific Investigation Division (SID) sampled that day, investigators suspected that someone had moved Sharon's body from the front porch while her wounds were still fresh, and possibly Jay's as well.

The officer, who collected and typed a total of forty-five blood samples from the house and front porch area, determined that a large spot near the entryway matched Sharon's, just three feet from another large spot on the front porch that matched Jay's.

A three-strand nylon rope, forty-three feet and eight inches long, and about three-quarters of an inch in diameter, was wrapped twice around Sharon's neck, went up and over a ceiling beam, and hung freely down to the floor. The other end was wrapped one and a half times around Jay's neck and went under his body and toward the fireplace. They couldn't be sure if the victims had been hanging at some point, or if their bodies had simply been arranged that way.

Either way, it was a truly horrific scene. With the rope tying, so many stab wounds, and so much blood, especially the red-lettered message on the white door, these murders seemed ritualistic. Like black magic.

———

The LAPD kept their only suspect, William Garretson, in jail for two days. But after putting him through multiple interrogations and polygraph tests—which he passed—they determined that they couldn't connect him with the crime.

He was finally released at 2:00 p.m. on Monday, August 11, and immediately returned home to Lancaster, Ohio. Within a week his mother had filed a $1.25 million claim on his behalf against the city of Los Angeles, alleging the violation of his civil rights by false imprisonment. The claim was ultimately rejected.

Although Garretson had told detectives that he couldn't remember hearing any strange noises or whether he'd let the dog out that night, he later admitted at trial that he'd taken the Weimaraner out the back door to do his business.

He was lucky to be alive.

CHAPTER 9

"HOW COULD ANYBODY
BE SO CRUEL?"

That same Saturday evening, seventeen-year-old Barbara Hoyt was watching *Hobo Kelly* on TV in the kids' trailer at Spahn Ranch when Sadie came in and changed the channel.

Seeing that the murders they'd committed early that morning were all over the news, Sadie ran to get some of the other girls. "Come watch television with me," she said.

She also called for Tex, but he didn't want to watch TV, and Charlie was asleep, so she asked Clem, who had been present when Charlie had given them instructions the night before, and again when they returned. Until they saw the news stories, Sadie didn't know who they had just killed, so she was thrilled to learn that their pregnant victim had been a movie star and the wife of the director of *Rosemary's Baby*—one of the "beautiful people," as Sadie called them.

In her mind, they couldn't have selected a better set of victims to generate the kind of widespread fear, paranoia, and unrest that Charlie was hoping for.

"The Soul sure picked a good one," she said, which prompted a nefarious group chuckle.

The fact that the murders were not only making national but international news was, to Sadie, nothing short of far out.

———

The rest of the city of Los Angeles, however, was having a very different reaction as everyone learned the initial grisly details about the Tate murders.

Everyone but businessman Leno LaBianca and his wife Rosemary, that is, who were away from the news for much of the day, waterskiing at Lake Isabella with Rosemary's kids, twenty-one-year-old Suzan Struthers and her fifteen-year-old brother Frankie.

Married for the past decade, Leno and Rosemary had driven up to the lake the previous Tuesday with their speedboat for Frankie and his friends to use. They'd gone back that Saturday to bring him home, but Frankie was having such a great time they decided to let him stay an extra day with his friend's family, who had a cabin on the lake.

Born and raised in LA, Leno was a University of Southern California graduate who didn't like to talk about personal or business matters. Quiet and conservative, the gray-haired, hazel-eyed forty-four-year-old ran the supermarket chain his father had founded in 1920, the State Wholesale Grocery Company.

Leno had taken over as the company's president after his father died, and sold five of its nine stores to Mayfair Market. The remaining four were profitable until 1962, when Leno, a frequent gambler, began taking salary advances.

By outward appearances, the couple was doing well as Leno bought the speedboat and invested in a stable of race horses and several real estate deals.

Leno had lived in his family's house on Waverly Drive as a boy, then moved back there to stay rent-free after separating from his first wife, with whom he had a son and two daughters. He returned there a decade or so later with Rosemary in November 1968, after purchasing the home from his mother with the proceeds of the sale of the couple's former house on Woking Way, once owned by Walt Disney.

His wife, a vivacious thirty-eight-year-old brunette, had been adopted as a child in Arizona, then moved with her new family to Fullerton, California. After years of waitressing, she, too, came to run her own business, the Boutique Carriage dress shop, right next door to Leno's supermarket on North Figueroa, and not far from their house on Waverly.

Rosemary had recently confided in a girlfriend that she felt a foreign presence in their home. "Someone is coming into our house while we're away," she said. "Things have been gone through and the dogs are in the house when they should be outside and vice versa."

When she questioned Frankie and Suzan, they denied any involvement. Although they knew that Rosemary often left her keys in the car behind the house, her description sounded an awful lot like one of the Manson Family's creepy crawlers.

Leno, Rosemary, and Suzan headed back to LA from the lake that hot Saturday night with their speed boat on a trailer, towed behind their Thunderbird.

Arriving in Los Feliz around one o'clock Sunday morning, Leno and Rosemary dropped off Suzan at her apartment on Greenwood Place, the façade of which would be featured on the popular prime-time series *Melrose Place* more than twenty years later.

From there the couple headed over to the newsstand at the corner of Hillhurst and Franklin to buy a copy of the Sunday *Los Angeles Times* and Leno's usual racing form. There, they chatted with the vendor about the frightening and bizarre murders that had shaken everyone while they were at the lake.

Rosemary started crying as they talked about the vicious killings, described in the *Times*' front-page headline as "Ritualistic Slayings, Sharon Tate, Four Others Murdered."

"How could anybody be so cruel?" she asked.

By the time she and Leno arrived home that night, it was so late that they left the boat attached to the trailer out front, and went inside to get ready for bed.

———

Earlier that evening, Charlie gathered an even bigger group—Leslie, Sadie, Clem, Katie, Linda, and Tex—to discuss his vision for the second wave of the killing spree. He said he wanted to leave dead bodies and stir up fear all over the City of Angels, but with one big difference.

"Last night was too messy," he said, explaining that the first crew had caused too much fear and panic in their victims on Cielo Drive. So, this time he was coming along to make sure it was done right. Show them how it *should* be done.

Linda didn't really want to go out again, but she also didn't want to refuse Charlie. Leslie, on the other hand, didn't need any convincing. She'd felt left out the previous night. She also wanted to show Charlie that she believed in him when he said that what they were doing was necessary for the betterment of society. Sadie asked Bruce to come along, but he declined.

Tex and Sadie snorted some more speed from the Gerber's jar, got dressed in their familiar uniform of dark clothing, and climbed into the same yellow Ford sedan with the others. Charlie, armed with a .45-caliber automatic and a bayonet, took the wheel and started to drive.

No one questioned him as he spent several hours cruising around Los Angeles, searching for just the right target. Sometimes, he had Linda drive instead. It took him quite some time to decide.

His first stop was a church in Pasadena. He got out and approached the building only to return to the car. He said he'd wanted to hang a priest upside down and kill him as a symbolic gesture, but he couldn't get in because the doors were locked.

The next stop was a residence. But after peeking through the windows, Charlie said that one was out too. "Man, there were pictures of children in that house," he said. "I just couldn't do that."

From there, they headed for Pacific Palisades, where Charlie thought a motorist in the sports car next to them looked like a good victim. But the light changed and the car sped off before he could shoot the driver.

In the early hours of Sunday, August 10, the group wound up in the hilly, middle-class neighborhood of Los Feliz, near Griffith Park and its observatory, where Charlie headed down the winding Waverly Drive and parked on the street.

"Charlie, you're not going into that house, are you?" Linda said, referring to his friend Harold True's old place, where the Family used to drop acid and party.

"No, I'm going next door," he said.

Just like he said, Charlie walked up the long driveway at the adjacent home, at 3301 Waverly. It had been vacant during their last visit, so some of them had sex there during True's party.

The modest Spanish-style house sat atop a grassy hill that sloped down to the street, with a long, steep driveway that ran up the hill and curled around behind the house. They could tell it wasn't vacant anymore, because a 1968 Thunderbird was parked out front, with a speed boat attached to it.

Charlie came back a few minutes later to get Tex. They walked back up the driveway and stood at a front window, where they could see a man inside, sleeping on the sofa. Then they headed around back, where they found the door unlocked, and walked right in.

As Tex stood nearby, holding the silver bayonet, Charlie used his gun to prod the heavyset man in blue pajamas who had fallen asleep on the couch reading the *Los Angeles Times* sports section.

"Who are you?" the man asked. "What do you want?"

"We're not going to hurt you," Charlie said. "Don't be afraid."

Charlie moved calmly about the tastefully decorated room, trying to make the man believe this was just a robbery. He'd already told Tex that he didn't want the victims to know they were going to die this time.

"Don't scare them like last night," he'd said.

According to Tex, Charlie took the leather thong from his neck, told the man to roll over onto his stomach, then had Tex tie the man's hands with the cord. Tex made sure to use a square knot, which would tighten if the man tried to fight back and pull his wrists apart. The man was sitting down, but he was a hefty guy, 230 pounds and five feet eleven inches tall.

Asked if anyone else was in the house, the man told Charlie that his wife was in the bedroom. Charlie left for a moment, brought her into the living room, and had her sit on the floor, next to her husband's feet. Trying to cover up, the woman had pulled a nice blue dress over her short pink nightgown.

Still speaking calmly Charlie asked what money they had in the house. The woman offered up a small box that had a few bills in it, maybe seven dollars.

"We'll give you anything you want, just tell us," the man told Charlie, adding that they didn't have much cash around, but he could get more. "Let me take you to my store and you can get as much as you want."

"No, we just want what's here," Charlie said.

Satisfied that he'd set his crew on the right track, Charlie took his gun, grabbed the woman's wallet from her purse, and started to head out.

"Make sure the girls get to do some of it," he told Tex. "Both of them."

Leaving Tex to guard the victims with his bayonet, Charlie went out to the car to send in Leslie and Katie.

"Do you believe in me enough that you believe this is something that has to be done?" he asked Leslie.

"Yes," she said.

After giving his little motivational pep talk, he dispatched her and Katie into the house with some clean clothes to change into afterward.

As the girls walked into the living room, the woman pleaded with her captors to take what they wanted and go. But she and her husband learned soon enough that this was not a simple robbery after all.

As Tex started issuing directions, he quietly told Katie to go into the kitchen and get some knives, then instructed her and Leslie to take the woman back to the bedroom and kill her.

Once the women were out of the room, Tex proceeded to stab the man multiple times, starting with a forceful thrust through the throat.

Charlie had told Tex to take two pillowcases off the bed, place one over each of the victims' heads, then wrap the electrical cords from nearby table lamps around their necks and across their mouths, securing them like gags.

While Tex did as he was told with the man in the living room, Leslie and Katie did the same to his wife in the bedroom.

Katie told Sadie later that she tried to reassure the woman—and herself—that they weren't going to hurt her. "Everything is going to be okay," Katie told the woman as she sat on the bed, essentially blindfolded by the pillowcase.

But her captors knew that Leslie was holding her down so Katie could stab her. Once they all heard the man making gurgling sounds in the other room, trying to breathe with his throat cut, the woman started fighting back.

"Leno! What are you doing to my husband?" she screamed, forcing her way off the bed. "Leno!"

Grabbing hold of the cord they'd tied around her neck, the woman swung the heavy lamp base around her, which briefly kept Katie and Leslie at bay. The lady of the house, who weighed 128 pounds and stood at five feet six inches, was a fiery opponent.

The swinging lamp, coupled with the calls to her husband, made it difficult for Katie to stab her. But Leslie managed to knock the lamp out of her hands and wrestle her back down onto the bed. When Katie went to stab her in the collarbone, however, the knife bent and broke off in the woman's shoulder.

Leslie jumped up, ran to the doorway, and yelled for Tex to help them. "We can't kill her! It's not working!"

Tex was still at it in the other room, hearing Charlie's voice in his head again. He felt nothing more for the man on the couch than he had for the victims on Cielo Drive.

These people are already dead, the remnants of a dying culture.

Then, remembering Charlie's instruction, *Do something witchy,* Tex finished off the man by ripping open his button-up pajama top and carving "WAR" into his meaty belly.

Responding to Leslie's call, Tex came in right away and took over with his bayonet, repeatedly plunging the blade into the woman's back.

Leslie had been preparing for this moment—she'd even taken Tex's class on how to stab people to death—but the reality of actually doing it was something entirely different.

As she stood at the bedroom doorway she felt overwhelmed, staring into space with her back to Tex, and listening to the guttural sounds coming from the woman as Tex stabbed her to death.

Even so, she knew that if Charlie had asked her to kill babies—or even herself—at that moment she would have done so. She had surrendered herself completely, morally, and ethically to him and his philosophy. She'd also subverted any part of her personality that might have stopped these killings from happening. So, instead of feeling like all of this violence was wrong, she criticized herself for not being able to participate in it as enthusiastically as Tex and Katie seemed to be.

Tex came up behind her, took her by the shoulders, and turned her toward the woman, who no longer seemed to be breathing on the bedroom floor.

"Do something," he said, handing her a knife.

Leslie did as she was told. With the woman's dress and nightgown pulled up to expose her lower back and buttocks, Leslie stabbed the woman sixteen times.

"Do something witchy," Tex told Katie.

Heading into the living room, Katie could see that the man on the couch wasn't moving anymore, so she took a pearl-handled, two-tined carving fork and jabbed holes all over his rather ample abdomen, leaving the fork protruding from his stomach. She also plunged the entire blade of a brown-handled steak knife into his neck and left it there.

It was the perfect act to symbolize the lyrics from the Beatles' song "Piggies," which Charlie had played for them many times:

Have you seen the little piggies . . . What they need's a d**n good whacking . . . Everywhere there's lots of piggies . . . Clutching forks and knives to eat their bacon.

As the coup de grace, Katie grabbed a piece of paper, crumpled it up, dipped it in the man's blood, and wrote "HEALTER SKELTER" on the fridge, misspelling the term. She also wrote "RISE" and "DEATH TO PIGS" on the living room walls.

Leslie and Katie washed up in the kitchen sink and rear bathroom, while Tex showered to rinse off all the blood. Tex told Leslie to give him the change of clothes they'd brought from the ranch, and even though she wasn't bloody, he told her to change and put on some clothes belonging to the woman they'd just killed. Charlie's orders.

She and Katie wiped the rooms of their fingerprints, then went into the kitchen. Tex was hungry so they took some cheese, chocolate milk, and watermelon from the fridge and had a snack, not bothering to throw the discarded rinds in the garbage.

The only living creatures in the house they did not harm were the three dogs, one of which followed Tex around everywhere he went. Tex patted him on the head before they left.

Outside, as dawn was breaking, Charlie and the others were long gone.

The trio walked until they reached the reservoir, where Tex tossed the bayonet as far as he could into the water, then they lay down under a tree and slept for a while.

———

Meanwhile, after leaving Tex, Leslie, and Katie at the LaBiancas' house, Charlie drove Linda, Sadie, and Clem northwest to Pacoima, mistakenly believing that it was a predominantly African American community. Driving one exit too far, they ended up at a gas station in Sylmar where Charlie told Linda to put Rosemary's wallet in the women's restroom.

Charlie hoped that a black woman would find the wallet and get caught using Rosemary's credit cards, leading the police to think the LaBiancas had been killed by the Black Panthers. But Linda hid the wallet a little too well—inside the toilet tank, where it remained for months.

It was early Sunday morning when Charlie continued on to an apartment building in the beach town of Venice, where one of Linda's old lovers lived. Charlie told her to knock on his door, get inside, then cut his throat and shoot him with Sadie and Clem's help.

But Linda still didn't want to kill anyone, especially after what she'd witnessed at the Tate house. She'd recently discovered that *she* was pregnant, but hadn't told anyone. She'd been horrified—and scared for her own life—when she learned that one of the victims had been so close to giving birth.

After Charlie dropped Linda, Clem, and Sadie at the apartment complex, Linda purposely led her cohorts to the wrong floor and knocked on a stranger's door. When the occupant opened up a crack, Linda apologized and said she had the wrong apartment. Then she, Sadie, and Clem left and hitchhiked back to the ranch.

———

Back at the reservoir, Tex, Katie, and Leslie woke up and dumped their bloody clothes before heading to the freeway to catch a ride back to the ranch.

Once they were safely at Spahn, Leslie took out the seven dollars in cash that the woman had given them, then burned the stolen clothes.

Now that it was over, Leslie felt as if her inner rage had been released, as if an immense burden had been lifted from her soul. Everything felt lighter. When one of George Spahn's dogs came over and licked her hand, he seemed to be smiling at her. She felt as if they'd done something right.

Leslie boasted to Dianne Lake, now sixteen, about what she'd done, hoping to impress the teenager with her story of repeatedly stabbing a woman who was already dead.

"The more I did it, the more fun it was," she said.

Tex told Katie to hide out for a day or so in a tent in the woods of Devil's Canyon, near the ranch. After Charlie came back, he took her and Leslie to stay with some friends in nearby Box Canyon at a cult Charlie had tried to take over known as the Fountain of the World.

———

Perhaps sensing her son was in trouble that day, Tex's mother reached out to one of his friends in LA. Tex hadn't called his family in six months, she said, and she was worried about him.

After Tex's friend got in touch, Tex used his mother's call as an excuse to get some time away from Charlie and the ranch. He told Charlie that the FBI had come to his mother's house looking for him, but really, he just needed a break from the chaos.

Charlie agreed that it was best for Tex to leave, and told him to hang out in the desert for a while. So Tex set off with Juan Flynn, the ranch hand, for an isolated outpost in Death Valley, where the Family had spent some time during the winter months, scouting things out.

When a couple of sheriff's deputies stopped them a couple of miles down the highway, Tex told them he was Charles Montgomery, the same name he'd used when he'd bought his 1936 Dodge truck. Montgomery was his mother's maiden name, but it was also the name of his second cousin, Tom Montgomery, the sheriff of Collin County, Texas. Tex found it especially amusing to give that name to law enforcement while he was on the lam for murder.

The deputies searched the truck for stolen property, but never found the two Volkswagen motors hidden in back. Nor did they realize they'd had in their brief custody the guy who had led the Manson Family in murdering seven innocent people in the past few days.

CHAPTER 10

"CALL THE POLICE!"

Rosemary LaBianca's son, Frankie, got dropped off at their house on Waverly Drive around eight thirty on Sunday night, August 10. He thought something was up right away because the car with the boat was still parked out front. He knew his mom and stepdad had driven home late Saturday, but they never left the boat out overnight like that.

As Frankie walked up the long driveway leading to the house, he could see that the lights were on in the master bedroom closet and kitchen. He tried to peer in through the kitchen windows, but the shades were drawn, which was strange. His parents never closed the shades either.

By habit, he tried to enter through the back door, but it was locked, so he tried knocking and got no answer. Seeing the water skis sitting on top of the fender of his mother's Thunderbird coupe by the garage, he figured his parents had come home from the lake and taken the skis out of the boat so they wouldn't get stolen. But why not put them away?

Then he went to the northwest side of the house, where he called out for his parents through the windows. When he still got no response, he decided to go call for help.

Something was definitely wrong and he wasn't going to chance climbing in alone to find out.

Planning to call his sister from a pay phone, Frankie walked a few blocks to the Charburger stand on Hyperion Boulevard. When he tried calling the restaurant where Suzan worked, her boss said she wasn't there that night, but he agreed to phone her at home and ask her to contact Frankie at Charburger.

After Suzan called Frankie back, and he reported what he'd seen at the house, she and her fiancé, Joe Dorgan, drove over to pick him up.

As the three of them pulled up to the house around 10:25 p.m. Suzan also noticed that the inside lights were on. Walking around to the rear of the house by the garage, Suzan pulled Rosemary's keys out of the ignition of her car.

Using the keys to open the back door, Joe and Frankie purposely left Suzan behind for her own protection. This was lucky, because the scene they discovered inside was worse than any nightmare they could have conjured up on their own.

Leno was lying on his back on the floor between two couches and the coffee table, with a bloody pillowcase over his head. The cord of the lamp on the table next to him was tied around his neck and across his mouth. The carving fork stuck into his stomach was the same utensil that Leno and his father had used to carve turkeys and hams at family dinners.

When Suzan tried to step farther into the house, Joe stopped her so she didn't have to witness the gore. "Everything's okay," he lied. "Let's get out of here."

But Suzan could see from the red words scrawled on the fridge that Joe wasn't telling the truth.

Rather than look for Rosemary, Joe started to call the police from the kitchen wall phone, but decided that he'd better not in case he disturbed fingerprints or other evidence the killers had left.

Traumatized, they ran to a neighbor's house, shouting, "Call the police!"

The neighbor, frightened by the disturbance, thought they were juvenile pranksters, so she didn't answer the door. She did call the police, but only to report the prank.

With no answer at the first house, Suzan, Joe, and Frankie ran across the street to try another neighbor. This time the homeowner let them in, but because they seemed so flighty and nervous, she decided she should call the police herself, repeating the story that Joe had told her: the neighbors had been stabbed.

———

Dispatched at 10:35 p.m., two officers from LAPD's Hollywood Division pulled up to the house in a black and white patrol car, where they were met by Suzan, Frankie, and Joe.

One of the officers tested the front door and found it unlocked, so he walked right in. But as soon as he saw Leno's body in the living room, he immediately came out to call for backup, an ambulance, and a supervisor while his partner secured the rear door.

The paramedics, who arrived five minutes later, pronounced Leno and Rosemary dead on arrival.

———

LAPD Homicide Sergeant Danny Galindo was still at the office typing up reports from the Tate murders when he got a call from a reporter just after midnight on Monday, August 11. Something about a knife sticking out of a murder victim's neck.

Minutes later, he got a call to head over to a double homicide in Los Feliz.

Galindo had been busy that week. Placed in charge of guarding the evidence at the Tate house, he'd stayed overnight there on Saturday. He'd tried to find a place to sleep near the front door, but there was so much blood on the floors and walls that the only clear spot he could find was in the back of the house.

Galindo arrived at the crime scene in Los Feliz around 1:00 a.m., where he was soon joined by another sergeant and two detectives assigned to assist in the investigation by a different homicide lieutenant than the one running the Tate team.

Within a matter of hours, more than thirty officers, detectives and their supervisors, photographers, and evidence techs had arrived at the house.

Although Galindo and the other detectives assigned to the LaBianca murder team were less experienced than those investigating the higher-profile Tate killings, they had seen enough cases to recognize that this was an unusually gruesome scene of torture and mutilation.

With the letters carved into Leno's torso and the shallow pairs of holes all over his abdomen, apparently made by the carving fork protruding from his stomach, this murder was more twisted than any they'd ever seen. By far.

Someone had placed a throw pillow over Leno LaBianca's head, which was still covered with the white pillowcase. Noting the electrical cord tied around Leno's neck, Galindo wrote in his report that he initially thought the victim had been "throttled," even though the blood from Leno's many stab wounds had seeped into the couch cushions and floor around his body.

That may have been because Galindo couldn't see Leno's throat wound or the brown-handled knife stuck into his neck that the reporter had tipped him about, which were covered by the pillowcase. One of the paramedics must have talked to the press.

Leno's wrists showed purplish bruising and ligature marks, as if he'd struggled against the thin leather cord wrapped around them. The lack of defensive wounds on his fingers indicated that he'd been tied up the whole time he was being stabbed to death.

As Galindo searched the rest of the house, he found Rosemary lying face down on the bedroom floor, amid signs of a struggle. Her head was also encased with a white pillowcase, secured in the same fashion.

The large bloody stain on the carpet below her toes indicated that she'd crawled two feet from where she'd been stabbed, which was as far as the cord around her neck let her go before it went taut and pulled two lamps, connected by the same cord, to the floor. Dollar bills were scattered around, as were some small items that likely had been knocked off the nightstands.

Rosemary's nightgown and dress had been pulled up to expose her lower back and buttocks, which were covered with stab wounds and scratches.

The investigators pulled several loose hairs from Rosemary's pink-polished fingertips, then wrapped her hands in plastic bags for further forensic analysis. They were later determined to be dog hairs.

Galindo found traces of blood in the kitchen sink and also on the floor of the rear bathroom. Under the wash basin, a roll of paper towels had been soaked with water and still had a reddish tinge of blood, which proved to be Rosemary's. Analysis of the messages on the walls and fridge showed they were written in Leno's blood.

At first nothing seemed to be ransacked or missing. In fact, after searching for five or six hours, Galindo determined that the killers had left many valuables in the house untouched, such as Leno's one-carat diamond ring and two of Rosemary's rings, which were adorned with many small diamonds.

The killers didn't take Leno's cache of weapons—several unloaded rifles, shotguns, and handguns—either. Nor did they take the metal case containing his coin collection; two bags of mint nickels, worth about two hundred dollars; or a gallon jar full of loose change, all of which were right out in the open.

Galindo and another sergeant finally found Leno's wallet, which contained some ID cards and a little cash, in the glove compartment of his T-Bird, as well as a black briefcase of business records in the trunk.

In the end, the only item they could determine was missing was Rosemary's wallet, containing her driver's license, her checkbook, and some credit cards. Her handbag was still sitting open on top of a liquor cabinet in the dining room, its contents disheveled.

If this was a simple robbery, the detectives wondered, why leave all these valuable items? And why stick around long enough to eat and leave watermelon rinds in the kitchen sink?

"It wouldn't indicate to me, as a policeman, that a ransacking had occurred for the purpose of stealing or burglarizing," Galindo testified later.

Because the Tate and LaBianca homicide teams had different supervisors, in those days the detectives didn't even think to compare notes, let alone recognize the parallels between the murders, which was odd given that Galindo—and the SID detective who collected blood samples—had been to both scenes.

Investigators lifted numerous latent prints at the house. After an extensive elimination process, they culled a few usable sets, which they spent the next couple of months comparing against more than forty-five thousand suspects'.

They also conducted handwriting analyses, trying to narrow the suspect list for the person who wrote the messages in blood by analyzing their height, and whether the author was left- or right-handed. They determined that whoever wrote "RISE" was at least five feet eight inches tall, because the message was printed a foot higher than that.

———

The pathologists who did the autopsies counted forty-one stab wounds on Rosemary's body and ten on Leno's, including the fatal thrust to his throat, which severed the carotid artery. Those in Rosemary's lower back were not as deep as the others and, because they didn't bleed much, indicated that the killer may have stabbed her repeatedly after she was already dead.

The cause of death was clear for both of them: massive hemorrhaging from multiple stab wounds to the neck and trunk or abdomen. But the motive for this senseless violent slaying was still a big question mark.

CHAPTER 11

DRUG BURN OR ROBBERY GONE WRONG?

Long before news stories or images went viral on social media, fear and panic about the series of brutal murders spread quickly through the neighborhoods of LA by phone, radio, and TV, followed soon afterward by newspapers and magazines.

Los Angeles was a town where suspense thrillers were filmed, but this was as if a horror movie had come to life. Never before had so many homicides come in such a quick succession or monstrous fashion.

This story was so shocking and sensational that it was splashed across the front page of newspapers nationwide, many of which ran their headlines—such as "Terror in L.A. Suburbs, 'Ritual' Murders Reach Seven"—*above* the masthead.

Although most readers took it all in, their insides churning, Sadie didn't bother to continue watching the TV news for reports on the second night of killings. "All I heard on the news was 'Tate, Tate, Tate,'" she said later. "I just shut it off."

The general population, however, wanted to learn as much as they could about what had happened, although at this point, no one had any answers, which left Angelinos feeling insecure, anxious, and frightened. All they knew was that one or more crazies were roaming around, breaking into people's homes in the middle of the night, shooting and cutting up innocent residents.

Knowing that the only suspect thus far had been cleared certainly didn't help, because that meant the real killers were still out there, and their motives remained a mystery.

It had already been a year of national social upheaval. As race riots raged and protesters marched in opposition to the unpopular war in Vietnam, Richard Nixon had taken his place in the Oval Office that January, and Sirhan Sirhan admitted in court that he'd shot and killed presidential candidate Robert Kennedy.

But these dangers were closer to home and harder to ignore. Mothers dragged their kids to the beauty parlor rather than leave them home alone, but they couldn't escape the gore even there. All they had to do was pick up a magazine like *TIME* and read the story "Nothing but Bodies" to be reminded of the grim details.

After learning that the owner of their local supermarket had been brutally murdered in his living room just a few blocks away, families living in Los Feliz felt like they were at Ground Zero.

This quiet, upper-middle-class neighborhood had always seemed so safe with its palm-tree-lined streets, lush green slopes peppered with one- and two-story Spanish-style or colonial houses, and yards well-tended by the doctors, lawyers, businesspeople, working musicians, and actors who lived there.

Before the murders, kids used to cut through the canyon to get to Griffith Park or hike up to the observatory. But not after the news broke.

"You guys are not going to that park anymore," their mothers decreed, some of whom sent their children to live with relatives in safer areas or outside the city limits entirely.

The wealthy hired extra bodyguards and bought alarm systems or watchdogs, which tripled in price. One gun store in Beverly Hills sold two hundred weapons in just two days. Actors like Steve McQueen began carrying a firearm at all times, including to the funeral of his close friend Jay Sebring.

But it didn't matter whether you were a middle-class Joe or a wealthy

Hollywood celebrity, hiding behind the security gates of your luxurious estate. The city at large was on high alert as everyone made sure to lock his doors and windows. No one felt safe—in his home or otherwise.

———

The police usually tried to prevent widespread panic by saying very little to the media, but in this case, LAPD's top brass flatly denied seeing any ties between the two sets of bizarre killings from the outset, noting that the victims lived in different parts of the city and didn't know one another.

"I don't see any connection between this murder and the others," one high-ranking official told the Associated Press (AP) at the LaBianca crime scene. "They're too widely removed."

Although one sergeant acknowledged "a similarity" between the two cases, he was in the minority. "Whether it's the same suspect or a copycat we just don't know," he told the AP.

Despite the seventeen sergeants and two lieutenants working the two cases within the LAPD, the Tate and LaBianca teams continued to work independently.

Still convinced the Tate murders were drug-related and tied to the lifestyles of the rich and famous, the detectives on that case saw no reason to share information with colleagues investigating what they saw as the unrelated murder of a businessman and his wife.

The media, on the other hand, did not hesitate to draw parallels between the two cases, noting that the detectives refused to even consider questions about such details.

"The strikingly similar features of both murder cases were numerous," a United Press International (UPI) story stated, noting that in both cases the killers viciously stabbed multiple victims multiple times and left messages written in the victims' blood.

Ironically, the pair of sheriff's detectives who *did* see a connection didn't follow up again with the LAPD after the LaBianca murders, though to be fair the investigators in that case purposely didn't release the fact that "HEALTER SKELTER" had been written on the fridge.

Both sets of murders would likely have been solved much sooner if that bloody phrase—which was also found scrawled in several places at Spahn Ranch and ultimately provided the prosecution with a motive for the murders—had been shared, at least among the detectives. It also would have helped matters if fewer egos had been at stake. Yet detectives failed to explore the very obvious connections the media had already pointed out.

———

As soon as William Garretson was eliminated as a suspect, the Tate homicide team began to pursue several theories.

For a time, detectives thought the ritualistic clues—such as the messages in blood, mutilation, and rope-tying—could have been linked somehow to Sharon and Roman's involvement in satanic and vampire-themed movies, but they soon discarded that theory.

Over the Labor Day weekend, Sergeant McGann, one of the lead detectives on that team, wrote up the first lengthy investigative report and a timeline of the victims' activities the day of the murders. He also laid out the three scenarios that he and his team were pursuing.

As they continued to gather background on the victims, McGann and his team ultimately rejected two of these original scenarios—that this was a robbery gone wrong or a hired killing—in favor of a third, that the murders were drug-related, which was underscored by the activities at the house the day of the murder that were directly related to doing or buying drugs. Based also on the victims' "loose" celebrity lifestyle and drug-infused parties, the "goodly amount of narcotics" found on the property—as one report put it—and Voytek's friendship with known drug traffickers and a Pan Am pilot, the detectives thought the slayings could have been a revenge killing related to the smuggling of drugs into the victims' Hollywood crowd.

Two traffickers had partied recently at the house and had talked to Voytek about being the first to try MDA, with which one of them apparently did supply him. Detectives went on to establish that the other trafficker came by the Tate house on Friday afternoon before the murders to share a bottle of wine with Voytek and discuss a larger MDA delivery, now that Voytek had some capsules to test.

Jay's receptionist told police that her ex-boyfriend, a playboy and a known drug dealer, had also delivered cocaine and mescaline to Voytek and Jay that day. Voytek and Jay told the dealer that they wanted more so he left to try to get some, but he did not return.

Born Thomas John Kummer in Detroit, Jay had used his four years as a navy barber as a stepping-stone to make his fortune in LA as Hollywood's master of men's hair design. By the age of thirty-five, he had already created iconic looks for celebrities including actors Steve McQueen, Warren Beatty, and Henry Fonda as well as musical artists Frank Sinatra, Sammy Davis Jr., and Jim Morrison.

Jay could earn as much as $2,500 for a single haircut, because his clients often paid for a round-trip flight to their shooting or performance locations. With this kind of money to burn, Jay Sebring lived in the fast lane, a fitting lifestyle for someone who had taken his new name from the Sebring International Raceway in Florida and loved to speed around town in his black Porsche.

Told by witnesses that Jay was a kinky ladies' man who was constantly high on coke, detectives knew he was at the very least a recreational drug user, based on the cocaine, pot, and "brown gummy substance" they found in his Porsche. And based on the large cocaine purchase he'd made earlier that week, they suspected he was dealing it as well.

The day before the murders, Jay told his receptionist that he'd just been "burned" on a buy of two thousand dollars' worth of bad cocaine. She told police that he'd probably have done almost anything to get back at the supplier.

Likewise, detectives learned that Voytek was not only a heavy recreational drug user, but he also planned to start supplying friends with MDA, the new party drug formally known as Methylene Dioxy Amphetamine. Police found ten capsules of MDA and some other pills in Voytek's nightstand, plus a stash of hash and a bag of pot in the living room.

When the victims' toxicology tests came back on August 22, MDA was found in the blood of both Voytek and Gibby, which bolstered the detectives' theory that the murders were drug-related.

During her daily afternoon visit with her psychiatrist, Gibby had discussed her drug use, which was tied to her disappointment with Voytek, whom she was trying to leave. Gibby was the daughter of Peter Folger, the president of Folger Coffee Co., and heiress to the coffee fortune.

After graduating from Radcliffe College in Cambridge, Massachusetts, Gibby worked at the University of California Art Museum in Berkeley and also at the Haight-Ashbury Free Clinic. She moved to New York and worked at a bookstore where the Polish novelist Jerzy Kosinski introduced her to Voytek.

She and Voytek started dating, then drove across the country to LA, where they'd been living together ever since. Gibby and Sharon had both invested in Jay's trend-setting hair business, but Gibby's main focus was on doing social work in Watts after the riots there.

Voytek's wealthy father had subsidized Roman's first film, so Voytek and Roman had remained close. And although thirty-two-year-old Voytek had tried his hand at writing and filmmaking, he wasn't very good at either avocation, so he was living off Gibby's family money.

With his contacts, his outgoing personality, and his constant invitations for people to come over to the house, selling drugs must have looked like a fast and lucrative way to make some cash of his own.

Because of her pregnancy if nothing else, Sharon Marie Tate was the most drug-free of the bunch. She'd been working hard to make a name for herself as an actress, starting out with bit parts on TV, including *The Beverly Hillbillies* and *Petticoat Junction*. Early on she had small parts in movies such as *The Americanization of Emily* and *The Sandpiper*, but her appearances were brief or deleted entirely.

She'd met Roman in the summer of 1966, when he hired her for his movie *The Fearless Vampire Killers*. Although she was engaged to Jay Sebring at the time, she fell in love with Roman, and that was that.

Jay, who had met Sharon at a studio preview three years earlier, was upset by the breakup. But after meeting Roman, Jay realized he actually liked the man, so the three of them stayed friends. Jay and Sharon remained quite close, and he often came over to the house, although he typically didn't stay the night.

When Sharon and Roman were married in London in January 1968, the media ate up their wedding and cake-cutting photos: Sharon wore a yellow taffeta mini dress with puffy shoulders and a mock turtle neck, and little white flowers in her hair. Roman sported a mod long-sleeved outfit, with a white ruffle at the neck. It wasn't long before Sharon got pregnant.

Her profile was on the rise after she costarred in the 1967 film *Valley of the Dolls*. But at the time of her death, she was still mostly known as Roman's beautiful wife. It was her murder that made her a household name.

———

The scope and emotional nature of this high-profile investigation added pressure to solve it—and quickly—which likely was the cause of some Keystone Cops–style mistakes. For example, police pulled sheets from the linen closet to cover the bodies, but didn't bring the sheets to the morgue.

Although the SID officer collected forty-five blood samples, he failed to take key specimens from pools of blood in the living room and on the front lawn and walkway. He also failed to run blood subtypes to differentiate between the victims, which caused problems later when the samples were too old to do so.

As officers walked through the numerous pools on the front walkway, they tracked blood in and out of the house on their shoes, which hampered the ability to properly determine the killers' and victims' movements.

One or more officers accidentally kicked three pieces of a broken wooden gun grip, sending two under a dining room chair in the living room, and one onto the front porch, which obliterated any usable fingerprints. No one would admit to displacing them from their original location.

That said, two usable fingerprints *were* collected at the house—one from the front door and one from the door in Sharon's bedroom that led out to the pool.

The detectives spent a good amount of time chasing down leads on a pair of horn-rimmed glasses found, lenses down and frames up, near the two blood-marked steamer trunks.

With the FBI's help, detectives were able to determine that the broken gun grip came from a .22-caliber High Standard Longhorn revolver, also known as a Buntline. Designed by Ned Buntline, only 2,700 of these rather rare guns had been made and sold by 1970, two of which were given to the famous Old West deputy sheriff Wyatt Earp.

As detectives pursued all kinds of leads over the next few months, they interviewed various gun and Buck knife vendors, optical lens manufacturers, as well as small- and big-time drug dealers who ran in the same circles as the Tate victims and sold drugs to other Hollywood celebrities. They also flew to Washington DC, Massachusetts, New York, and even Ocho Rios, Jamaica, but most of the leads didn't pan out. Missing some crucial information, the investigators were looking too far afield when the killers were right there in their own back yard.

———

Roman Polanksi learned of his wife's death while he was still in London, working on a screenplay. He had been planning to fly home in a few days.

Because he'd been talking daily with Sharon, he'd thought it was her calling. But it was his agent on the phone that Saturday, crying.

"My reaction first was, naturally, no reaction, stunned disbelief," Roman recalled later.

In shock, he went for a long walk with some friends, but he was so overwrought that they called a doctor, who gave him a sedative to make him sleep.

Flying back to Los Angeles as soon as he could, he sobbed much of the way in a friend's lap. The house was still a crime scene, but it was too traumatic for him to sleep there anyway. He went into seclusion, staying with friends.

Although Roman said publicly that the police were "quite human and wonderful," other sources said he was frustrated by their lack of progress so he and some friends, including actors Warren Beatty, Peter Sellers, and Yul Brynner, put up a twenty-five-thousand-dollar reward for information leading to the arrest of his wife's killers.

Rudi Altobelli, the owner of the now tainted house, was still in Rome at the time of the murders. He returned to LA immediately, but was so upset that his former tenant, Terry Melcher, invited him to stay in his guesthouse in Malibu. Altobelli remained there for six months, until he could handle going back to his own place on Cielo Drive.

CHAPTER 12

RAID AT SPAHN RANCH

The Manson Family showed up on law enforcement's radar almost by accident. During the summer of 1969, property owners and car dealers near Spahn Ranch had been complaining to the sheriff's department about a group of dirty hippies who were living in squalor at the ranch, and had amassed a suspicious collection of Volkswagen buses, dune buggies—and guns.

The neighbors didn't know the half of what was going on, but they were certainly scared by the armed hippies who patrolled roads at night, shooting off their weapons and generally harassing and threatening people.

After the complaints started coming in, sheriff's deputies came out to the ranch more often. As they, too, were confronted by these aggressive armed men, their suspicions were also aroused by the odd mix of cars and auto parts they saw scattered around the property. At the same time, the LASD was also hearing reports of vehicles and parts being stolen from local dealers.

Detectives can be territorial, protective, and unwilling to share investigative details with other agencies. But in Los Angeles County— California's largest in terms of population—information sharing was and still is even more crucial, because the many different geographical sub-regions fall under the jurisdiction of so many separate and also overlapping law enforcement teams.

While the LAPD was responding to the series of senseless slayings that had sent waves of panic across the city, separate teams of investigators at the LASD were looking into a suspected auto theft ring at Spahn Ranch as well as the murder of Gary Hinman in Topanga Canyon.

At this point the LASD didn't know that the crimes in their jurisdiction were related to one another, let alone to the homicides that the LAPD were investigating with separate teams that still weren't talking to each other.

That said, both agencies were looking into the murder of a sixteen-year-old boy whose body had been found in Topanga and suspected his death might be connected to the hippy group at Spahn. However, neither agency had come up with any solid leads so far.

Frank Retz, who owned the adjacent parcel, urged George Spahn to force Charlie and his unbathed runaways and twentysomething do-nothings to leave. He even enlisted one of the longtime ranch hands, Donald "Shorty" Shea, to try to help move the eviction along any way he could.

But George was caught between two conflicting forces. Several of Charlie's girls, who lived in a trailer next door to his house, cooked and cared for him. He particularly liked Lynette Fromme, the redhead with whom he'd struck up a special friendship.

George was the one who gave her the nickname "Squeaky," which is how she is referred to by the media even today. Some say that George named her after Squeaky, his red mule; others say the name stemmed from the timber of her voice or the high-pitched sounds she made when George touched her leg.

Gossip had it that Lynette also spent time in bed with George, rumors she fed with affectionate gestures, such as stroking his shoulders while standing behind his chair at the table, and also by bragging about what a good lover he was.

Lynette helped George see what she wanted him to, never letting on that she was Charlie's eyes and ears, too, always looking out for his and the Family's interests and keeping him informed.

Nonetheless, George ate up the attention, largely oblivious to what the Family was up to at the ranch—and beyond.

———

Starting in July, sheriff's deputy William Gleason conducted a five-week investigation into the suspected criminal activities at Spahn Ranch, which involved collecting community complaints as well as reports by LASD and LAPD officers, city firefighters, and two informants.

Gleason was told by a "confidential reliable informant," who had been staying at the ranch since July, that he'd seen weapons in practically every building. Men were carrying loaded guns at all times, he said, even keeping them at arm's reach while they slept. He also said he'd been threatened by Charles Manson, the leader of the approximately twenty-five young people in the group.

Initially, most of what Gleason knew about Manson was what he'd gleaned from the ex-con's rap sheet: The thirty-four-year-old was still on parole from federal prison after serving two back-to-back sentences for stealing US Treasury checks, auto theft, and pimping. Booking records showed Manson was five-feet-seven, weighed 140 pounds, had brown hair and eyes, a tattoo of a woman's head on each arm, and a one-inch scar over his left eye, but no convictions on violent crimes.

Gleason, whose duties also involved collecting intelligence on criminal motorcycle gangs, noticed that Manson and Danny DeCarlo had been arrested on suspicion of rape against DeCarlo's wife at Spahn in June, but the charges were dropped.

By August 13, Gleason had learned enough to label Charles Milles Manson as suspect #1, the leader of an armed auto theft ring, citing a number of incidents to back up his claims in a search warrant affidavit.

LAPD officer Dale Butler, who worked in the county jail and also ran an auto business, reported that Manson was having his men install engines and other parts into dune buggies that Manson had bought from him for $2,300 in a wad of hundred-dollar bills.

Manson had also purchased an engineless dune buggy from Butler, who had placed a VW engine into it himself. The rest of the VW was subsequently stolen from Butler's storage yard.

During the investigation, the LAPD got a bird's-eye view of the operation by flying helicopters over the ranch and the hills three miles north, near Devil's Canyon, where they saw dune buggies, VW buses, parts, and engines—out in the open and hidden under sleeping bags on a flatbed truck. A firefighter later found Butler's stolen car body there, and was threatened by several members of Manson's group.

On another occasion, Manson bragged to two LAPD uniformed officers at the ranch that he and his friends had plenty of weapons. Also boasting that he'd done time for auto theft, he said his friends had rifles trained on them at that very moment—standard procedure whenever the law set foot on "their" land.

Manson was so brazen that he even called the LAPD to arrange to pick up three loaded "Panama" clips for a .30-caliber carbine that he said had fallen out of his dune buggy on the highway.

During a mini-raid in the early hours of July 28, LASD deputy Samuel Olmstead spoke to a man who identified himself as Charles Milles Summers, a member of the Satan's Slaves biker club. He said he was acting as a lookout because the group was anticipating an attack by the Black Panthers. Gleason later learned that Summers was actually Manson.

"We got into a hassle with a couple of those black motherf***ers and we put one of them into the hospital," Summers told Olmstead. "Join up with us. Those guys are out to kill you just like they are out to kill us . . . If we join together we could solve this problem."

Manson explained that a black man had come to ride a horse at the ranch and "made advances" toward some of the women in Manson's group, so several of his men beat up the guy. Thinking the black man had been sent by the Black Panthers, Manson said he thought the Panthers were going to come back en masse and attack the Family in retaliation.

A sheriff's deputy later reported that top brass at the LASD had been very secretive about preparations for the raid, asking for information to be submitted in memos with a cover sheet so no one else could read them, and also issuing a verbal "hands off" order not to arrest Manson and his group at Spahn. This frustrated many of the deputies who had wanted to pursue Manson's numerous parole violations and believed that for some unknown reason the ex-con was being protected "in a fire-free zone."

A couple of days later, a city firefighter patrolling the ranch talked to a man named Jack in front of a building, where several "heavy-caliber" rifles were visible inside. After seeing two men and two women shooting guns from a parked car nearby, the firefighter asked Jack if he knew them.

"Oh, yeah, they're some of our people," Jack said. "We have a guard at each road in with a rifle and a telephone. So anyone comes in, we'll know."

After visiting the ranch to get a lay of the land on August 4, Gleason wrote up the search warrant affidavit to show he had probable cause that a felony had been or could be committed by using items Manson had collected: "stolen automobile parts, including but not limited to VW frames, engines, transmissions and carts thereof, and automatic pistols and rifles."

Summers, aka Manson, was listed in the affidavit as one of two informants, the other being the confidential informant who fingered Manson as the group leader.

Noting the intel that the ranch was equipped with telephones and an alarm system, Gleason got a judge to sign off on a warrant on August 13, with permission to serve it during a surprise raid while the group was sleeping. But for whatever reason, the LASD waited three days to take action.

———

On August 13, Linda left Spahn in a ranch hand's car. Charlie had instructed her to give a message—"Everything's going to be alright"—to Bobby and Mary, who were still being held in separate jails. But instead, Linda headed east to Taos, New Mexico, where her husband was staying. As long as she didn't go to the police, she figured her baby Tonya would be safe at the ranch.

Two days later, biker Alan Springer brought a group of his Straight Satans brothers to the ranch to pull out their boy, Danny DeCarlo. The last time Springer had visited the ranch, he'd found DeCarlo passed out in the filthy bunkhouse, which was thick with flies and lined with a cache of guns: a .45-caliber automatic, a 9-millimeter Polish Radom, a 1903 Springfield rifle, an M-1 semi-automatic carbine with an M-2 stock on it, a 12-gauge police rifle gun, a .22 rifle, and a machine gun.

None of the weapons belonged to any Family member in particular, but Charlie really liked the Buntline, which he obtained in a trade for DeCarlo's truck with a friend of Bruce's. DeCarlo, who didn't authorize the trade, was not pleased. When the gun disappeared only a few Family members knew that Tex had thrown it into some bushes after the Tate murders.

DeCarlo, Springer, and some of the other bikers had been hanging out at the ranch at Charlie's urging, having sex with the girls. But after hearing Charlie's whole spiel about tearing society apart, most of them thought he was nuts. Springer believed DeCarlo was being brainwashed, and therefore needed to be removed for his own safety and brought back to Venice, where he belonged.

The night Springer came to rescue DeCarlo, he and his buddies stood on the boardwalk, looking for a fight. They wanted to rip up the place and beat down the hippies, but all they did was hassle a few of them and take a gun off Clem.

Sadie didn't help matters, trying to act tough. "We can take care of the Straights like we took care of them five piggies," she said.

DeCarlo tried to keep the peace and get his brothers to leave before anything serious happened. "Let's go down and have a beer," he said, shooing them toward their motorcycles with the hope they would head down to the Valley.

Before they left, the bikers found a missing sword that had belonged to one of their brothers. Charlie had bragged how he'd cut off a guy's ear with it. The group took the sword back that night to return it to its rightful owner, but they couldn't persuade DeCarlo to come with them. So, he was at Spahn with the rest of the Family when the sheriff's deputies showed up an hour later.

———

It was 5:45 a.m. on August 16 when 102 sheriff's deputies converged on Spahn Ranch in two helicopters and twenty-five patrol cars and motorcycles.

A group of deputies approached the front door of what appeared to be the main building, knocked, and announced themselves and their warrant. Seeing and hearing people moving around, they marched inside when no one responded.

They found eight sleeping bags on the floor in another building, from which the occupants had fled, apparently after being alerted by the alarm. Half a dozen or more bayonets were stuck into the wall near a box with two hundred rounds of .32-caliber bullets and a military-style crank field phone, similar to others they found in buildings nearby. Was this their not-so-sophisticated alert system?

"Where's the rest of your group?" Deputy Olmstead asked a scruffy suspect.

The young man pointed toward the east. "Over behind them rocks," he said.

"Let's go wake them up," Olmstead said.

The only way to get to them, over the rugged terrain and dirt roads, was by dune buggy, the suspect explained.

The posse of deputies soon realized that many of the hippies were scattered around the property—in trailers, in ramshackle shacks, and out in the hills. Their leader was also nowhere to be found.

"Where's Charlie?" the deputies asked, but no one answered.

They finally found him, hiding under a building, and had to pull him out to arrest him.

By the end of the search, the deputies had found five children and twenty-six young people, most of whom ranged in age from teens to midtwenties. Eleven of them had been sleeping in one room with three rifles, two of which were fully loaded.

Rounded up and arrested, the hippies were packed into vans, booked at the Malibu station on charges of grand theft auto, and taken to the county jails. What the LASD didn't know at the time was that most of them were using aliases and gave fake ages, which complicated proceedings enormously.

Several arrestees were teenage girls, who were taken to Juvenile Hall, while one ten-year-old and four infants were placed into foster care, including Linda Kasabian's eighteen-month-old daughter, Tonya; Sadie's ten-month-old son, Zezozose; and Charlie's son with Mary Brunner, sixteen-month-old Michael.

In addition to auto theft, Charlie was also charged with burglary. DeCarlo was charged with assault with a deadly weapon after reaching for a loaded .45-caliber handgun during his arrest.

It did not escape Charlie's notice that Shorty Shea was not among the arrestees. George Spahn, who wasn't arrested either, told authorities later that he had become scared of Charlie and his group—especially when he could hear them sharpening their knives.

———

Several ironies came to light after this raid, which in hindsight made it seem like more of a training exercise or public relations exhibition. They also underscored the blind spots and poor coordination by the various law enforcement agencies.

After a patrol visit to the ranch before the raid, a city firefighter reported seeing a car he described as "a grubby, ranchy looking hippie type vehicle"—a dark red-and-white VW bus parked up in the canyon, hidden in some bushes.

It's unclear whether any law enforcement agency ran a license plate check on the car, but at the time no one connected it to the two stolen cars in the APB the LASD had sent out after the murder of Gary Hinman, whose decomposing body had been found by two detectives about two weeks earlier.

The LASD had already charged twenty-one-year-old Bobby Beausoleil for Hinman's murder but still had not connected Bobby to the suspected auto theft ring at Spahn—even after he'd listed the ranch as his address when he was booked into the LA county jail on August 7.

Among the nine vehicles and motorcycles scattered around the ranch that were impounded that day was a yellow 1959 Ford sedan with the license plate GYY 435. It would be months before authorities realized that this car had provided transportation to three of the Family's murder scenes.

Meanwhile, the media continued to tie the Tate and LaBianca murders to each other, and now to the raid as well. The day after the raid the *Los Angeles Times* published three separate stories on the same page, connecting the dots into a portrait of crime that law enforcement officials still refused to recognize.

The story headlined "Night of Horror: Anatomy of a Mass Murder in Hollywood" discussed possible motives for the murder on Cielo Drive, including narcotics, the study of black magic, and the "rough trade" lifestyles by some of the "Tate-Polanski crowd." It also noted that local authorities were trying to track four suspected drug traffickers who had either visited the Cielo house or were associated somehow with the murder victims.

The story about the LaBiancas being given their final rites quoted police describing the murder as the work of a "copycat killer," one of the scenarios Manson had hoped to create.

But in yet another inexplicable bungle, the Spahn Ranch search warrant was deemed faulty because the LASD had waited three days to serve it. So all twenty-six arrestees from the raid, including all the Tate and LaBianca killers except Tex, were released "for lack of evidence."

CHAPTER 13

"I FELT I COULD CONQUER THE WORLD."

Charlie Manson had been falling through—and taking advantage of—cracks in the system his entire life. His grandmother, Nancy Maddox, was a devout Nazarene who raised four children as a young widow in Ashland, Kentucky. Despite Nancy's efforts to raise her kids right, her fifteen-year-old daughter Kathleen rebelled, falling in love with twenty-four-year-old Colonel Walker Scott. Colonel, which was a family name, was by various descriptions a laborer working on a local dam project, a man working cons with his older brother, Darwin, or possibly both.

Although he came from a good Baptist family in the nearby town of Catlettsburg, Colonel got Kathleen pregnant, then "didn't stick around long enough to watch the belly rise," as Charlie put it in his autobiography.

Nancy sent her pregnant daughter to give birth in Cincinnati, about two hours from Ashland, where Kathleen went looking for a man to give her unborn baby a name. She set her sights on William Manson, who worked at a dry cleaner's there, and they were married on August 21, 1934, just across the Ohio River in Campbell County, Kentucky.

Even though the date on their marriage license predates Charlie's birthday on November 12, 1934, by four months, he spent his life claiming the more colorful story that he was born an illegitimate bastard child, saying, "I was an outlaw from birth."

The marriage didn't last long, but even as William Manson was filing for divorce Kathleen was already making other financial arrangements.

Eleven days before William's divorce petition was granted in April 1937, citing Kathleen's "gross neglect of duty," she won a judgment—for a lump sum of twenty-five dollars, plus five dollars a month—in a bastardy lawsuit against Charlie's biological father. But Kathleen had to return to court to try to garnish Colonel's wages for back support payments.

As an adult, Charlie often told tales about Kathleen's failures as a parent, one of which has become quite well-known: Charlie was sitting in her lap in a café one afternoon when the waitress joked that she had no children of her own and would buy Kathleen's son from her for a good price.

"A pitcher of beer and he's yours," Kathleen replied.

The waitress brought Kathleen a batch of suds, which she downed before walking out, leaving her toddler behind. Charlie's uncle had to search for the waitress for several days before he could locate her and bring the boy home.

———

Criminal behavior was also a family trait. Charlie's paternal uncle Darwin Scott went to federal prison twice, but incarceration struck Charlie even closer to home. When Charlie was four, Kathleen and her roommate picked up a stranger, Frank Martin, in a beer parlor in North Charleston, West Virginia. As he paid for their drinks, they saw a stack of bills in his wallet and called Kathleen's brother, Luther, with a scheme.

The young women took Frank dancing at several bars, where they casually met up with Luther, as if he were a stranger. Proposing to continue the festivities, Luther and Kathleen asked Frank to drive them home to get some belongings. But before they left the last tavern, Luther surreptitiously pocketed a large ketchup bottle filled with salt.

As Frank was driving through an isolated area in his Packard convertible, Luther had him pull over, then smacked him in the head with the bottle. Luther grabbed Frank's wallet and the twenty-seven dollars inside it, leaving the poor man in a ditch, and driving away in his car.

After tracking down the stolen convertible, police arrested the threesome several days later. Kathleen confessed, but Luther refused to snitch on his partners. Nonetheless, he and Kathleen were convicted of armed robbery and sentenced to five years at Moundsville State Prison.

Charlie's first acquaintance with correctional institutions came when he visited his mother at Moundsville. Kathleen told him that while she was assigned to clean the area near death row, she unexpectedly witnessed a hanging as she hid in a broom closet. That story stuck with him, taking on a particular resonance when he was sent to death row himself at San Quentin State Prison in 1971.

While Kathleen was in prison, Charlie stayed with his grandmother in Ashland. But after only a few weeks, she sent him to live with his aunt and uncle, closer to his mother in Moundsville.

When Charlie came home crying after his first day of school, his uncle Bill made him put on his cousin's dress the next morning, and sent him on his way. "The other kids teased me so much I went into a rage and started fighting everyone," Manson wrote in his autobiography. "I took my lumps and shed a little blood, but in that school I became the fightin'est little bastard they ever saw."

His uncle didn't make him wear a dress again.

———

After Kathleen was paroled in 1942, she and eight-year-old Charlie moved from state to state. As she continued to run into trouble with the law, Charlie landed in a few foster homes.

Kathleen didn't earn much as a cocktail waitress, but she managed to get him a guitar and singing lessons. She stopped the lessons, she said later, when she felt he was becoming "overconfident" and "conceited" about his abilities as he sang solos with the church choir.

While his mother dated a series of men, Charlie let it be known by skipping school and running away that he didn't like these "uncles" hanging around. In 1947, when Charlie was thirteen, she went before a judge to claim that she couldn't afford to provide her son with a good home. The judge made the teenager a ward of the court and shipped him off to the Gibault School for Boys, a Catholic school in Terre Haute, Indiana.

For the next ten months, Charlie was miserable. Not only did he miss his mother, but he also claimed he was whipped with leather straps and paddles for repeatedly wetting the bed. Impatient to see Kathleen, who rarely visited him, he ran away to go see her, thinking she'd be thrilled. Instead, she shipped him straight back.

Until the day he was released at nineteen, Charlie repeatedly ran away from every single facility in which he was placed.

"You've got a juvenile, you lock him up in juvenile hall," he said, looking back years later. "He don't know anything. He's got no parents and he's got nobody telling him the truth, everybody is lying to him. So the only thing he can do is run away, so that's all I did . . . And every time I ran away, they just got me and put me in a harder place to get away."

One time he took off from Gibault, he made it all the way to Indianapolis, 160 miles away, where he survived by stealing food, cash, and a bicycle, which landed him back in court. At a hearing attended by his mother and a priest, Charlie convinced the judge to send him to the famous Father Flanagan's Boys Town in Nebraska.

The hearing made it into the newspaper, which described him as a "dead end kid" who was getting another chance to make good.

"I think I could be happy working around cows and horses," Charlie innocently told the judge, as he smiled and shook the man's hand. "I like animals."

But after only four days at Boys Town, Charlie escaped with another boy, stealing and crashing a car. They were ultimately captured in Indianapolis, where they did robberies for the other boy's uncle.

Back in court, the next judge had no choice but to send Charlie to a more secure facility, the Indiana School for Boys in Plainfield, Indiana, where his escape attempts only increased in number.

Small for his age, Charlie was not even five feet tall and weighed less than sixty-five pounds, which made him a prime target of older bullies. He claimed that he was repeatedly abused and beaten by guards, and was also gagged and brutally raped by teams of boys at the encouragement of one particularly sadomasochistic guard, who compounded Charlie's anal injuries by manually assaulting him with a handful of chewing tobacco juice mixed with wet, fermented grass feed from the dairy.

But Charlie was a fighter. He got his revenge on two of his young rapists by clubbing one of them in the head while he slept, and framing the other one for the crime by leaving the weapon—a foot-long metal window crank-opener—in his bed. After word got around, no one tried to rape Charlie again.

At sixteen, Charlie got more ambitious. This time, he and two older boys, one of whom had already killed a man during a hold-up, drove a stolen 1950 Studebaker across four state lines, violating the federal Dyer Act before being captured in Utah, heading for California.

Sent to the even higher security National Training School for Boys in Washington DC, Charlie asked to be transferred to the Natural Bridge Honor Camp. After undergoing psychotherapy for three months, he got his wish in October 1951 and came up for early release.

But as his parole hearing approached, he held a razor to a boy's throat, sodomized him, and lost his chance for parole. He later claimed that the "victim" was a gay and willing partner who agreed to have sex with Charlie as long as he could pretend that Charlie had forced him if anyone found out.

"We got caught," Charlie wrote in his autobiography. "I was not only listed as a homosexual, but one with assaultive tendencies."

After this incident, Charlie felt he had nothing to lose, so he had relations with another boy, and this time admitted it was rape.

His attitude changed, however, after he was transferred to two federal reformatories in Petersburg, Virginia, and Chillicothe, Ohio, where his behavior and study habits improved. Although he still had trouble reading, he raised his education from a third-grade to a seventh-grade level.

Charlie was nineteen when he was finally released from the juvenile institutions on May 8, 1954, returning to live with his aunt and uncle in McMechen, where he obediently attended Nazarene church services with his grandmother.

Pursuing unpopular odd jobs that wouldn't require revealing his criminal past, he pulled weeds and pumped gas, and also shoveled manure and fed horses at the then-Wheeling Downs racetrack. After being locked away for many years, he still felt like the same small child he was when he'd left.

In a marked contrast to the counterculture leader he would grow into, the young Charles Manson gave the quiet, conventional life a try, marrying the first girl with whom he ever had sex.

He met Rosalie "Rosie" Jean Willis, an Irish cafeteria waitress with nice skin, in a card room as he was trying to turn his paltry wages into a small fortune.

As they fell in love, he later wrote, "A huge void was being filled. For the first time in my life, I felt I could conquer the world."

Charlie was twenty when he married fifteen-year-old Rosalie in Marshall County, West Virginia, on January 17, 1955. For many years afterward, Charlie would say that Rosie was the only woman he ever truly loved, and the only person he ever really cared about.

But the honeymoon didn't last long. The young couple didn't have much money, and neither of them had a proper education, so Charlie fell back on the only income-bearing avocation he'd ever learned: taking stolen cars across state lines, again violating the federal Dyer Act.

In July, he and Rosalie headed to Los Angeles in a Mercury sedan he'd stolen in Bridgeport, Ohio. His wife, a coal miner's daughter from West Virginia, had always wanted to see California.

When Charlie was arrested two months later, he admitted that he'd actually stolen four or five other cars as well, pleading guilty in a hearing before US District Court judge Harry Westover that October.

In the first of many times in the coming decades, Charlie's mental competency was questioned in court as his probation officer and federal prosecutor said he "may be presently insane or otherwise so mentally incompetent as to be unable to understand the proceedings against him or properly to assist in his own defense . . . [and] unable to distinguish between right and wrong."

After being examined by a psychiatrist, Dr. Edwin McNiel, Charlie was described as "quiet, pleasant and cooperative." He exaggerated his mother's criminal record, saying she'd been in prison several times. Claiming that he'd been locked up for being mean to her, he admitted to engaging in homosexual relations since he was fourteen, and even to physically abusing his now pregnant wife.

"She has been the best wife a guy could want," Charlie said. "I didn't realize how good she was until I got in here. I beat her at times. She writes to me all the time. She is going to have a baby."

McNiel concluded that Charlie was sane, but had "an unstable personality" and an "unfortunate background" of unhealthy environmental influences. But noting that Charlie felt he had "developed a new understanding of his own problems and why he always wanted to run away," and had "asked for a chance to try to get along in the community," McNiel made a hopeful recommendation to the judge to consider probation with "careful supervision."

Judge Westover responded by giving Charlie a five-year suspended sentence with five years' probation, and released him on November 7, 1955.

But the die was cast. Launching another lifelong behavioral pattern, Charlie gave in to an apparent compulsion to break the law, and most likely an unconscious desire to return to the familiar safety of a locked facility, which he expressed repeatedly in subsequent years. So he hit the road and headed out of state without getting permission, violating his parole and missing several court hearings.

Arrested in Chicago on a slew of warrants in March, he was sent back to Los Angeles. Judge Westover still gave him a break, however, modifying his five-year suspended sentence to only a three-year prison term.

CHAPTER 14

DOING HARD TIME

By late April 1956, Charlie Manson was behind bars at the Federal Correctional Institution, Terminal Island, in the San Pedro neighborhood of Los Angeles.

In the meantime, Rosalie had their baby and named him Charles Milles Manson Jr. The two of them lived nearby with Kathleen for a while, surviving on welfare checks.

At first, Rosalie wrote letters to Charlie and brought the baby to see him in prison, but her visits and letters soon tapered off, then stopped altogether. Kathleen finally had to break the news to him, that his wife and son had moved out and were living with a truck driver. Charlie was understandably upset.

Although he was expecting an early parole date at an upcoming hearing, he couldn't wait that long to talk to Rosalie, so he attempted to escape on April 10, 1957. But he didn't get far. He was caught trying to hotwire a car before he even got out of the prison parking lot, and lost his chance for an early release.

Rosalie, who was eager to start over with her boyfriend, Jack White, couldn't wait to have another baby. She was already pregnant by the time she filed for divorce on July 8, citing Charlie's criminal record and abuse.

"Since the marriage, defendant has treated plaintiff with extreme cruelty, and has wrongfully inflicted upon her grievous bodily and mental injury and suffering," she wrote, requesting permanent custody of their child.

Charlie was served with the papers a week later, but did nothing to contest the divorce or custody arrangement, which Rosalie won by default the following year.

Charlie's mother blamed his future treatment of women on this first failed relationship. "I think the business with Rosalie really hurt Charles," Kathleen said in 1971. "I think [Rosalie] was the only woman he ever really loved, and from then on, he never respected women."

With Rosalie gone, Charlie focused on the next stage of his education: learning how to become a good pimp and have your ladies bring home the bread. He also set his mind to learn some new things, so he signed up for a Dale Carnegie leadership-building course, which was popular among prisoners.

After serving twenty-nine months of his three-year term, Manson was released on September 30, 1958, six weeks before his twenty-fourth birthday.

———

Back on the outside, Charlie tried a number of odd jobs, including going door to door to set up appointments for salesmen hawking freezers and frozen food plans. Claiming the salesmen "double-crossed and short changed" him, he soon gave up attempting to earn a legitimate income.

Instead, he decided to try out his prison pimp schooling and run some women, including his girlfriend, Leona Rae "Candy" Stevens, aka Leona Rae Musser, as prostitutes around LA. When the pimping didn't produce the easy money he anticipated, he fell back on his old standby—stealing.

But he wasn't much better at that either. On May 1, 1959, Charlie was arrested for pilfering two US Treasury checks from the mailbox of Leslie Sever, made out to her and her husband, Ollie, who had died two and a half years earlier.

Charlie signed the backs of the checks, and successfully cashed the first one, a thirty-four-dollar check made out to Leslie, at a gas station.

But when he tried to cash Ollie's $37.50 check at a Ralph's market, the clerks questioned him and he took off running. The clerks caught and detained him until the police arrived.

Charlie admitted to the crime, then later denied confessing. Despite the small amounts he stole, this was no petty crime. He now faced charges of stealing mail and forging signatures with the intent to defraud the federal government, with fines of up to two thousand dollars and a five-year prison term for each count.

Hoping he couldn't be prosecuted if he destroyed the evidence, Charlie quickly shoved one of the checks into his mouth and swallowed it when the Secret Service agents holding him in custody weren't looking.

Charlie's next tactic was to ask other inmates, and probably Leona, to handwrite respectful letters in his name to the judges presiding over his case, including Judge William Mathes. The ploy worked—at first.

These letters described his trademark story—the woes of being institutionalized and having no money or education—but with a new twist: his attorneys were greedy, incompetent, and trying to do him wrong. It's unclear whether these claims were sincere or were simply part of his burgeoning strategy to manipulate whenever possible, but they served as seminal precursors to the tactics he employed years later during his high-profile murder trials in LA.

When Charlie's attorney asked for a psychiatrist to examine his client, Dr. McNiel, who had assessed him four years earlier, was selected.

Now twenty-four, Charlie admitted his guilt to McNiel, but failed to elicit another hopeful recommendation. McNeil reiterated much the same opinion as before, but with a new chilling prognosis: "[Charlie] does not give the impression of being a mean individual. However, he is very unstable emotionally and very insecure. . . . In my opinion, he is probably a sociopathic personality without psychosis. Unfortunately, he is rapidly becoming an institutionalized individual. . . . I certainly cannot recommend him as a good candidate for probation."

Angus McEachen, the chief US probation officer for the LA office, agreed. "Defendant certainly has displayed no ability or willingness, perhaps both, to get along on the outside for any length of time," he wrote in the pre-sentence report.

Undeterred, Charlie came up with another plan. He sent Leona to try the "my wife and I are going to have a baby" trick on his probation officer, a ploy that had worked in 1955. If they would let Charlie go, Leona pleaded with the officer, they could get married and make a good life. She repeated the same emotional appeal for the judge in the courtroom, where she cried and asked for leniency. Charlie and Leona actually did get married in 1959.

Charlie also entered into a plea agreement, admitting guilt to one count of "uttering and publishing" the Treasury check "with intent to defraud," in exchange for dismissal of two other counts.

In the end, Manson's ploys were surprisingly successful. Overlooking the psychiatrist's and probation chief's recommendations, Judge Mathes apparently responded to the letters and "heartfelt" pleas from Charlie and his wife. He gave Charlie one more chance, suspending the ten-year sentence and giving him five years' probation.

But after being miraculously released back into the real world on September 28, 1959, Charlie wasted no time in throwing away his good fortune. Working as a bartender, he became sexually involved with two teenage girls and was arrested for grand theft auto and using stolen credit cards.

Somehow managing to escape punishment for these misdeeds, he continued his crime spree by stealing a Triumph convertible that December and headed to New Mexico with Leona and another of his girls. While the girls were turning tricks, Charlie hung out with the Yaqui Indians, played Russian roulette with an unloaded gun, and took psychedelic mushrooms. He and the girls were charged with driving the stolen car and engaging in prostitution across state lines.

But then Leona turned against him. As part of a deal to get her own charges dropped, she testified as a "material witness" before a grand jury in April 1960 and blamed him for taking her out of state. Arrested in Laredo, Texas, in June, Charlie was shipped back to jail in LA.

When Judge Mathes reinstated the original ten-year prison term, Charlie appealed.

Leona, who truly was pregnant this time, came to visit Charlie in jail. But after that he never saw her again, or their son, Charles Luther Manson.

At sentencing, Charlie expressed an unusual desire to return to prison, to which Judge Mathes acquiesced. "It may save the government the trouble of prosecuting you for these other offenses," Mathes told Charlie, referring to allegations that he'd had sex with the two teenagers. "It may save the government a little expense. But you want to go to prison. You have just asked for it, and I am going to accommodate you."

Judge Mathes dismissed Charlie's appeal and sent him back to federal prison on May 29, 1961.

———

Charlie settled in easily at McNeil Island Penitentiary in Washington, where he befriended Alvin "Creepy" Karpis, a former member of Ma Barker's gang during the Great Depression and a "Public Enemy #1" taken alive by the FBI. It was Karpis who taught Manson how to play steel guitar.

Charlie picked up his criminal education where he'd left off, with nothing but time to sit and listen to the stories of the system-wise inmates like Karpis and Mafia members from the East Coast like Frank Costello, whom Manson called gangsters of "the old underworld, where they made all that moonshine stuff."

Although Charlie later referred to the judges, police, and correctional officers who tried to make him follow the rules as his "fathers," his true role models were these old-timers, who shared body-burying tips and pimping stories with him.

"I learned all the things they learned," he said.

Despite his learning disabilities, Charlie took this time to study various philosophies and religious beliefs he discussed with other inmates who had better reading skills. Tenets he gleaned from Dale Carnegie's *How to Win Friends and Influence People*, Dr. Vincent Peale's *The Power of Positive Thinking*, the sci-fi novel *Stranger in a Strange Land* by Robert Heinlein, and Scientology founder L. Ron Hubbard were among his favorites. All of this impressed his prison evaluators.

But Charlie dedicated most of his attention to improving his guitar-playing skills and to writing dozens of songs. When a fellow prisoner, music producer Phil Kaufman, heard him singing on the yard, he thought Charlie had a good voice, albeit self-taught.

"He was rather like a young Frankie Lane. He had that kind of lilt in his voice," said Kaufman, who told Charlie to go see a friend of his at Universal Studios in LA when he got out.

—

In 1964, Leona informed prison officials, who then notified Charlie, that their divorce—filed in April 1963 on the grounds of "conviction of felony and extreme and repeated acts of cruelty"—had been granted.

Writing Judge Mathes for advice on crafting his parole plan, he claimed that he could have gotten out much sooner, but he had no one on the outside and no job lined up. By the time he was released in 1968, he wrote, he still would have no one to turn to.

"You told me more than once my future was in my own hands," Charlie wrote. "Is it? Has it ever been?"

Mathes had been right when he said Charlie wanted to go back to prison, he wrote. Only this time he really wanted to get out and he hoped the judge could accommodate him once more. When the judge gave him probation, he said, it was like being in a boxing ring with his hands tied, because he didn't know how to live in "the strange world out there." He needed some help untying his hands, or there was no sense even trying.

Charlie's query went unanswered. In June 1966 he was transferred back to Terminal Island in LA to prepare for his release, with no parole plan other than to try to sell the songs he'd written behind bars.

CHAPTER 15

THE FIRST FAMILY
MEMBERS

After seven years behind bars, Charlie could see that the culture had changed dramatically when he rejoined the outside world on March 21, 1967, at 8:15 a.m.

He took a local bus from the prison to the probation office in downtown LA, where he asked to have his case transferred to the San Francisco office, then immediately headed north to the Bay Area.

Thousands of young people, proudly wearing the moniker of "hippies," were going barefoot, eating vegetarian diets, actively rejecting the materialism and authority of the establishment, and heading in droves to Haight-Ashbury in San Francisco. Berkeley, a community across the bay from the Haight, also drew many hippies, and was an attractively affordable and nonjudgmental place for an ex-con like Manson to live.

After the Free Speech Movement in 1964–65, the University of California, Berkeley was still roiling with student demonstrators and political activists who joined forces with high-profile figures such as Martin Luther King Jr., Allen Ginsberg, and Muhammad Ali in protesting unnecessary deaths of American soldiers in the hugely unpopular Vietnam War.

Street musicians and vendors lined the rollicking sidewalks surrounding the Berkeley campus, where students walked to class along rolling green lawns, open plazas, and classical-style buildings. It was here that Charlie met twenty-three-year-old Mary Brunner, a quiet, unassuming, and rather plain young librarian from Eau Claire, Wisconsin, who worked on campus.

Within a month or so he and Mary had moved into a two-bedroom apartment in town together, and she became the first member of what would ultimately be known as the Manson Family.

———

Parole officer Roger Smith was responsible for closely monitoring a caseload of thirty of the most high-risk probationers in the Northern District, including Charles Manson. For the next year, he either saw Charlie every week in his San Francisco office or made a surprise visit to wherever his nomadic ward said he was staying.

Charlie enjoyed telling Roger jokes and stories, but mostly he just liked to talk. Their discussion topics often touched on the philosophical and religious ideas he'd picked up in prison. One book in particular—Heinlein's science-fiction novel *Stranger in a Strange Land*—seemed to be a seminal influence on him as Roger watched Charlie slowly gather a group of young, vulnerable, and troubled female confidantes who looked up to him. The hero of Heinlein's story, Valentine Michael Smith, came to Earth after being raised by martians. And like Charlie was said to do, Smith exercised his special psychic powers to control other people's minds, wooing a group of highly sexual men and women into his inner circle to recruit others, and preaching a philosophy that death was meaningless because the soul survived in the afterlife.

During Roger's weekly meetings with Charlie, he gleaned that his parolee "didn't have a great affection for African Americans," which Roger attributed to Manson's time in prison, where inmates generally keep to their ethnic groups. He also gathered that Charlie thought he was helping the physically and emotionally abused girls he collected by telling them how beautiful and wonderful they were.

Charlie's disjointed rants, which became a trademark behavior, prevented Roger from getting a word in edgewise. Roger saw this tactic as a way of keeping control of the conversation.

Although Charlie occasionally asked Roger for permission to travel—to LA to play music or to Washington State to see his mother—he frequently took unauthorized out-of-state trips without Roger's knowledge, with and without the girls, to Nevada, Texas, Mississippi, Alabama, Arizona, and New Mexico and even across the border into Mexico.

———

Mary mistakenly thought she was going to have Charlie to herself—until he invited a young, offbeat nineteen-year-old named Lynette Fromme to join them.

Cute, petite, and freckled, the redheaded Lynette was into normal teenage activities such as dancing and reading poetry, but she was known more for wild, bizarre acts such as shooting her arm multiple times with a staple gun. Her Redondo Union High School classmates voted her "Personality Plus."

The troubled teen's home life had become pretty dismal after her father stopped speaking to her at thirteen. Although they still lived under the same roof, for the next three years they communicated only through her mother.

Lynette went on to date Bill Siddons, who later worked as road manager for the Doors. She also tried going to El Camino Community College, but ended up dropping out.

Then, in early 1967, her parents kicked her out of the house. She was sitting on a curb in Venice, looking forlorn, when a bus pulled up and parked. Charlie got out and came over to her.

"Your parents threw you out, didn't they?" he asked.

"How did you know that?" she asked, stunned.

He's a genius, she thought. *He must be psychic.*

Charlie waited about thirty seconds before walking away. "I can't make up your mind for you," he said.

He was halfway down the block before she grabbed up her meager belongings, ran after him, and got onto the bus. Lynette stuck by Charlie and remained one of his most loyal followers for the next fifty years.

———

It didn't take long for Charlie to find his way to the Haight, where a hundred thousand hippies converged during the Summer of Love in 1967. With them came the musicians—and the psychedelic drugs.

The Grateful Dead drew many hippies as followers, and, like Carlos Santana and Janis Joplin, played at open-air concerts in nearby Golden Gate Park, where most attendees were high on LSD.

A number of kids experiencing bad acid trips that summer prompted Dr. David Smith, a twenty-eight-year-old physician with specialties in pharmacology and addiction, to open a free clinic, partially funded by benefit concerts in the park. Located two blocks away, the clinic drew volunteers including Abigail Folger and, later, her mother as well. It still operates today.

Dr. Smith was introduced to Manson and his burgeoning communal group by Roger Smith (no relation), who described his probationer as someone who was "part of the scene," with a van in the park and an apartment on Cole Street in the Haight.

"This is Charlie and his girls," Roger told Dr. Smith, whose clinic treated the first Family members and its first offspring.

———

It was no coincidence that Mary got pregnant during the Summer of Love, a quick escalation in her new relationship with the ex-con, which troubled her midwestern family enough to fly to California to investigate.

When her parents and some other relatives showed up at Roger's office, their faces were fraught with worry. "They're talking about getting married," they said. "What can we do? Is there anything you can do?"

Roger said he understood their concerns, but his hands were tied.

"Legally, there's absolutely nothing I can do to intervene," he said. "She is an adult and there is no crime being committed."

As Roger got to know Mary better, she seemed like "a very decent human being in a circumstance that she couldn't control," who would have preferred to have Charlie to herself. But at the time, Roger didn't see Charlie as someone dangerous for her or the other girls to hang out with.

By June, Mary had quit her library job, which enabled her to go on the road when Charlie wanted her to.

On one trip to LA Charlie stopped in Mendocino County, where the Reverend Dean Moorehouse picked him up while hitchhiking and took him to his house to meet his wife and his fourteen-year-old daughter, Ruth Ann, nicknamed Ouisch.

Moorehouse gave his piano to Charlie, who then traded it for a 1961 Volkswagen microbus he saw in the neighborhood. Ruth Ann's father was not pleased when she then ran away from home to join Charlie and the girls on the bus, so he called the police.

On July 28, 1967, Charlie was arrested near Hales Grove for obstructing the arrest of a runaway. As he was being booked he listed his occupation as "minister," got a thirty-day suspended sentence, and went on his way.

When Charlie and Moorehouse met up again, he gave the minister some LSD, which changed Moorehouse's perspective. So much so, he became one of Charlie's disciples, soon joining him, Ouisch, and the girls in Topanga Canyon and preaching the Manson philosophy to recruit new Family members.

Charlie and his growing Family moved from place to place until they got evicted or hit the road again in their VW bus. When they outgrew the minibus, he found a yellow school bus for them.

———

Charlie met nineteen-year-old Patricia "Patty" Krenwinkel that September in the LA area, where she was living with her older sister Charlene in Manhattan Beach.

"There's this guy, he's playing guitar. Why don't you come and meet him?" said Charlene, whose friend Billy had served time with Charlie at Terminal Island.

Patty didn't mind that he and Billy had criminal records. Charlene, who had run away, gotten pregnant and married at fifteen, and was on heroin by sixteen, had also been in jail.

In comparison, Patty was a good girl. As a serious and gentle child, she had won a national piano audition, studied the Bible, and went to church. Growing into a caring, reserved, and polite teenager, she'd earned a service commendation and joined the National Wildlife Federation.

But she felt unattractive. Overweight, tall, and gawky, she had more body hair than her peers, her features were lumpy, and her big ears poked through her long hair. Additionally, her parents' marriage was rocky, and Patty soon turned to drugs. Prescribed diet pills by her doctor, she thought nothing of popping the Benzedrines or the Seconals that Charlene gave her or of adding marijuana and alcohol to the mix.

After her parents divorced, Patty finished high school and eventually made her way to Manhattan Beach, hoping to settle in with Charlene. After working in sales at a dress shop and at JCPenney, she took a job as an insurance processor.

While she and Charlene were at Billy's house that fall day in 1967, Charlie coyly asked Patty if she had a place to stay. Charlene offered up their apartment and he accepted, turning his charms on Patty.

The next night, she couldn't stop crying as he made love to her. He knew just what to say to open her heart. "I'm ugly, you're ugly," he told her, "but you're beautiful to me."

She'd been looking for a boyfriend, and she thought this thirty-two-year-old troubadour with the dark, mirthful eyes wanted her as his girlfriend.

"All Patti ever seemed to want was someone to love and take care of her and make her feel needed and wanted," a high school friend wrote to Patty's trial attorney years later. "She was definitely non-violent; and she was definitely not promiscuous."

A couple of days later, Charlie said he was going to drive to Washington to go see his parole officer, look for his mother, and record his music. He asked if she wanted to come along.

"I can see that you're not happy, that your sister is out of control, that she's an addict," he said.

To Patty, Charlie was the first person to really *see* her and her troubled life. He seemed like her salvation, offering her a convenient way out of a difficult transitional living situation.

He also seemed much stronger and self-assured than her, better able to handle the world, and more knowledgeable. She listened to his words and let herself believe they were true.

"I love you," he said.

Maybe he's the one, she thought. *The one I can eventually settle down with. The one I can eventually marry.*

Charlie gave Patty a new name, Katie, and made her feel special.

But within a few days of being on the road together, Katie learned that she was going to have to share their new life together. Charlie had another woman, Lynette, waiting for him in LA. After the trio drove to the Bay Area together, they met up with yet another woman, Mary, who was carrying his baby.

He shrugged this off by saying that babies didn't "belong" to their mothers or fathers; child-raising duties were to be shared by the communal group, which could mold them the way Charlie wanted.

"Charlie was into this philosophy that children are born perfect and all knowing, and adults are the ones who screw them up with possessiveness," Roger Smith recalled.

By then Katie had fallen in love with Charlie, who continued to whisper sweet nothings to her as the group drove up the Pacific Coast. "You're the only one," he told her. "I love you the most."

So she hung in there, discovering the joy of travel and communal love as she shed her conventional upbringing.

"I seem to find that with each new day the world becomes more beautiful," she wrote to her "Dearest Father," Joseph. "Life is to be experienced and that is what I am doing. I am happy."

Katie told her dad that she and her new friends had earned some food money by washing windows at a gas station near Seattle. She also asked him to sell her Dodge Dart to repay the charges she'd run up on his gas card.

As they bummed around in their bus, she and her friends sang outside coffee shops for tips. She knew it was wrong to keep charging up her dad's credit card, but continued until he cut her off.

That didn't bother Charlie, though. He frowned upon any mention of her family. Told her to forget what her parents had taught her and to break from her past.

She so wanted to please him she accepted this new life willingly, still holding out hope that he would be *her* man in the end.

As time went on, he introduced hash and LSD into their lives, becoming the conductor of her perception, her "master of illusion," and everything that came along with that.

———

The flashes of violence came on slowly and surprisingly.

The first incident occurred after a few months on the road, when Charlie pulled Katie's hair and shoved her face into a wall in Sacramento because he thought she was laughing at him. She'd thought she was laughing *with* him.

Charlie was immediately apologetic. "Sorry," he said. "Let me take you out. Let me make love to you."

Shocked, Katie hadn't seen the meanness underneath that impish smile. She was able to get past it for the next six months, until he started talking about the coat hangers he once used to beat the women who worked for him.

To survive on the road, he said, they needed money and a place to stay, which meant that she and the other girls had to sleep with whoever he told them to. Raised to believe it was the woman's job to make a relationship work, Katie saw the act of complying with Charlie's orders as doing her part for the communal group.

She'd already become so enmeshed in the Family mind-set she

couldn't see that Charlie had essentially turned her and the other young women into working girls.

But the sad fact was that she felt she deserved this treatment, "that I wasn't going to be able to find someone better than I had." So she stayed.

———

Susan Atkins was nineteen and high when she met Charlie in November 1967. As she stood in the kitchen of her three-story communal house in the Haight, she heard someone playing the guitar.

Walking into the living room she saw a small dark-haired man with tattoos and an angelic demeanor, performing for a circle of girls. He offered her the guitar to play, but she didn't know how.

When someone put on a Jefferson Airplane record Susan danced for the man, luring him to get up and dance behind her. His hands on her hips, they moved as one—in ways that even she, as a topless dancer, hadn't experienced before.

"You are beautiful, you are perfect," he said, looking into her eyes. "I've never seen anyone dance like you. It's wonderful. You must always be free."

After they exchanged names, he motioned to the other girls that it was time to go and they obediently followed him out.

Two days later, Susan ran into him again. As he led her to his pad, she felt honored. All her housemates were infatuated with him.

"Have you ever thought about making love with your father?" he asked.

No, she said. Although she was embarrassed to admit it, she had thought about it. A few times, in fact.

Susan had grown up in San Jose with an alcoholic and physically abusive father who drank even more after her mother died of breast cancer when Susan was thirteen. He soon abandoned Susan and her two brothers.

Charlie told her to disrobe, stood her in front of a full-length mirror, and turned her naked body to face forward.

"Look at yourself," he said. "There is nothing wrong with you. You are perfect. You have always been perfect."

He told her to imagine that he was her father, saying it would help her work through her daddy hang-ups, which, somehow, he had magically sensed.

The interlude didn't last long, but it was the most beautiful and fulfilling sexual experience she'd ever had.

The next day he returned in a school bus with two girls, Katie and Mary, saying they were going to paint it black and travel around in it. But Charlie waited until that afternoon to invite her along. "Well, are you going to go with me or aren't you?" he asked.

Susan immediately packed a suitcase with two days' worth of clothes, some keepsakes from her late mother, and off they went. She rarely had any more intimate time with Charlie, who often chose Lynette over the other girls.

Charlie gave Susan a new name too—Sadie Mae Glutz—to help her shed her old persona and become someone new. He killed her to release her, he said, so she could be truly free.

Sadie didn't have a problem with the crimes that he expected her and the others to commit, or with him telling her to sleep with other men, because she'd already done all of that before they'd met.

She'd already seen herself as "the best shoplifter in the neighborhood" by the third grade. Essentially orphaned with no parental supervision, she'd dropped out of Los Banos High School at fifteen, and later claimed she'd been molested.

Heading for San Francisco, she got a job working the phones in an office. When her boss said he couldn't pay her, she agreed to have sex with him for a car, spending money, and rent for her apartment for a few months.

After that, she bounced back and forth between the city and her hometown, waitressing, babysitting, and housecleaning, until she found her next adventure: a road trip to Oregon with two young men in a "new" car—code for stolen. As the men committed a series of armed robberies, the trio hid out at campgrounds and stole from other campers.

Their crime spree lasted until a state trooper pulled them over near Salem and arrested them for possession of a concealed weapon in September 1966. Unabashed, Sadie turned to the trooper and said, "I should have killed you."

Sadie was convicted of the weapons charge as well as a pleaded-down misdemeanor for the stolen car. After three months in jail, she got two years' probation and her case was transferred back to Santa Clara, California. However, no probation officer monitored her case, because her records got lost.

Back in San Francisco, she entered an amateur topless "go go girl" contest. That led to a regular gig at the Galaxy Club, which hired her to pretend to be an audience member who jumped on stage to strip for the crowd.

Drinking too much, smoking hash, and using psychedelic drugs at eighteen, Sadie also worked as a cocktail waitress and slept with wealthy guys for money.

But most men disappointed her. As soon as she realized she was in control, she immediately lost interest and moved on. That is, until she met Charlie, after which, she proclaimed, she was "completely content."

Sadie loved Charlie no matter what he said or told her to do, even though the harder she tried to please him, the more he told her not to.

"Do it for yourself. I don't care about you," he said. "I just love you completely."

Such a statement might seem ambiguous or contradictory to people outside the group, but to her it made total sense. It also kept her motivated to earn his approval and demonstrate her love. As their guru, he demanded that. But she actually seemed to thrive on his control over her.

"Charlie is the only man I have ever met . . . on the face of this earth . . . that is a complete man," she testified later.

CHAPTER 16

"DENNIS WILSON: I LIVE WITH 17 GIRLS"

In early 1968, Charlie told Roger that he wanted to transfer his case down to LA. He'd made some good contacts in the music industry there and wanted to pursue them. Roger submitted the paperwork to his counterparts in the Southern District and thought that was that.

After he finished his doctoral program and left probation work, Roger and Dr. David Smith opened a clinic for speed addicts in the Haight, a walk-in basement with some couches and an office in back. He was surprised when Charlie showed up to visit with five of his girls some months later. No other former probationer had done that before.

As the girls gushed about how Charlie's fame in the music industry was just a matter of time, they didn't look stoned, disheveled, or in any trouble. Just happy to crow about his successes.

"He's singing with the Beach Boys and Terry Melcher, and he's going to get a contract," they said.

Regardless of whether a contract was ever a real possibility, Manson certainly had reason to continue pursuing his dream. In a 1968 interview in the *Record Mirror*—entitled "Dennis Wilson: I Live With 17 Girls"—the Beach Boys drummer said of Charlie, "When I met him I found he had great musical ideas. We're writing together now."

When Roger tried to press Charlie for more information, he was his typical noncommittal self. "Oh yeah, playing some gigs here and there," he said.

While Charlie was staying in Topanga Canyon, he met up with his prison pal, music producer Phil Kaufman, who was released in March 1968 after serving five years for importing marijuana.

For a time, Kaufman was happy to partake of the sex and drugs that Charlie provided, but then he went on his way. Charlie did go see Kaufman's friend at Universal Studios, but nothing came of it.

———

Dennis Wilson's months-long episode with Charlie and the Manson Family started with his innocent meeting of two young hitchhikers named Katie and Ella Jo, whom he picked up twice in Malibu that spring.

The second time, Dennis took them back to his house and chatted with them for a few hours, sharing his recent experience with the Maharishi. In turn, they told him about their guru, Charlie Manson, who had recently gotten out of prison after twelve years. They thought Dennis should meet him.

When Dennis got home from a recording session in the wee hours that night, a man emerged from the back door to greet him. Dennis was understandably scared, so Charlie, who was in his foot-kissing period, got down and kissed Dennis's feet.

"Do I look like I'm going to hurt you, brother?" he asked.

Dennis walked into his house to find a dozen of Charlie's friends inside, most of them girls.

By this time, Charlie had collected small pockets of people, who were staying in different places, and were often taxied back and forth by Lynette Fromme, who served as a "den mother" of sorts for the Family. Some stayed at a place known as the "Spiral Staircase" house in Topanga Canyon, and some were at the Spahn Movie Ranch in Chatsworth.

But now that they'd found this groovy new pad in Pacific Palisades, a former hunting lodge owned by cowboy political humorist Will Rogers,

Charlie started directing his people to send girls and drugs to Dennis's house. The more he could bring to the party, the better chance he had of getting that record deal.

———

Catherine Share was one of those new girls. She was staying with Bobby Beausoleil at his place in LA when a man wearing a cowboy hat and a beard drove up with two young girls in a beat-up car. No one made introductions before Bobby sped away on his motorcycle, but it was clear that Catherine was supposed to get into the car with them.

The girls, who turned out to be Lynette and Ouisch, said nothing as they all drove toward a lavish house in the Palisades, where the cowboy pulled up to a security gate, punched in the security code, and drove inside the compound of wooden logs, glass, and tall eucalyptus trees.

"This is your dream, isn't it, girl?" he asked Catherine. "Start living it."

Inside, young, attractive people were swimming in the pool—lots of girls with bare breasts, passing joints around.

The cowboy disappeared and reemerged clean with wet hair, wearing loose yoga-style pants and a silk robe. She soon learned they were Dennis Wilson's clothes and this was the rock star's house. But the cowboy seemed so comfortable there, it was as if he were welcoming her into his own home.

"Hello, I'm Charlie Manson," he said, as if they hadn't already met.

They had sex that night, just as Charlie did with all the new girls. And once he was satisfied with his assessment, Catherine was initiated into the Family as Gypsy.

———

Some of Dennis's friends were happy to join the scene with Charlie and the girls, which included groovy, psychedelic group sex sessions, facilitated with hash, LSD, and strobe lights. In a practice the Family continued at Spahn Ranch, a few men lay naked on the floor of a room full of nubile teenage girls and young women, where everyone touched and made love to whomever was nearby, regardless of gender. It was, as one female Family member described, as if they were all "like just one."

Meanwhile, Charlie tried to make the most of his new connections with Dennis's friends—famous musicians like Neil Young, talent manager Rudi Altobelli, talent scout Gregg Jakobson, and music producer Terry Melcher—even tagging along to night clubs with some of them.

Young, a singer-songwriter, saw something in Manson's music, but he wasn't sure what. "It was beautiful, it was just a little out of control," he said.

Jakobson was impressed enough by Charlie's songwriting talents to talk him up to Melcher, who had met Charlie at the house a couple of times.

———

Sharmagne Leland-St. John-Sylbert, who was one of Jay Sebring's girlfriends, wasn't impressed by Charlie or his musical abilities. She first heard him play in a tall office building at 9000 Sunset Boulevard, which housed some of the most influential music firms of the 1960s and '70s. Her boss, Jim Dickson, manager of the Byrds, had an office there, down the hall from Beach Boys manager Nick Grillo.

On her way to work one morning, Sharmagne passed Charlie in the hallway. His hair stringy and dirty, he was sitting barefoot and cross-legged in jeans on the floor, playing an acoustic guitar outside Grillo's door. It wasn't unusual to see groupies and wannabe performers hanging out in those hallways, waiting to be discovered.

When she headed to the bathroom a few minutes later, she thought he was gone. But as she tried to get into the bathroom, she felt the door pushing toward her. He came out, saying nothing as he walked by.

Inside, she was shocked to see words scrawled in lipstick on the light-colored tile wall, sexually explicit and demeaning references to a woman involved with Byrds member Chris Hillman.

A year or so later, Sharmagne was mourning Jay's death as she watched a news conference about the Tate slayings on TV. When they showed a photo of Manson's face, she recognized him immediately.

Holy smokes, that was the guy sitting outside the Beach Boys' door! she thought. *Creepy.*

"His face was everywhere, always, for the next few months," she said. "It was always there."

———

Mike Love, another member of the Beach Boys, didn't fall for Charlie's shtick either. Dennis invited Mike to the house one night for "dinner," after which Charlie initiated a group sex session. It wasn't Mike's scene, so he left the room.

Charlie immediately burst into the bathroom, where Mike was showering. "You can't do that," he said, clearly annoyed. "You can't leave the group."

Mike just ignored him, but Dennis fell victim to Charlie's wiles. Recognizing that Dennis felt like a low man in the Beach Boys hierarchy of talent, Charlie told the drummer how talented he was; Dennis responded with mutual encouragement.

Charlie had more than enough charisma and troubadour charms to win over young men who were far more vulnerable than Dennis—lost souls with no direction, looking for love, validation, and acceptance. Like Charles Watson, a twenty-two-year-old from Texas.

In the spring of 1968, Watson was driving his truck along Sunset Boulevard toward Malibu when he stopped to pick up a hitchhiker who introduced himself as Dennis Wilson of the Beach Boys. Dennis told Watson he was thumbing a ride because he'd crashed his Ferrari *and* his Rolls Royce.

Watson hadn't heard of Dennis, but he'd definitely heard of the famous all-male singing group. He was even more impressed when he saw Dennis's expansive home in the Palisades and was invited inside.

As Watson walked into the kitchen, Dennis introduced him to the Reverend Dean Moorehouse, a pot-bellied bald man with a long gray beard, who sat at a table with some young girls.

"There's someone you should meet in the living room," Moorehouse said, taking him to a small man with big energy who was playing the guitar and singing on the couch, surrounded by more girls. The man looked up at him and smiled, exuding a gentle, welcoming warmth.

"This is Charlie," Moorehouse said. "Charlie Manson."

Watson was the son of a service station–grocery store owner and his wife, a domineering woman nicknamed Hot Rod Speedy Lizzie, who had laid out life plans for Watson, the youngest of their three children. Groomed to be a passive follower like his father, Watson did what he was told, which was to study marketing at North Texas State University.

Lured to the glamour of the Sunset Strip while working as an airline baggage boy, he'd left Texas State during his junior year to move to LA. He briefly enrolled at Cal State Los Angeles, dropping out this time to sell wigs in Beverly Hills.

Quitting that job as well, he resorted to hocking wigs and marijuana out of his truck, but he eventually just stuck to selling drugs.

Soon, he wasn't as worried about pleasing his parents, or figuring out what to do with his life. Sitting in Dennis Wilson's living room that afternoon, his mind opened up and he felt at peace, as if he belonged there. As if he were part of something bigger than himself.

He also liked feeling pampered by the girls, who served the men cheese and avocado sandwiches. Listening to Charlie's songs about love, Watson felt the music speaking to him.

As Watson was leaving that night, Dennis invited him to come back to hang out and swim in the pool. Before he knew it, Watson had his own room there.

His drug experimentation progressed to peyote, speed, and LSD as he absorbed the Manson philosophy: the key was to lose your ego and join with others as one entity, so each of you would "cease to exist" independently. Charlie even wrote a song with that title.

Watson felt a bond with Charlie, his philosophy, and his girls—a deeper kind of love, connection, and freedom than he'd ever achieved through sex alone. He also felt the material world slipping away.

Charlie slowly worked his way into Watson's head. Possessing little self-confidence, Watson later concluded that he'd fallen under a sinister form of sorcery the day they met, and that Charlie's music was a "ritual of magic, a formula of words, chants, recited for my deception. While smoking hash with Manson, unknowingly I chose to open my mind to evil and to give myself as the sacrifice. A coincidental meeting with the shaman that I will regret for the rest of my life."

After Watson moved with Charlie to Spahn Ranch, George Spahn nicknamed him "Tex" because of his Texas accent, and also because, well, there could only be one Charlie at the ranch.

———

Despite Charlie's charms, his lack of education and his years in reform schools and prisons put him in a whole different class from people like Dennis Wilson and producer Terry Melcher. In the end, he couldn't help being himself.

Always looking for an angle, Charlie and his Family constantly worked Dennis for handouts, food, clothes, and money. For months, Dennis was generous and complied with their requests, even giving Charlie nine or ten of his gold records.

As Dennis later told prosecutor Vincent Bugliosi, he treated the whole Manson crew to penicillin shots to treat their gonorrhea. He paid for studio time and also set up recording sessions at his brother Brian's studio so Charlie could put down some of his original songs.

But when Dennis finally reached the limit of his generosity, he didn't know how to get Charlie and the girls to leave the house. So he took off in August and moved in with his friend Gregg Jakobson, leaving it to Gregg to evict Charlie and his crew.

Charlie responded by sending a threat to Dennis. Handing Gregg a bullet, he said, "Tell Dennis there are more where this comes from." Not wanting to scare Dennis, Gregg never delivered the message.

Although none of Charlie's studio recordings ever made it into distribution, the Beach Boys did use one of Charlie's songs on their *20/20* album, which was released in 1969. Charlie had titled the tune "Cease to Exist," but when the album came out, he was furious to discover that

Dennis had rewritten some of the lyrics, changed the title to "Never Learn Not to Love," and taken full writing credit for it. It stung even more when the Beach Boys played the tune on *The Mike Douglas Show*.

"I gave him a bullet because he changed the words to my song," Charlie explained later.

Because the Manson crew had stolen and damaged so much of Dennis's property—trashing the house and crashing Dennis's uninsured $21,000 Mercedes Benz, for an estimated total loss of $100,000—Dennis hadn't felt obligated to give Charlie a shared credit, let alone any royalties.

Dennis eventually shared his experiences with Bugliosi, but he refused to testify at trial, fearing for the safety of his seven-year-old son and himself, especially after Charlie found Dennis again and threatened him personally.

"I'm the luckiest guy in the world, because I got off only losing my money," he said.

CHAPTER 17

SEARCHING FOR
A NEW HOME

After being forced out of Dennis Wilson's house in the late summer of 1968, Charlie tried to move more of his followers to Spahn Ranch under the same work-for-rent arrangement, but was told they couldn't stay, so he kept looking for another place.

In the meantime, at least some of the runaway teens and young adults had a roof over their heads at the ranch, where a place to sleep, a packet of cigarettes, and three squares a day—even out of a dumpster—seemed a fair exchange for one of their parents' credit cards and shoveling some manure.

Charlie took an immediate liking to one of these kids. Steve Grogan, a seventeen-year-old ranch hand, was already living in a shack at Spahn when Charlie had first arrived earlier in the year. As usual, Charlie gave him a new name—Clem Tufts—and he, too, became a trusted Family member.

Clem had started visiting Buddhist monasteries, as well as meditation and encounter groups, on his own at fourteen, exposing himself to different kinds of programming. After dropping out of school in the tenth grade with the romantic notion that he could find more meaning in life by leaving his blood family behind, he was already primed for Charlie's preaching.

Although he was open to skirting the law, he'd never been arrested for any violent offenses. His past charges ranged from possession of one marijuana joint to shoplifting a pair of socks, prowling, and stealing money. But he always went free or received only probation.

He soon fell under Charlie's domination, surely facilitated by the group leader's encouragement to use psychedelics. Clem's escalating drug use eventually turned his brain into scrambled eggs, making him seem unsophisticated and naïve. Thus his other Family nickname: Scramblehead.

But as he and the few other male Family members jockeyed for position in the hierarchy, they were just as insecure as the female members, trying to fill their dark emptiness with drugs and the emotional crumbs of acknowledgment that Charlie threw his "children."

Tex came to see Clem as Charlie's favorite, noting how he followed Charlie and the girls around like a dog, with a dumb smile on his face, and repeated whatever Charlie said. Clem didn't even seem to get into trouble when he took Dennis Wilson's Mercedes on a joy ride and crashed it.

As Charlie saw it, Clem needed very little programming, because he did what he was told. But like most of the girls in the Family, serious criminality did not come naturally to him. He seemed so innocent and childlike, and Charlie loved children.

———

Mary Brunner gave birth to their son on the Family's bus on April 1, 1968, and Charlie named the boy—his third son—after his Heinlein hero, Valentine Michael Smith. Mary had no midwife or doctor present, and only marijuana to smoke for pain during labor, which was complicated by a breech birth.

But focused on charming Dennis Wilson and his friends into recording his music, Charlie sent the boy away with his mother, Sadie, Katie, and a couple of other girls to Mendocino County. He told Mary he wanted the group to look for a permanent home there, but he also didn't want to overwhelm Dennis with bringing too many people over to the house, especially mothers and babies.

Continuing the Family way of life in Mendocino County—doing drugs and giving them to underage kids—this female contingent rented a house in Philo. But they proved to be a bad fit for this small town.

On June 22 the worried mother of a seventeen-year-old called the sheriff's office, asking for a deputy to check out her son. He'd taken a blue pill from some women at a "hippie house," which made him shake, feel nervous, think his legs had turned into snakes, and see flashing lights when he closed his eyes.

The deputy promptly arrested the five women, most of whom gave aliases but admitted to giving the teenager LSD after the cop found more drugs in the woodshed.

Just two months earlier, Mary had been arrested in Ventura County for contributing to the delinquency of a minor after the Family's bus stalled and she and several other members camped out nude in a ditch with the newborn. Coupled with the earlier arrest, Mary's arrest in Philo prompted authorities to take her child.

At Mary's request, social workers gave her son to Charlie's former probation officer, Roger Smith, and his wife, in a temporary foster care arrangement.

Because Charlie hadn't seen the need for pre- or postnatal care for the boy, including circumcision or immunizations, the Smiths had their hands full.

After determining the boy's foreskin was too tight, the Smiths had him circumcised even though they knew his parents wouldn't approve, because it brought the boy some pain relief. They also obtained a birth certificate for him, another "injustice" that angered Manson, because it represented the mainstream culture he'd rejected.

After two months in the county lock-up in Ukiah, Mary pleaded guilty to misdemeanor possession of LSD in exchange for a suspended three-year sentence and probation, and was released.

When it came time to return the boy to Mary, Roger's wife handed him over to a man who showed up in a Jaguar XKE. Terry Melcher had loaned his Jaguar XKE to Tex at least once, so it's possible Tex made the pick-up.

Like Mary, Sadie also got off with probation. She, too, had since become pregnant to add a child to the Family. After she and Mary were released from jail in September, they rejoined the group at Spahn Ranch.

———

Like Sadie and Katie, nineteen-year-old Leslie Van Houten was looking for someone all-knowing to steer her rudderless life. She, too, thought she'd found him in Charlie Manson.

Leslie was staying in the Haight that summer when she met Gypsy, Bobby Beausoleil, and his girlfriend Gail. She went on the road and panhandled with them as they traveled aimlessly up and down the California coast for several months.

While Bobby and Gail fought in the front seat, Gypsy talked endlessly to Leslie in the back about a Christlike figure who ran a commune on a ranch in LA. She said they really needed to get down there and be with him, because he had all the answers. To join, all Leslie had to do was to "drop out" of society.

Leslie agreed, and later that summer she and Gypsy showed up at Spahn to meet the fabled guru, who had managed somehow to get the rest of his Family settled in at the ranch. At first Charlie was angry that Bobby didn't come back with them. But he soon calmed down and showed his gentle, loving side to Leslie.

Leslie had sex with Charlie only a few times. He didn't continue to make love with her because he seemed to view her as Bobby's girl—or maybe as a draw to keep Bobby coming back to the ranch.

Bobby viewed himself as his own man and would later claim that he never was an actual member of the Family. Nonetheless, he spent a good amount of time living with the group, bringing new young girls to Charlie, and participating in his orchestrated orgies.

Leslie was one of the prettiest girls in the Family. In addition to being a homecoming princess, she also played baritone sax in the marching band at Monrovia High School. The brunette's coy eyes reflected her dependent personality, a lack of boundaries, and some dark, hidden pain.

Leslie's parents had divorced when she was fourteen, and like Katie, the breakup affected her deeply. At fifteen, she was smoking pot, dropping acid, and doing speed. She felt abandoned when her father got remarried and moved to Manhattan Beach, leaving his seventeen-year-old daughter with the mother who forced her to have an illegal abortion in the fourth month of her pregnancy, told her to be quiet, then buried the fetus in the backyard.

For years afterward, Leslie tried to cope with the forced abortion by calling it a miscarriage. "It took away my personality. I lost a lot of who I felt I was," she recalled.

Planning to become a nun at a yoga ashram after high school, Leslie ended up instead at Spahn Ranch, where Charlie Manson told her to break with the beliefs that her parents had instilled in her. He introduced her to a new way of looking at the world and a new group of friends who looked out for one another. They adopted Charlie's language, and used it to mock one another to help stay on his program.

As she was drawn in by Charlie's talk of love, the drugs, and the music, she also let him strip away her identity and indoctrinate her.

It didn't take long, but soon Leslie didn't want to leave the Family, and she couldn't even when she tried. For her and these other lost souls, this was their destiny.

———

That summer, while Charlie was still exploring other possible homes than Spahn Ranch for the Family, he came across a rural settlement in nearby Box Canyon, where he encountered the remnants of the late Krishna Venta's cult.

Many years earlier, Venta had established an outpost for his group of followers, the Fountain of the World. Like Charlie, Venta had a small-time criminal record and had also convinced his members that he was Jesus Christ. Before he was killed in a suicide explosion set by two cult members in 1958, Venta had been trying to gather 144,000 followers in a hole in the desert, where they would hide out until the blacks won an anticipated race war with the whites.

Charlie befriended a preacher at the Fountain named Jon Fisher, who that summer was reading transcripts of Venta's lectures from 1948. As they discussed Venta's teachings, Charlie said he especially liked what were known as Venta's "Golden Gems," and this one in particular: "No one is to blame for the things that come upon me; for they are all of my own making."

Also inspired by Venta's teachings about reincarnation, Charlie decided that because his last name was Manson he was literally the "son of man," or Jesus Christ.

In a scheme to take over the Fountain outpost as its new ruler, thereby absorbing all of its members into his Family, Charlie agreed to a ninety-day probationary period while he and some of the girls stayed there. But he was soon ejected for smoking pot with cult members.

After the Tate and LaBianca murders, the FBI and other authorities visited the settlement to interview the cultists about Charlie's time there.

"The remaining Fountain members lied to the police, claiming Manson had only stayed three days," Fisher later wrote in his memoir. "And we certainly didn't tell the police that we had preached to Manson the idea that Krishna Venta was gathering the 144,000 Elect to hide in the desert during the Final Battle."

CHAPTER 18

"SOMEBODY DROPPED THE BALL."

The Los Angeles federal probation office, which was responsible for monitoring Charlie Manson in 1968 and 1969, really had no idea what he was up to as he repeatedly exaggerated his celebrity connections and sugarcoated the truth. The officers also didn't seem to try to independently confirm his progress reports.

Even Roger Smith noticed that something was awry. After Charlie's case was transferred to LA, Roger was concerned that his former probationer didn't seem to have a new officer monitoring him, or if he did, that Charlie wasn't really on his radar.

"Somebody dropped the ball," Roger said. "He had to see me every week. I was enough on top of him he didn't get out of control, but left to his own devices and access to unlimited amounts of acid and control over those girls, it's absolutely no surprise that he spiraled out of control."

It seems that Charlie managed to snow the entire LA office about his whereabouts and activities—and the chain of command up to the US Parole Board in Washington DC as well—through a series of misrepresentations, lies, and manipulations.

In July 1968, for example, he told his probation officer that he "thought it best for everyone" if he moved out of Dennis Wilson's home, when in fact he'd been evicted.

When the officer came to check on Charlie's "new" digs at Spahn Ranch on October 3, he was satisfied to find Charlie dressed in western clothes and "performing well as a cowboy." He fooled the officer into thinking that the laid-back rural setting "provided him with enough activity to do something worthwhile, and that he was distant enough from any negative influences," as Angus McEachen, head of the LA probation office, put it.

A month later, Charlie called the officer to request permission to leave Spahn and relocate to Myers Ranch near Trona in Death Valley, claiming he was bored and that Myers "would be a good change. He was anxious to continue with ranch life as a means of not taking on too much responsibility and thought in that respect it would be simple for him to stay out of trouble," McEachen wrote.

Charlie never mentioned that the Family had already been out to the desert—driving to the bottom of Goler Wash in a green school bus the girls painted and decorated inside with silks, satins, and tapestries to look like a harem den. As they hiked over to nearby Myers Ranch, which was owned by the grandmother of Family member Catherine "Cappy" Gillies, they spotted Barker Ranch along the way. When it was warm enough, they went nude, one of Charlie's rules.

Charlie also didn't disclose that he gave one or more of Dennis Wilson's gold records to Cappy's grandmother to persuade her to let him and some friends stay for a while at the Barker cabin, which Charlie had hoped to purchase.

While Charlie told teenage Family member Brooks Poston that they were searching for a city of gold buried under the desert, he told his probation officer that he was gold prospecting and that he'd discovered "a vein of gold bearing ore in one of the mountains at a high altitude." He said he'd filed a claim on the mine with two other prospectors, but Brooks later told authorities that it was he and a gold prospector, Paul Crockett, who had filed those claims.

Based on such statements, McEachen was conned into feeling optimistic about Charlie's future. "He is courteous and polite with us, and would like to remain in our district," he wrote. "There have been no further negative reports about subject and it may be that subject will continue to improve in his conduct."

Charlie lied about his income as well. Long after Dennis had cut ties with him, he claimed that the Beach Boys were paying him advances on royalties for two songs that would be on their next album—five thousand dollars on one, and another that was under discussion for "a personal settlement."

By then, Charlie and some of the Family had relocated back to the San Fernando Valley, specifically to a canary yellow house on Gresham Street in Canoga Park that they called "the Yellow Submarine." But he never mentioned that move either.

———

Charlie and Family member Paul Watkins were on an acid trip at the Yellow Submarine when Charlie started riffing about the black man: "Blackie" had been suppressed, he said, subjected to cruelty and slavery, and it was time for his karma to change. The militant blacks—groups like the Black Muslims and Black Panthers—were going to rise and kill all the whites.

"A revolution is coming," Charlie said in what became a Family catchphrase.

The Family needed to prepare for this revolution, he said, by going into the city and saving white children. Better still, they should have a bunch of kids themselves and expand the Family to 144,000 chosen people out in the desert, where they would wait it out for 150 years, living in a bottomless pit.

By then the revolution would be over and Blackie would be done killing. However, the blacks wouldn't know how to lead, so they would willingly let Charlie take over, quite satisfied to return to being servants like they used to be.

"The only thing Blackie knows is what Whitey has told him or shown him," Manson said.

As Charlie developed his premise in the coming months, he wove the tapestry of his own LSD-enhanced prophecies with threads from Beatles lyrics from the White Album, Krishna Venta lectures, and references from the book of Revelation—an odd mix of concepts that his Family came to accept without question as Manson mysticism.

Charlie saw parallels everywhere: Beetles, locusts, and the Beatles were all related. The Bible's Revelation 9 was a corollary to the Beatles song "Revolution 9." The biblical breastplates of iron were the Beatles' electric guitars. There were five angels in the Bible, just like the original Beatles. Now there were just four and Charlie was the fifth, *Exterminus* or the Destroyer, as in Revelation 9:1: "And the fifth angel sounded, and I saw a star fall from heaven unto the earth: and to him was given the key of the bottomless pit."

He said he was "tuned in" as he repeatedly played the songs "Helter Skelter" and "Revolution 9," listening for deep meaning, especially in the eerie echoing line, "number nine, number nine, number nine."

In February 1969 he moved the Family members at Gresham Street back to Spahn Ranch, and sent Brooks Poston, the young Family member, back to Barker Ranch to keep watch over Charlie's desert outpost in Death Valley while he prepared the others to join him there later that summer.

———

When the various contingents of the Family reconvened back at the ranch, Charlie seemed much more intense, especially to those who had not heard his earlier rants at the Yellow Submarine.

As he brought the others up to speed about the coming revolution, he said the Family had to step it up and band together even more in preparation.

Katie's usual duties were to cook or take care of the children, but Charlie changed it up. One day he told her to dress in dark clothing, go with Tex to an auto showroom, and drive off with some dune buggies. So that's what she did.

Charlie escalated the psychological push as well: "We had to be one philosophy, one thought. We were one him," Katie recalled. "And we would be able to survive somehow."

When Leslie wasn't high, she kept busy with her tasks and chores. She and the others practiced creeping up on one another, took karate lessons, and learned survivalist techniques like canning food that would last for years in the desert.

To keep the momentum going, they turned the Lone Star Saloon into a nightclub, painted the walls black, and renamed it Helter Skelter, a song off the White Album. They also drew the words on a glass Sparkletts jug inside the club, and wrote slogans on the trailer's cabinet door: "1 2 3 4 5 6 7, All Good Children Go to Heaven," a lyric from the Beatles album *Abbey Road*, and "Helter Skelter Is Coming Down Fast," a combination of lyrics from that song.

But by June, Charlie was getting restless. He took Paul Watkins aside and said Blackie needed some help starting the revolution.

"I'm going to have to show him how to do it," he said.

———

Meanwhile, the LA probation office was still completely unaware of Charlie's true whereabouts. Although by May he'd been back in LA for several months, he was still reporting that he was living on a ranch near Trona. He also said he'd earned five hundred dollars from Gregg Jakobson "of Beverly Hills" for a music gig and working as a "caretaker and songwriter." Charlie waited until June—four months after his return to Spahn Ranch—to inform the authorities.

He occasionally asked if he could leave the state for a period of time. Still falsely claiming to be working with the Beach Boys, he was granted permission to play with them in Texas in May and June. Charlie lied again later, saying he didn't go because the group had gone without him.

Charlie kept the probation office at bay by admitting to the occasional minor offense, presumably to seem honest. After all, no probationer is a perfect angel. For example, he said he was arrested for being drunk in Canoga Park on June 3, and paid a twenty-dollar fine. And two months later, amid the chaos after the Tate-LaBianca murders, he reported simply that he was arrested for auto theft on August 16. He never mentioned the sheriff's raid at Spahn, only that he'd gotten a thirty-five-dollar traffic ticket.

Angus McEachen, LA's chief probation officer, finally began to catch on to Charlie's games after being informed that a colleague from the Division of Alcohol, Tobacco and Firearms (ATF) had obtained a warrant for Charlie's arrest. The warrant was based on information that Charlie had purchased two firearms from the Surplus Distributing Company in Van Nuys, using a fake ID: a short-barreled rifle on July 2 and a 9-millimeter Polish Radom handgun on July 14.

Bruce Davis confessed years later that it was he who purchased the 9-millimeter that day, using a fake ID with the name of Jack McMillan. Bruce claimed he bought the gun for target practice, so he "could be like the other guys" at the ranch. That same weapon was used during the three-day torture session that ended in Gary Hinman's murder two weeks after the purchase.

In September 1969, McEachen faced reality, telling his counterpart in San Francisco that he was skeptical of Charlie's unverifiable income claims, and that they shouldn't give him the benefit of the doubt after he'd violated the conditions of his release by buying firearms and consorting with other ex-cons. But by then it was too late. The murders had already occurred and Charlie had fled to the desert.

When Charlie's probation officer finally went to Spahn to do an in-person check, he reported back that a young woman named Lynn—who described herself as "George's housekeeper"—said Charlie no longer lived at the ranch.

The gun store employee, who had identified a photo of Manson as the buyer of the illegal firearms, subsequently decided that he'd been wrong, so the ATF had to withdraw its warrant. It's possible that Charlie was with Bruce that day, and the clerk misremembered who actually bought the weapon, but it's also possible that the Family threatened the clerk into changing his story.

If Charlie had been picked up sooner for any of his numerous probation violations, Hinman and the eight other victims murdered by the Manson Family might still be alive today.

CHAPTER 19

LOOKING FOR

TERRY MELCHER

Charlie was nothing if not persistent in the pursuit of his musical recording dream. Earlier that spring, one afternoon in late March, he had visited the house on Cielo Drive in an attempt to contact Dennis Wilson's friend, music producer Terry Melcher.

Shahrokh Hatami, a photographer who took portraits of Hollywood celebrities, models, and actresses, was doing a shoot there with Sharon Tate while she was packing to join her husband, Roman Polanski, in Rome. Hatami was concerned when he saw Charlie outside, uninvited and yet walking so confidently into the yard.

When Hatami met him on the stone path to ask what he wanted, Manson said he was looking for someone whose name the photographer didn't recognize.

"This is the Polanski house," Hatami said. Agitated, he suggested the visitor try the guesthouse via the "back alley," referring to the dirt path farther from the house, which also led around to the rear.

Hearing voices outside, Sharon came to the door to see scruffy-looking Charlie standing about eight feet away. "Who is it, Hatami?" she asked.

Charlie left in a bit of a huff and, after finding no one home at the guesthouse, left through the front gate a few minutes later. He returned that night, and this time Rudi Altobelli, who owned the three-acre property, was at home in the guesthouse.

Charlie had already met the talent manager at Dennis Wilson's place in the Palisades, where Dennis had played Altobelli some of Charlie's music to which the manager had offered a minimal remark: "Nice."

When Charlie asked him where Terry Melcher was that night in March, Altobelli said, "He doesn't live here anymore."

Charlie said he knew that, but wanted to know where he could find him.

Altobelli replied that Melcher had moved into his mother's house in Malibu, but lied that he didn't know the address.

When Charlie said he'd like to come back and talk more, Altobelli lied again, saying he'd like to, but he was leaving for Rome and wouldn't be back for a year. "I have a couple of clients making a movie," he said.

When Charlie said that he, too, was going to make a movie and a record, Altobelli replied that he'd heard Charlie was talented, but he was upset that Charlie had gone to the main house and disturbed the tenants. With that, Charlie took off.

The next day on the plane to Rome, Sharon asked Altobelli about "the creepy looking guy" in the yard the day before.

When Altobelli recalled this event later, he noted that Sharon, Jay, Voytek, and Gibby had all been at the main house that night. Charlie would have had to walk by them—and likely observed them through the big picture window in the living room—on his way to the guesthouse.

———

In May, Gregg Jakobson, a talent scout who scoured LA and the nightclub scene looking for writers or performers for Terry Melcher's production company, suggested that he and Melcher drive out to Spahn Ranch to check out Charlie's group to possibly record and film them. Jakobson had been calling Melcher for several weeks about it, describing them as a "musical act quite out of the ordinary," with too many members to come to Melcher's office.

When Jakobson and Melcher got to the ranch, Melcher estimated there were at least forty young people hanging around. "They were everywhere, mostly young women, and they all seemed to be part of the same group. They all sang together with Charlie Manson," Melcher later testified.

While Charlie played the guitar, the girls sang and banged on tambourines. After listening to a dozen of Charlie's original tunes, Melcher made some noncommittal compliment to be polite, his usual practice during an unremarkable audition.

"That is a nice song," he said.

Then he handed out all the money he had in his wallet, about fifty dollars, because the kids looked so skinny and dirty. He thought many were probably runaways and could use some food.

Melcher thought Manson's music, and the entire setting, really, was "rather peculiar to the pop music business, to say the least."

Shortly after the trip, a friend told Melcher that he was going to spend the summer traveling around in a mobile recording unit, collecting performances by various Native American tribes. Melcher brought the friend to the ranch a week later to see if the Manson "tribe" would fit into the project.

But Melcher wasn't interested in recording Charlie's music himself. He just felt bad for the group. They were such a sorry lot.

Nonetheless, Charlie came away from the experience believing that Melcher had made a promise to record his music, then reneged on it.

"He did wrong. He lied," he said later. "What does a contract mean to you? When you make a contract you keep your word or you lose your life."

———

Charlie had no trouble drawing young women into the Family. But finding men—ones he could trust and count on to accept his programming and to carry out his instructions—proved to be more challenging. He was always on the lookout for new prospects, men who were willing to "procure" whatever the Family needed and had the skills to carry out his orders. Men like Tex and Bobby.

Even when he found one, though, he often had a hard time keeping him around. Bruce Davis, whom he first met through a mutual friend in Topanga in late 1968, became one of these, and like Tex, he eventually took on a leadership role in the Family.

Charlie and Bruce had more than a few things in common: a southern upbringing, a curiosity about Scientology and other religions, issues with their parents, an interest in music, a taste for drugs, and a history of being raped and sexually abused. But perhaps most importantly, Bruce also had a self-described "criminal mind" and little respect for authority, having committed insurance fraud even before he'd met Charlie.

Born in Louisiana and raised in Alabama and Tennessee, Bruce was the son of an alcoholic pipefitter-welder who had abused him enough that Bruce didn't even attend his funeral.

After attending the University of Tennessee for a year, Bruce dropped out and, ironically, followed in his father's footsteps, working as a welder on a pipeline. The job brought him to LA, where he was arrested in Malibu for possessing marijuana while trying to buy some. He spent ten days in jail, but the charges were dropped because he'd had no drugs on him. He lost his job anyway.

Hurt and angry at the establishment, Bruce saw himself as "a counter-culture dropout and an outlaw." When Charlie invited him in late 1968 to his place in Topanga, Bruce was impressed—by Charlie's women, the way his people did "exactly what he wanted," his musical talent, and believe it or not, his ability to juggle.

Bruce looked at Charlie and his setup, and thought, *Boy, this is all right.*

Although Bruce had already used diet pills and NoDoz as a teenager, he waited to try marijuana until he was twenty-three. From there, he graduated to hallucinogens like LSD, mescaline, and psychedelic mushrooms, mostly on the weekends, to numb feelings of anger, resentment, and self-pity.

He enjoyed the benefits of staying with the Family for more than a month until his unemployment checks ran out, but then didn't try to find another job. As his drug use increased, he knowingly used stolen cars and credit cards instead.

"It was sex, drugs, and rock and roll, and I was hooked," Bruce said. "Charlie was a person that had things I wanted—girls and drugs—and he treated me like, I thought . . . I was being respected."

Viewing Charlie as a father figure, Bruce adopted him as his own, mistakenly thinking the admiration he felt for Charlie was mutual.

"I never told him that," he said. "Of course I never told anybody that, really."

Still, Bruce soon decided it was time to move on, no hard feelings. It was all peace and love when he left to hitchhike up north, returning briefly to Tennessee to visit his family, then off to Europe with a small inheritance from his father's death.

He landed at the Church of Scientology headquarters in London, where founder L. Ron Hubbard had first established his religious organization in 1952, hoping to achieve "a drug-free, crime-free and flourishing future for all."

However, Bruce couldn't follow the rules and got kicked out after a few months for using drugs. When he returned to LA in April 1969, Charlie and one of the girls met him at the airport.

And by then, everything had changed.

———

When Charlie said they had to get ready for Helter Skelter, Bruce didn't really buy into it because he didn't think it made much sense. But he went along because he liked the idea of "dropping out" even more by escaping to the desert.

That's when Bruce's welding skills came into demand as he and Tex, who was a good mechanic, retrofitted the dune buggies with stolen VW parts and mounted guns on them in preparation for the move.

At twenty-six, Bruce was one of the oldest Family members. When Charlie left the ranch on one of his jaunts, he left Bruce in charge.

Bruce, who kept track of the stolen credit cards, saw himself as a survivor. As long as he stayed out of trouble, he thought, nothing else mattered, and everyone else was on his own. He knew enough not to hurt or kill someone, because that was against the law and he could go to prison.

I can roll with this and I can get warm, but not get burned, he thought.

Bruce hated Charlie for the things he did, the trouble he got the Family into, and the lies he told. But he also loved Charlie for the lies he told—specifically the ones about how great Bruce was. He became hooked on hearing them. It was the kind of positive feedback he'd always wanted, but never received, from his father.

"Part of me knew better," Bruce recalled later, but "it wasn't enough to move me."

———

Like Bruce, Tex also left Charlie and the Family for a short time. While living on the ranch from August to December 1968, Tex became scared by his continual use of hallucinogens and the loss of contact with his parents, so he left to live with a friend in LA. After his friend got drafted, Tex went back to selling drugs and got romantically involved with his friend's girlfriend, Rosina. But Charlie kept calling, asking him to come back.

When he was away from Charlie, Tex dressed up in nice clothes, but he just wasn't pretty like Bobby. He was insecure about his appearance and his ability to make women want him, and he wasn't strong enough to fight Charlie's pull. So, in March 1969, he answered Charlie's call back to the ranch, where he took on more of a leadership role in the Family even as his drug use increased.

After boiling and chewing up some belladonna root, he became confused, disoriented, and assaultive. He also had hallucinations.

"I began talking to space people in space language," he said.

On April 23, the police found him in a car, high and acting strangely, so they arrested him and took him to jail, where he was attacked by another inmate. He had to get stitches for a deep gash above his right eyebrow.

Tex was booked and fingerprinted, then released. This set of prints ultimately became the first key piece of physical evidence that helped the prosecution team catch the Tate and LaBianca killers.

———

Danny DeCarlo, the Straight Satans biker, never fully joined the Family, but Charlie came to depend on him as well.

Charlie had a three-wheeler motorcycle with a blown engine that needed fixing, so he asked DeCarlo to handle it. An expert at rebuilding Harleys, DeCarlo said yes. After four years in the Coast Guard, DeCarlo also considered himself something of a gun expert.

In March, Charlie asked him to stay on at the ranch. He wanted some protection, tough guys to maintain the weaponry and to help keep watch for outsiders and for cops in particular. He hoped that by offering DeCarlo and his buddies sex and drugs, he could get some of them to stick around.

But DeCarlo was the only one who stayed for any length of time. He didn't get paid, but he liked life at the ranch enough to hang out there, having sex, drinking too much beer, playing the radio loud, and passing out drunk in the bunkhouse.

At 3:15 a.m. on March 30, two sheriff's deputies responded to a disturbance call at Spahn and arrested him and Charlie for assaulting DeCarlo's twenty-four-year-old wife "with intent to commit great bodily harm." Charlie was held at the Malibu station on a possible rape charge.

During a meeting with the victim, the prosecutor said he didn't see enough evidence to support a "great bodily harm" complaint, but was willing to file a simple battery charge. When she declined to pursue it, Charlie escaped punishment once again.

In June, Charlie and DeCarlo went to Jack Frost, a war surplus store in Santa Monica, where Charlie bought two walkie-talkies and two field battle phones circa World War II. He also bought five plastic five-gallon gas containers, and more than 150 feet of thick, strong three-strand nylon rope to tow broken-down cars or dune buggies at the ranch—or whatever else Charlie might come up with.

Nevertheless, when the LASD found all these items during the raid on Spahn Ranch on August 16, they thought they were looking at a simple auto theft ring.

CHAPTER 20

THE MURDER OF
SHORTY SHEA

Everyone in the Family knew that Charlie Manson didn't like ranch hand Donald "Shorty" Shea. For one, Shorty had married a black topless dancer in July, and Charlie didn't like the races mixing.

When Shorty didn't get picked up during the sheriff's raid at Spahn, Charlie's animus for the guy grew even stronger, because he suspected that Shorty had ratted them out to the law. Taking the cue from their leader, the rest of the Family concurred.

Born in Boston, Shorty was a stocky guy—five feet eleven inches tall and 190 pounds—who had worked at the ranch on and off for fifteen years, taking the occasional role as a stuntman.

He cut an unusual figure at Spahn. When he was in the air force in the mid-1950s, his ankles had been crushed and hips shattered in a parachute jump. In addition, he had a withered arm that was shorter than the other.

But he loved horses, having three of them tattooed on his chest, along with a rose. More recently, he'd added the figure of a woman to his upper left arm with the words "I'll always love you, Niki."

Shorty had been married once before, in 1961. He and his first wife moved with their three children to Spahn to train horses, then moved to Boston in 1965, where they divorced.

In 1956, after multiple stints in reform school, twenty-one-year-old Manson was sentenced to three years at Terminal Island Penitentiary, the first in a series of prisons he would see in his life.

(Courtesy of the US Bureau of Prisons)

In 1968, Manson brought his Family to Spahn Movie Ranch in Chatsworth, California, where they cared for the horses and grounds in exchange for permission to live as they wished.

(Anonymous / AP / Shutterstock)

In a photograph often imitated today, Family members posed with Straight Satans biker Danny DeCarlo in a cave on the grounds of Spahn Ranch: (Left to right) DeCarlo, Catherine Share, Mary Brunner, Chuck Lovett, Jennifer Gentry, Catherine "Cappy" Gillies, Lynette Fromme, Sandra Good, and Ruth Ann Moorehouse.

(Courtesy of the Photo Collection at the Los Angeles Public Library)

Sharon Tate wore a yellow-taffeta mini dress when she married Roman Polanski in London in January 1968.

(Evening News / Shutterstock)

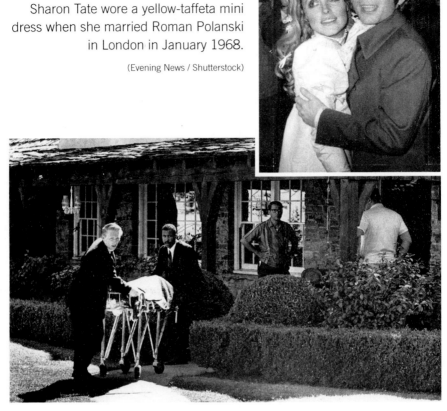

Sharon Tate's body was taken by investigators from her rented house on Cielo Drive in Benedict Canyon, where she and four others were killed on August 9, 1969.

(AP / Shutterstock)

Below: Leno and Rosemary LaBianca were murdered at their home on Waverly Drive in Los Feliz on August 10, 1969.

(Anonymous / AP / Shutterstock)

The hunt for evidence in the aftermath of the killings took place on foot and by helicopter in the Hollywood Hills as well as other locations.

(Courtesy of the Photo Collection at the Los Angeles Public Library)

Crews searched for additional bodies in multiple sites, including a 35-foot well at Spahn Ranch.

(George Brich / AP / Shutterstock)

When arrested at Barker Ranch in October 1969, Manson wore buckskin clothing sewn by Family members and laced-up by leather thongs similar to those used to tie Leno LaBianca's wrists during his murder.

(Anonymous / AP / Shutterstock)

Charles "Tex" Watson was held for months in Texas before extradition to Los Angeles to face trial for seven counts each of first-degree murder and conspiracy to commit murder.

(George Brich / AP / Shutterstock)

The three Manson girls on trial for murder—(left to right) Susan "Sadie" Atkins, Patricia "Katie" Krenwinkel, and Leslie Van Houten—often smiled and laughed while walking to court.

(George Brich / AP / Shutterstock)

Linda Kasabian, initially indicted on seven counts of murder, was later given immunity as the prosecution's most important witness.

(David F. Smith / AP / Shutterstock)

Manson Family girls, holding constant vigil outside the courthouse, shaved their heads after the verdict: Nancy Pitman (aka Brenda McCann), Sandra Good, Catherine "Cappy" Gillies, and Mary Brunner.

(Wally Fong / AP / Shutterstock)

Mary Brunner—the Wisconsin librarian who became the first member of the Family and the mother of Manson's son Michael—was a reluctant but crucial prosecution witness.

(George Brich / AP / Shutterstock)

Prosecutor Vincent Bugliosi, thirty-five, had lost only one of his previous 104 felony cases when he was assigned to the Tate-LaBianca trials.

(AP/Shutterstock)

Manson never realized his dream of becoming a rock star, despite his connections to Beach Boys drummer Dennis Wilson and producer Terry Melcher. He continued to play guitar and record music in prison.

(Trinity Mirror / Mirrorpix / Alamy Stock Photo)

Afton Burton began visiting Manson when she was eighteen and soon became known as Star Manson. She obtained a license for their prison wedding in 2014, but it expired as his health declined.

(Polaris Images)

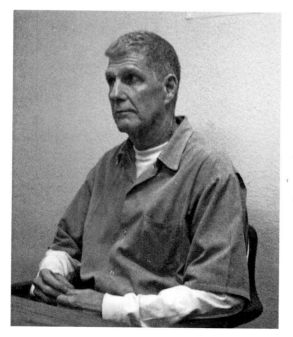

In 2016, seventy-year-old Tex Watson was denied parole for the seventeenth time. He will be eligible again in 2021.

(Photo by Lis Wiehl)

Charles Manson spent the vast majority of his years behind bars, moving from juvenile detention facilities to county jails and federal and state prisons. Clockwise: in 1968, in 1985, in 1996, and in 2017, three months before he died.

He returned to LA broke, so broke that he was constantly pawning his prized pearl-handled guns, two .45-caliber Colt Dakota revolvers with 7.5-inch barrels. But he always got them back. He pawned one of them for the last time at the Hollywood Collateral Loan Association on July 25, the other three days later.

The guns weren't really his to begin with. He'd borrowed them for a bit part in a film shoot in Arizona in 1968, leaving a camera as a deposit and promising to return the pistols. But Shorty told a friend that he'd never give them up. No matter what.

———

The "Niki" tattoo was inspired by his second wife, Magdalene Velda Fury, a dancer he'd met at the Cab-Inn in Carson, Nevada, where he was the manager. The couple got married in Las Vegas, then came back to LA together.

When Shorty brought his new bride to the ranch to meet George and Pearl, he also introduced her to Tex, Lynette, Gypsy, and Charlie.

Pearl, who had known Shorty since he'd arrived at Spahn fifteen years earlier, noted later that the couple's visit "made the hippies mad."

One Saturday night shortly thereafter, Shorty was walking on the boardwalk when a five-inch knife went flying by his head and stuck point-first into the saloon door, missing him by about two feet. Shorty looked around and saw Charlie standing nearby.

When Shorty confronted him, Charlie replied, "I might as well kill you, because your wife's brothers will do it anyway. Why did you marry a black woman?"

Shorty related the episode to Magdalene as soon as he got home that night. But he had a tempestuous relationship with her too. They'd been married for only six weeks when he left her in the middle of the night after an argument.

He called her the next day to tell her that everyone at the ranch had been arrested in a raid. "I'm going up there to stay and take care of the horses," he said, telling her to call one of his good friends if she needed to reach him. He also wrote her a letter a few days later, saying he hoped they could reconcile.

In the meantime, Shorty lived at the ranch in his car, a white 1962 Mercury he'd recently acquired from a friend, and kept all his belongings in it: a suitcase, two foot lockers, and a brown gun case.

A couple of days after the raid, Shorty ran into a producer with whom he'd previously bunked at the ranch. "I'm glad you're here," Shorty told him. "I think they're trying to kill me. Someone threw a knife at me. Can you loan me a few dollars?"

Shorty said he might go back to work at the Leslie Salt Mine near San Francisco for a while, but he needed to leave in the next few days or he wouldn't have the money to get there.

One night, Shorty got drunk and asked Pearl if he could stay at her house; he felt he was in danger and didn't like being around the weird hippies. She told him she didn't have room for him, but suggested he find a place to sleep amongst a group of Family members.

Pearl then got into her car and was about to leave when she saw a blue vehicle pull up. Charlie, Tex, Bruce, Clem, and another guy quickly jumped out and spread out along the boardwalk near where she'd left Shorty. Pearl thought it was odd; she'd never seen those guys move so fast. But she didn't look back; she just kept on driving.

———

After the charges from the sheriff's raid were dropped and the Family members were released from jail, five of them—Gypsy, Brenda, Clem, Lynette, and Barbara—were sitting on a rock outside the Longhorn Saloon when they saw Shorty walk around the corner of George's house, bend over, and peer underneath.

"That Shorty is sneaking around again," one of them said.

"Yes, but he'll be taken care of," Brenda said.

The same night that Shorty talked to Pearl on the boardwalk, Barbara was getting into bed in a building near the creek when she heard a scream. She sat up, thinking she might have imagined it.

But the screeching started up again and kept going. She could tell that the long, agonizing shrieks of pain were coming from the creek, another one of Charlie's favorite spots to do target practice. She also knew Shorty's voice, and she was sure it was him. Scared to move, she lay quietly until the screaming stopped.

———

Magdalene called the ranch about a week after receiving Shorty's letter and asked to speak to him.

"Shorty went to San Francisco early this morning," said the woman who answered the main ranch phone in George's house, a duty that Lynette usually handled.

Magdalene tried calling Shorty's friend as he'd instructed, but he didn't know anything about a trip to San Francisco. He'd thought Shorty was still at Spahn.

But after the night Shorty talked to Pearl, none of his friends saw him again, and it took years before they found out what had really happened to him.

———

The details of how Shorty was murdered were fuzzy for years, because the killers purposely exaggerated the details at Charlie's direction. But over time, Clem and Bruce gradually revealed some kernels of truth so at least the outline of the story is known. It has since become obvious that Clem minimized what happened to protect everyone but Tex, and although Bruce also downplayed his role for many years, he has recently been more forthcoming, and has incriminated Charlie in the slaying as well.

Clem, Bruce, and Tex were standing on the boardwalk one day when Charlie told them that Shorty had been working to get the Family evicted, so he had to go. *Not* them.

"Shorty is a snitch," Charlie said. "We're going to kill him."

That same day they asked Shorty to drive Clem, Tex, and Bruce to get some spare car parts. Clem joined Bruce in the back of the car, and Tex rode in front with Shorty. The plan was to wait until Tex gave the signal, then they would all jump Shorty and kill him.

Shorty drove about a quarter mile before Tex told him to pull over toward an embankment. When Shorty refused, Tex took out his knife and Shorty did as he was told.

Clem knew he was supposed to hit Shorty with a pipe wrench, but he couldn't. It wasn't in him to hurt someone else. But he was scared. He always felt as though he was being watched at the ranch. If he didn't do what Charlie had instructed, Charlie could just as easily order him killed.

The kid kept watching for a car to come along and distract them so he wouldn't have to do it, but when none came, he finally took the wrench and halfheartedly struck Shorty in the back of the head. Not hard enough to knock him out, the smack only served to surprise Shorty and kick him into survival mode.

Leaving the engine running, Shorty used his stuntman tricks to slide out the passenger side of the car. Tex was already outside, so Clem had to climb from the back into the driver's seat to stop the car from going over the embankment.

By the time Clem got out, Tex already had hold of Shorty, and together they dragged him down a hill to a ravine.

Bruce stayed in the back seat for several more minutes until Charlie pulled up in another car. "C'mon," Charlie told him, leading him down the embankment about twenty yards to join the others, where Tex was stabbing Shorty.

"Charlie, why are you doing this?" Shorty asked, knowing he was the leader.

"Here's why," Charlie said, knifing Shorty after deeming that he had come to the state of fear-enhanced total awareness that Charlie referred to as "Now."

As Shorty was slumped over, with his head bent forward, Charlie handed Bruce a machete and pointed at the nape of Shorty's neck. Bruce touched the machete to Shorty's skin, but couldn't bring himself to chop off his head as Charlie was indicating. He'd only come along for the ride;

he didn't want to go against Charlie, but Tex and Clem were both bigger than him.

Still, he recalled later, "I couldn't do what he wanted me to do."

When Bruce dropped the machete, Charlie handed him a knife with a long, thick blade, which Bruce used to slice into Shorty's right shoulder, cutting him from armpit to collarbone.

Years later, Clem said Shorty was already unconscious when he knifed him twice in the chest, and Bruce said he was pretty sure that Shorty was already dead when he sliced his shoulder, as if that lessened the heinousness of their acts of mutilation.

But as Bruce finally admitted, "It wouldn't have mattered to me if he were dead or alive at the time. I was going to do what I did and I did it."

Once Shorty was dead, Clem pulled his body over to the side of the ravine and covered it with leaves. After driving back to the ranch, Clem waited until dark to return with a shovel to bury the body deeper in the soil.

Later that night Charlie woke up Gypsy and told her to get into a car with him, Clem, Brenda, and Bruce. They drove Gypsy to the bridge near the railroad tracks, where Shorty's Mercury was parked halfway into the road. Gypsy followed Charlie's orders to ditch the car in the Valley, then thumb her way back to the ranch, leaving the Mercury on Gresham Street, near the Yellow Submarine house.

Over the next few days, Bruce's initial feelings of shock and shame were replaced by a numbness and a foggy state of denial as he "tried to rationalize what [he] had done."

———

Seeing an opportunity to instill more fear into the Family, Charlie told Clem, Bruce, and Tex to tell everyone in the group that they'd chopped off Shorty's head, cut his body into nine pieces, and buried them all over the ranch.

Always the good soldier, Clem did as he was told, exaggerating the savagery and callousness of the killing to Paul Watkins and others. "Charlie told me to cut his head off, so I had this big machete and I chopped his head off and it went, bloop, bloop, bloop and rolled over out of the way," he boasted, adding that warm blood splattered all over his body. "It was real groovy."

"Do you feel guilty?" Paul asked.

"Any guilt that I have is something I have to work out with myself," Clem said.

Bruce backed up the gruesome tale as well. "Charlie stabbed him, then we all took turns," he told Paul. "Shorty got to Now. [Clem] cut his head off with a machete. We stashed the body under some leaves. It was dark. Clem came back later with some girls. It was at night and the moon was full and the girls buried him. We had to put him out of the way. He knew too much."

Charlie did his share of talking up the murder too. "Shorty couldn't keep his mouth shut," he told gold prospector Paul Crockett at Barker Ranch later that summer. "It's hard to kill a man that's brought to Now. I had to cut his head off."

When Charlie asked biker Danny DeCarlo about the proper chemicals to dispose of a body, DeCarlo explained that lime would preserve it, but lye would dissolve it.

Charlie's ploy worked. Most everyone—including juries in future murder trials—believed the stories that they had beheaded and dismembered Shorty Shea. In the short-term, the tales also had the intended intimidation effect within the Family, even as Charlie and those involved in the murder tried to cover their tracks.

When Gypsy put on a blue shirt she'd found in the bunkhouse, Charlie confronted her.

"Where did you get that shirt? That's Shorty's," he said, telling her to get rid of it.

"If anyone asks about Shorty, tell them he went to San Francisco," Bruce told the others.

Bruce didn't give any explanation to DeCarlo when he gave the biker Shorty's two pawn tickets for the pearl-handled guns, which DeCarlo redeemed in Hollywood, using the alias Richard A. Smith.

DeCarlo said later that he didn't know the guns belonged to Shorty until he redeemed the tickets. He kept one of the revolvers and gave the other one to Charlie, who returned it two weeks later. But after learning that Shorty had been killed, DeCarlo dumped the weapons at another pawn shop in Culver City.

CHAPTER 21

HIDING OUT IN
DEATH VALLEY

After the August 16 raid at Spahn, Charlie decided it was time to start making the move to Death Valley as planned. He sent Family members in several waves to set up camp before he got there and to bring more guns and supplies after he joined them.

Charlie and his new favorite girl, seventeen-year-old Stephanie Schram, got arrested at the ranch again on August 23—this time for trespassing and drug possession—just days after they were released from jail after the raid. The cops sent Stephanie to juvenile detention until they figured out her real name, then called her parents in Anaheim to come collect her.

But they couldn't keep her away from Charlie. Stephanie reached out to him a couple of weeks later, and he picked her up on September 10 with Lynette and Clem. Taking her briefly back to Spahn, he had someone rent him a red Toyota Land Cruiser with a stolen credit card, then drove her and some of the other underage girls to meet the others in Inyo County.

Charlie left the rental car near Goler Wash, then some of the group trekked nine miles down the wash to Barker Ranch, a journey across sand and rugged terrain they had to make on foot because most of their dune buggies had been seized during the raid.

It took them about three days to reach their destination and join the others staying in the small cabin at Barker Ranch in the Death Valley National Park; another group was staying at nearby Myers Ranch.

There was a lot of talk about the killing the Family had already done, and the killing they were going to do. If any people from the city approached them out there, Charlie wanted them dead.

Stephanie overheard Sadie bragging that she had stabbed a guy in the leg and killed some other people. "Sadie's always talking about killing, you know, death of some kind or, just doing weird things," Stephanie told detectives later.

Tensions had been high at Spahn, but here in the desert they escalated even more. Extremely paranoid now, Charlie had them traversing back and forth between the two ranches in the remaining dune buggies, which were equipped with rifles and radios.

He was also growing increasingly frustrated. The crew that had participated in the murders was falling apart, emotionally overwrought, and hungry. There were no supermarket dumpsters nearby to scrounge for food and no drug suppliers.

Manson still had them preparing for the inevitable: they stockpiled fifty-five-gallon tanks of gasoline and barrels full of clothes and food, which they buried under the sand. They also brought in ammunition and posted armed guards and lookouts for the cops or the revolution, whichever came first.

As Manson was giving a lesson on how to stab people one day, he looked directly at Stephanie. "Are you okay?" he asked. "Can you do this?"

"Sure," she said, trying to fake it.

She'd already learned her lesson the hard way. Back at Spahn, when she'd told Charlie the truth—that she wanted to go home—things got ugly. He beat her up, took her into a room, and threatened to kill her with a big knife. She now knew that she needed to go along with the program, or at least pretend to.

"If it really came upon me to kill I wouldn't know how," she replied.

"Well you have to. If you're going to cut them from their neck, cut them from one side to the other," he said, demonstrating how to slice from ear to ear, plunging the knife in deep and wiggling it around to cut as many vital organs as possible. "Stick it straight into their ear, or in their eyes if you can."

Then, Charlie said, she should take their skulls, boil them in a pot, and set them all up on display.

———

Barbara, the seventeen-year-old runaway, woke up one morning in September at Myers Ranch to hear Sadie and Ouisch talking. Sadie mentioned that "Tate" was the last one to die, calling out for her mother. She also said something about Tex stabbing "Abigail" as she called out for God.

Coming on the heels of hearing Shorty's agonizing screams, Barbara finally determined it was time to get out. As soon as she saw an opening, she and another girl made their escape, walking sixteen miles to the nearest settlement, where she caught a ride back to her grandmother's house in LA. Back with her mother in Canoga Park, Barbara lay awake all night with a knife by her side for protection, yet her mother still didn't believe Barbara's outlandish stories about the Family. Not yet, anyway.

———

Around the same time, Charlie and some Family members were coming back from the hot springs when they saw that "they"—the government, the enemy—had torn up the road and filled in some of the springs with an earthmover.

The Family fixed the road so it was passable again, then the men set fire to the tractor loader in retaliation for disturbing the natural environment, an act of ecological terrorism known as monkey wrenching.

The US Park Service rangers who discovered on September 9 that vandals had torched their forty-thousand-dollar tractor loader, burning the seat and some of the wiring, were none too pleased. They traced the unusual tire tracks leading from the loader over to Hunter Mountain, where they found a partially stripped Ford sedan, hidden in the trees, surrounded by female clothing.

Soon after that, a local resident reported to the park service that he'd seen a group of hippies hanging out and also driving a couple of dune buggies and a red Toyota Land Cruiser. He gave them the Toyota's plate number.

When California Highway Patrol officer James Pursell ran the plate through a statewide database, he found that it was actually registered to an old Dodge truck—a red flag.

On September 29, park ranger Dick Powell asked Pursell to drive down Goler Wash with him to investigate. They arrived that afternoon at the Barker Ranch cabin, where a dune buggy, missing its engine, was parked out front.

Two young girls came outside, saying they were just visiting. The cabin occupant was a prospector, who had gone for supplies. So, Pursell and Powell headed toward Ballarat to try to track him down.

As the officers traveled down the canyon, they stopped two guys in a military truck loaded up with gear coming toward them, a forty-ish miner named Paul Crockett—the prospector the girls had described—and his young assistant, Brooks Poston, who had left the Family earlier in the year to work for Crockett. The truck was filled with auto parts, lamps, oil, batteries, hoses, and belts, which Crockett said didn't belong to them.

Asked why they were hauling the supplies up the canyon, Crockett paused thoughtfully. "I thought my life depended on it," he said.

When Crockett said the battery in his truck was dying and he feared it wouldn't start again, the officers agreed to meet at the cabin to continue talking.

There, Pursell was fascinated to hear the men describe the strange happenings they'd been witnessing: sex orgies, drugs, and a guy wearing a white robe leading his group in nighttime rituals and chanting. The group also patrolled the area at night, driving dune buggies and carrying guns, as if they were commandoes, protecting their territory.

Then Brooks, an aspiring musician, picked up his guitar and began strumming. His soft melancholy music only heightened the surreal tone of the story.

Just what in the world do we have up here? Pursell wondered.

———

On their way out, Powell and Pursell encountered a cluster of seven women, some of them naked, who tried to hide behind creosote bushes as the men approached.

Asked what they were doing, the naked leader replied with a sarcastic quip that was typical Lynette: "We're a Girl Scout troop from the Bay Area. Would you and the ranger like to be our scoutmasters?"

Pursell and Powell took the girls back to their camp, where they observed a red Toyota Land Cruiser and dune buggy, along with some sleeping bags, all covered with tarps clearly intended to hide the group's presence.

While Pursell tried to coax the girls into revealing where they were from, Powell took off running after a young man and managed to catch him. It was Tex, who identified himself as Charles Montgomery and claimed he didn't know the girls, who had picked him up hitchhiking.

Pursell took down the cars' VIN numbers, then left with Powell. All they had in the way of communication with the outside world was a park service radio, which meant they were totally isolated. They had to drive thirty miles before they could make contact with their superiors and call in the VIN numbers. Both cars proved to be stolen; the Toyota was a missing rental from Encino in the San Fernando Valley.

After waiting several hours for further instructions, they were directed to remain overnight at the mouth of Goler Wash and wait for backup. The plan was to return to Barker Ranch at daybreak to conduct a surprise raid.

With only a government-issued jeep as shelter, neither of them wanted to lie in the sand with the scorpions and snakes, so they lay across the seats and tried to get some sleep, worrying they might be shot dead by morning.

———

Once their backup arrived at 4:30 a.m., the men returned stealthily to Barker Ranch as a group. While the other officers waited in hiding, Pursell and Powell quietly hiked down to the cabin and knocked on the door.

When Brooks and Crockett answered, they seemed genuinely spooked to see them. After the officers had left the previous afternoon, they said, Manson had burst into the cabin with a shotgun, then blasted off two rounds outside.

"They thought that Dick and I had been killed," Pursell recalled.

After Charlie's shotgun blast, Tex had dug into a trash pile to retrieve an engine, which he quickly installed into the dune buggy out front. Then he, Manson, and the others hightailed it out of there.

Pursell and Powell found two more dune buggies in the area that day, which also turned out to be stolen. But because they had no way to get them back to headquarters, they disabled the vehicles and left them in the wash.

A day or so later, Brooks and Crockett hiked out of the area, caught a ride into the settlement at Shoshone, and headed for the nearest sheriff's substation, where they gave a recorded statement to Deputy Don Ward of the Inyo County Sheriff's Office.

However, when Ward played the tape for his boss, "the sheriff didn't believe it, and at that point decided that the sheriff's office wouldn't be involved in anything," Pursell said later, summing up the department's hands-off approach in this case for decades to come.

Unwilling to give up, Ward brought the tape to Pursell. After comparing notes, Pursell, Powell, and their superiors decided to proceed on their own, assuming they were looking at the same type of crimes that the LASD had suspected before raiding Spahn Ranch.

At the very least, Pursell said, "We definitely had an auto theft ring."

———

The night of October 9, Pursell, Powell, and a group of officers gathered near Barker and Myers Ranches to ready for another early morning raid at both locations.

Descending on Barker at 4:00 a.m., they gathered up Clem and a couple of other armed men acting as lookouts, then startled Katie, Gypsy, and Leslie into running out of a small outhouse like bugs by throwing a rock onto the tin roof.

Inside the cabin, they found three more women—Sadie, Lynette, and one other girl.

Hitting Myers simultaneously, the officers gathered up and arrested Sandy, Ouisch, and Brenda, among others. Between the two ranches, they also picked up two sunburned babies belonging to Sandy and Sadie.

The ten girls and three men, many of them wearing knives on their belts, were taken into the town of Independence and booked on charges of auto theft, arson, and possession of stolen property. They all gave aliases, which again complicated matters for investigators.

Because the officers found a sawed-off shotgun and a .22-caliber pistol at the ranches, several of the arrestees were also subject to weapons charges. And after finding more sleeping bags than bodies accounted for, Pursell and the authorities decided to conduct one more raid.

———

Later that day, two seventeen-year-old girls came out of some bushes and approached the officers who were still processing the scene at Barker Ranch. Kathryn "Kitty" Lutesinger and Stephanie Schram said they were running away from the Manson Family and needed some help.

Before coming to Barker, Kitty said, they'd been living with a group of thirty to forty hippies and some members of the Straight Satans motorcycle club at a place called Spahn Ranch in Chatsworth. Their leader, Charles Manson, directed the hippies to rob and steal for him.

Kitty said she was five months pregnant by one man in the group, a guy named Bobby Beausoleil, who was already in custody in LA for murdering Gary Hinman. She'd heard a story that Manson had directed Bobby and two other women, one named Sadie, to go to Hinman's house and take money from him; a fight broke out and the victim was killed.

The Inyo County authorities relayed the information to their colleagues in LA County, who said they were interested in talking to Kitty to see if she could fill in some crucial missing pieces in their Hinman murder investigation.

———

Two nights later, on October 12, Pursell, Powell, and another ranger approached the cabin at Barker one more time. It was already getting dark, too late to wait for backup to arrive, so Powell stood ready to shoot while Pursell announced himself at the back door.

After he ordered the occupants to come out with their hands on their heads, a line of three girls and four young men, who had been sitting around the kitchen table, walked outside.

As Pursell entered the cabin, the kitchen was dimly lit by a candle in a cup on the dining table. With his gun in one hand and the candle in the other, he cautiously entered the teeny adjacent bathroom, where he looked around until he spotted a strand of dark hair sticking out of the cabinet doors under the sink. He saw fingers emerge as the doors opened to expose a short man, wearing a leather shirt and pants, curled up inside.

"Hi," the man said affably, smiling a little.

"Who are you?" Pursell asked.

"Charlie Manson," he said.

Pursell arrested him and the others outside, including Bruce Davis, and put them into his truck to transport into town.

On the ride, Manson explained to Pursell that they were hiding out in Death Valley, waiting for a race war to start.

"He told us that the blacks were going to win," Pursell later recounted to *Los Angeles* magazine. "He told us that because we were number one, cops, and number two, white, we should stop right there, let them loose, and flee for our lives."

All told, the officers arrested twenty-seven people, including Charlie, who was booked as "Manson, Charles M., aka Jesus Christ, God."

———

On October 15, Angus McEachen, LA's chief probation officer, asked Inyo County sheriff's officials to hold Manson in Independence on an arrest warrant for his numerous probation violations.

The law had finally caught up to Charles Manson, but the authorities still had no idea about the full extent of his activities. McEachen's hold, however, helped keep him locked up while the various teams of detectives and the Los Angeles County District Attorney's Office worked their investigations.

CHAPTER 22

CONNECTING THE DOTS

Following up on the tip from Inyo County authorities, LASD Deputy Guenther and Sergeant Whiteley drove 240 miles northeast to Independence to discuss the Hinman case with Kitty Lutesinger.

During their interview, Kitty said she'd heard Charlie telling some of the girls about the recent killing of a cowboy named Shorty. She confirmed that she was carrying Bobby Beausoleil's baby, but she was vague about other details in the Hinman case, giving only first names for two girls whom she said were either involved or might have more information—a Marnie or Mary and a Sadie.

Guenther and Whiteley returned to Independence the next day after learning that investigators had been holding a Sadie Mae Glutz in jail there since arresting her in the Barker Ranch raid.

When they questioned Sadie about Kitty's statement, she told the detectives two different stories about how Gary Hinman was murdered, neither of which was true.

After they confronted her partway through her first false story, she relented. "All right, I'll tell you what really happened," she said. But that only led to another tale with some half-truths and many red herrings. It also didn't incriminate Charlie in any way. Sadie said a girl named Marnie might have more information about that murder, but she refused to say anything more, let alone repeat her statement on tape.

Based on Sadie's and Kitty's statements, and the fact that all the arrestees were Family members who had also been living at Spahn Ranch, the investigators decided to segregate Sadie and charge her separately. They took her to the sheriff's station in San Dimas, where they booked her for first-degree murder in the Hinman case. From there, she was transported to the Sybil Brand jail in LA.

———

One interview led to another, as the detectives tracked the aliases and questioned Brooks Poston, Paul Watkins, and Paul Crockett about their interactions with Charlie and the Family at the Spahn and Barker ranches since 1968.

Slowly, new leads began to surface as the witnesses also recounted similar accounts of Charlie, Clem, and Bruce boasting about the brutal group murder of Shorty Shea. Some said he was killed for badmouthing them; others said he simply knew too much.

Brooks, who had come with the Family from Spahn Ranch to Death Valley in late 1968, had been living and working with Crockett in the desert for most of the past year. Brooks said Manson had tried to get him to come back into the fold, suggesting that he cut the Inyo County sheriff's throat while he slept. But Brooks resisted.

"He's talked about killing off the people in the desert . . . and if any police came up, he would kill them and leave their uniforms laying out as if the body had just disappeared from it," Brooks said.

———

Tired of pretending to be someone else, Katie finally told investigators her real name was Patricia Krenwinkel. But once they started asking her specific questions, she clammed up.

"We were both firmly convinced she knew of a killing, but we did not know which killing," Guenther said.

With nothing to hold her on, they had to release her.

After neither of her parents—her father in LA and her mother in Mobile, Alabama—knew how to deal with her jumbled thoughts and Manson programming, she ended up living near her mom's with a group that was similar in some ways to the Family she'd left behind. "I ran into some people who were, you know, drug addicts, and I felt comfortable there," she said.

In the meantime, Lynette called Katie several times, telling her to be patient. The Family didn't know what the plan was yet, but they would let her know as soon as they did.

———

Shortly thereafter, the LAPD and the LASD finally began sharing information. As a result, the two agencies started to connect the dots, noting the parallels and connections between the several sets of murders that they'd refused to see for months, despite the media's observations early on.

As one investigative report put it, "All three murders have the unique characteristic of the suspect using the victims' blood to write on the wall. This characteristic takes on a greater significance in that in each instance the words make reference to 'pig' in one form or another." The report also noted that knives were used in all three murders, and that a pillow was placed over one of the victims' faces in both the Hinman and LaBianca murders.

———

In late October, Sadie was in dormitory #8000 at Sybil Brand, where she passed the time by telling tales to her fellow inmates, violating the Family's "no snitch" pact as she confided in Virginia Graham and Ronnie Howard.

Graham, a former call girl behind bars for a parole violation, initially didn't know what to think of the unstable woman with all the crazy stories. Neither did Howard, a call girl formerly convicted of extortion and forgery, who was back in jail for forging a prescription.

Sadie's ramblings started when she and Howard were placed in adjacent beds, usually after dinner. "We're next to each other for a reason," Sadie said.

As they discussed their past acid trips, Sadie said she felt more alert and aware when she was high on LSD. But now that she'd "done everything there is to do," there was nothing left. She said there wasn't much that could shock her, but she could tell Howard a few things that would really blow her mind.

"You can't shock me either," Howard replied, "but try me."

"You remember the Tate deal?"

"Yes."

"I was there. We did it."

"Who is we?"

"The four of us. Charlie, Katie, Linda, and myself."

"Oh, really. Anyone can say that."

"No, I'll tell you."

Sadie began describing the night that she and the others killed Sharon Tate, referring to Charles "Tex" Watson as "Charlie," which Howard didn't realize at the time. As Sadie also talked about the LaBianca slayings, she didn't seem to be holding anything back, boasting that she got a sexual charge from stabbing the victims.

"Especially when you see the blood spurting out, it's better than a climax that you never had, the whole world is like one big intercourse. Everything is like in and out, like smoking, eating, stabbing."

Asked if it was like a drug habit, Sadie replied, "Yeah, the more you do it the better you like it."

"What about the Tate place, did anybody scream?"

"Yeah, the first time I stabbed Sharon Tate, it felt so good, she screamed," Sadie said. "It did something to me, sent a rush through me and I stabbed her again."

"How many times?"

"I don't remember, I just kept stabbing her until she stopped."

"What happened to the baby?"

"I wanted to take it with us."

"How would you have done that?"

"We would have had to cut it out of her."

"Why didn't you?"

"I went back inside to write 'PIG' on the door and when I dipped the towel in her blood, I wanted to cut the baby out but everything happened so fast . . . I just ran out of there."

"Why did you do this?"

"We wanted to do something to shock the world."

Sadie said the cops had gotten it all wrong with another case too. They'd said *she* had been holding this hippie down, which was crazy because the guy weighed two hundred pounds. It was really *Bobby* who held the guy down while *she* stabbed him.

———

On November 5, 1969, Family member John Philip Haught, aka Zero, who had been arrested in the desert raids and then released, allegedly shot himself playing Russian roulette in Venice—with a fully loaded gun, which didn't fit the rules of the game.

Witnesses, including Bruce Davis, told police the same story, that Zero picked up the gun and shot himself while lying on a mattress next to one of the girls. Although Bruce said he subsequently picked up the gun, investigators found no fingerprints on it or its leather case, yet they still ruled the death a suicide.

On November 18, Vincent Bugliosi, a thirty-five-year-old ambitious deputy district attorney, was excited to learn that he'd been assigned to work with a more senior prosecutor, Aaron Stovitz, as co-counsels on the Tate and LaBianca murder cases.

In the DA's office, which employed 450 attorneys, Stovitz was head of the trials division, and Bugliosi was an up-and-comer, who had won all but one of the 104 felony cases he'd tried during his five years with the office.

When Bugliosi heard about Zero's death, he immediately questioned the suicide story. His suspicions were raised further when a young man mysteriously disappeared shortly after telling a *Los Angeles Times* reporter that he had been at the house the day a female Family member had murdered Zero.

Oddly enough, Sadie knew details about the incident with Zero, even though she was in jail when it happened, and passed them on to Ronnie Howard.

"My girlfriend just told me that this guy killed himself playing Russian roulette," she said, explaining that he'd died in mid-orgasm while a girl held on to his wrist.

"Imagine how beautiful to be there when it happened!" she exclaimed.

Still unsure of Sadie's credibility, Howard compared notes with Virginia Graham until November 12, when Graham learned she was being transferred to the women's prison in Corona that afternoon. Once Graham was gone, Howard was on her own.

Howard tried to nail down a few more details with Sadie, then tried to convey the information to a female sergeant at the jail. After getting shut down, she became further convinced that the information was important, so she waited for a chance to use a pay phone away from the jail and the sergeant's eyes to call the LAPD.

———

On November 17, Ronnie Howard met with detectives from the Tate and LaBianca teams, Sergeants Michael McGann and Frank Patchett, following up with them again a week later. As they reviewed her conversations with Sadie, Howard was clearly confused about some details, mixing up the Tate and Hinman murders, and Charlie Watson with Charlie Manson. But she said she was sure Sadie never said anything about "a fella named Shorty" or the murder of a sixteen-year-old boy.

"She just told me that there were eleven murders that the police will never solve," she said, adding that Sadie did say they'd killed a guy and cut off his head.

Asked if Sadie had done that alone, Howard said, "No. She said, '*We* cut his head off.'"

"Did she seem kind of sad or remorseful?" Patchett asked.

"No, she thought it was funny," Howard said. "That is why this [other] girl said, even if they do convict her, they'll probably send her to a mental institution."

"Did she sort of recruit you, I mean, tell you that 'Helter Skelter' means this and this and this?"

"It means you have to die in order to live."

———

In yet another egregious mishandling of the investigation, the LAPD almost lost one of the murder weapons.

Back in September, ten-year-old Steven Weiss had been fixing the sprinklers when he found a gun on a hill in his backyard in Sherman Oaks. A fan of TV cop shows, he was careful to pick up the gun by the tip of the barrel to preserve any fingerprints.

He and his father, Bernard, called the LAPD's Van Nuys Division to report the finding, but the officer who came to collect it didn't show the same care. The Weisses were horrified as he put both hands all over the weapon. They were also shocked when they had to show him how to disarm it, and as he removed the two bullets and seven casings, he touched them too. So much for protecting the evidence.

Three and a half months later, Bernard called the police to remind them of the gun he'd handed over, because it sounded identical to the missing Buntline firearm used in the Tate murders that he'd just read about in the newspaper.

Sergeant McGann's team had distributed bulletins with photos—as far and wide as Canada—that they were looking for that particular gun, but somehow the Van Nuys division had missed it.

Similarly, it was a KABC-TV news crew—not the police—who used their investigative skills and common sense to locate the bloody clothing that Tex and the girls had tossed out of the car after the Tate murders, about a mile and a half from the Weiss property.

Civilians also found a knife off Mulholland Drive in late December and turned it over to authorities. Lab tests showed that it, too, may have been used in the Tate murders.

The police did do some good detective work, however. Sergeant Patchett tried to interview Charlie Manson in a small corner jail cell in Independence, but got nowhere. Asked if he knew anything about the Tate or LaBianca murders, Charlie replied, simply, "No."

So, Patchett had a go at interviewing Leslie, who was still insisting that her last name was Sankston. He didn't get much more from her either, other than confirmation that Sadie had been involved in the Hinman murder.

Foiled again, Patchett took the opportunity to examine Manson's belongings, specifically his clothing from the day of his arrest at Barker Ranch. As he looked over the buckskin pants, vest, and boots, he removed a long leather thong from one of Manson's boots and a shorter one from his pants.

Back at the LAPD Property Room, he compared them to the leather thongs used to bind Leno LaBianca's wrists. To the naked eye, they looked like a perfect match.

CHAPTER 23

THE DOMINOES
BEGIN TO FALL

Jury selection for Bobby Beausoleil's trial started quietly and with little fanfare on November 13. Because the detectives had yet to connect him to the Manson Family's activities, his trial was assigned to a Superior Court judge in Long Beach, about twenty-five miles from the main criminal courthouse in downtown LA, where his codefendants would be tried later.

Both sides had agreed that Bobby would not face the death penalty, but rather a maximum life sentence and a chance for parole.

Represented by a deputy public defender, Bobby made it through five days of trial—through closing arguments and jury instructions—before the proceedings screeched to an unanticipated halt.

The prosecutor asked for a private meeting in the judge's chambers to request permission to re-open his case based on some late-breaking evidence: LAPD detectives had just learned that Sadie had been talking to her cellmate Ronnie Howard about the Hinman, Tate, and LaBianca murders. The judge granted the motion, but kept Bobby and the jury in the dark, saying only that the trial was being continued for a week.

—

The detectives had learned new information from Straight Satans bikers Allan Springer and Danny DeCarlo as well. While the Family was still at Spahn Ranch, DeCarlo said, Charlie told him they knew a guy named Gary who had twenty thousand dollars, and they were going to try to "get it off of him."

DeCarlo said Bobby also told him how the whole weekend with Gary Hinman went down: After Bobby called Charlie to alert him that Gary wasn't cooperating, Charlie came over and cut up the man's ear. Sadie and Mary were there too.

Then Bobby called Charlie a second time. "You better take care of him," Charlie said. "You're going to have to kill him, that's all there is to it." So that's what Bobby did, DeCarlo said, stabbing Hinman with the knife he wore in a leather sheath on his belt.

After the Spahn raid charges were dropped, DeCarlo said, he'd gone out to the desert with Tex and Bruce. But after only four days there, he'd decided he was done with the Family for good and returned to LA.

Based on what DeCarlo told detectives, he became a key witness, not only in Bobby's trial, but in the Tate-LaBianca case as well.

———

When Bobby's trial resumed on November 24, the prosecution reopened its case and called several new witnesses, including DeCarlo. However, the testimony wasn't enough to win a conviction.

After deliberating a little more than a day, the jury foreman announced that the panel had reached an impasse: eight in favor of conviction, four for acquittal.

The judge declared a mistrial after questioning the jury. Determining that the jury didn't believe DeCarlo, the DA's office blamed the loss on the prosecutor's failure to properly prep him to testify. Next time, they vowed, would be different.

In the meantime, the dominoes against the Manson Family continued to fall.

That same week, Leslie Van Houten, who had been transferred from the Inyo County jail in Independence to Sybil Brand in LA, gave up a few more details.

To get these Family members to talk, investigators had to claim they had more incriminating evidence than they actually did—although some detectives used their legal ability to gain leverage over witnesses more than others. Some investigators lied, while others threatened a death sentence or the permanent loss of female witnesses' children if they didn't testify.

Leslie clearly didn't want to incriminate any of her fellow Family members. But once she learned about the death of Zero, whom she hadn't seen since the Barker raid, and also that Sadie had been talking up a storm, she became upset—or disarmed—enough to disclose names of the two girls who had gone with Sadie to the Tate house.

It took until November 30 for the LAPD to realize it had a fingerprint on file that matched the latent print found on the Tate house's front door, six inches above and to the left of the knob. This was a huge discovery for the prosecution team—its first piece of physical evidence in the case linking the Family to the murders.

The latent print was a match with Tex Watson's right ring finger print, collected during his arrest back in April. He'd since been released from the Independence jail as Charles Montgomery, and had flown back to be with his family in Copeland, Texas.

After determining Tex's true identity, they called the authorities in Tex's hometown, linked the alias to his cousin, Collin County sheriff Tom Montgomery, and notified him that they were looking at Charles Watson for murder.

The Tate-LaBianca prosecution team still didn't have enough evidence to prove its case in court. But by the morning of December 1, Vincent Bugliosi decided they had just enough to issue warrants to arrest Patricia "Katie" Krenwinkel, Linda Kasabian, and Charles "Tex" Watson for first-degree murder.

Sheriff Montgomery disclosed the warrant to Tex's uncle, a sheriff's deputy at the jail, who then called Tex's father. Convinced that Tex couldn't have killed anyone, his father and uncle picked him up at his apartment and drove him to the McKinney jail, where he turned twenty-four the next day.

When Tex had needed an attorney to represent him after he was arrested for stealing typewriters as a fraternity prank, his family had hired Roland Boyd, who got the charges dropped. Now, four years later, they hired Boyd's firm again to defend Tex against a far more serious set of accusations.

Boyd immediately filed paperwork fighting the request to extradite Tex to LA, arguing that he couldn't get a fair trial in California due to the unprecedented level of publicity about the case.

For a while, it worked.

———

The same day that Tex was arrested, Katie was driving to her aunt's house in Mobile when the cops pulled her over and arrested her too.

After taking her fingerprints during the booking process, the local police sent them to the LAPD, where investigators found a match: Katie's left little finger fit with the latent print discovered on the door in Sharon Tate's bedroom that led to the pool.

Bingo. A second key piece of physical evidence.

But Katie wouldn't agree to come back to LA to face trial either—until February 1970, when she not only stopped fighting extradition but asked to be returned to California. She'd finally succumbed to the pleas in Lynette's letters, urging her to participate in the Family's "united" defense.

———

Linda Kasabian was the only one of the three suspects to surrender voluntarily.

Three days after she'd taken off for New Mexico, the LASD had detained her daughter Tonya during the raid at Spahn Ranch and placed her into foster care. Linda was eventually able to get the child back through the courts.

Reunited, mother and daughter hitchhiked across the country to see Linda's father in Florida, then headed north to stay with her mother and stepfather in New Hampshire.

After learning a murder warrant was out for her arrest, Linda surrendered to the state police at her mother's house in Milford, a town of 6,600 people, on December 2.

As she was leaving the house with the officers, Linda turned to her mother and said, "All I ever wanted was what you've got—a husband, love, a home and children."

However, her mood changed abruptly once she got to court. "I don't care if the whole world comes down, I'm not talking," Linda told police after pleading guilty to being a fugitive from justice.

Turned over to authorities from LA, she was flown west the next day and booked into Sybil Brand.

———

As Sadie's jailhouse stories were filtering into the LAPD and LASD, her lawyer, Richard Caballero, was trying to get her a deal with the DA's office.

Although her allegiance to Charlie kept her from jumping at the chance to cooperate, she eventually agreed to tell her story on a two-hour tape, which Caballero shared with Bugliosi and a team of detectives on December 3. In one key statement to her lawyers, Sadie said Charlie sent the group to the house on Cielo Drive because the former home of producer Terry Melcher "represented a symbol of rejection for him."

The next day, on the eve of grand jury proceedings, Sadie and her attorney had a lengthy discussion with the prosecution team in the office of the DA himself. Caballero asked for immunity in return for Sadie's cooperation in helping to solve the Hinman, Tate, and LaBianca murders, but said he was unsure if she would testify "for fear of the physical presence of Charles Manson" and his codefendants.

The prosecutors acknowledged that Sadie's cooperation thus far had been vital to the case. As long as they determined that she'd testified truthfully, they said, they wouldn't use the information that she'd provided against her, nor would they seek the death penalty. Whether they sentenced her on lesser charges would depend on how cooperative she continued to be in the future. But they could not—and would not—grant her immunity.

Sadie accepted the deal and agreed to testify before the grand jury.

———

While Sadie had bragged to her cellmates that she'd fatally stabbed Sharon Tate, she told the grand jury that she couldn't bring herself to do anything but hold the pregnant woman while Tex did the deed. She said she'd *wanted* to cut out Sharon's baby but couldn't do that either.

The Cielo Drive house had been chosen as the target, she said, because Tex had been there before and knew the outline of the property. And when they got back to the ranch, Charlie wanted to know why they were done so soon.

But she still didn't incriminate Charlie in the murders, saying he had simply given her a knife and some dark clothing to wear, and instructed her to follow Tex's orders. Still characterizing Charlie as some sort of deity, she said the words out of his mouth came from "the Infinite."

CHAPTER 24

FORCED TO COOPERATE

In early November, Detective Guenther and Sergeant Whiteley of the LASD realized after some more digging that Mary Brunner was the Mary they'd been searching for in connection with the Hinman murder.

They learned that she had not only violated probation on a forgery conviction, but she'd also had a baby with Charles Manson. At the very least, they figured she probably had useful information, so they tracked her down in her hometown of Eau Claire, Wisconsin, where she'd gone after being released from Sybil Brand in September.

On December 4, while Susan "Sadie" Atkins testified before the grand jury, Guenther and Whiteley flew to Wisconsin to question Mary.

Lieutenant Roger Brown of the Eau Claire Sheriff's Department, who had known the Brunner family for twenty years, suggested the detectives meet Mary in the lounge at the Holiday Inn. Brown thought she might refuse to talk if they tried to interview her at the sheriff's office or the college where she worked.

When Mary came in with Brown, the two detectives were waiting at a small cocktail table near the bar. She sat at a table next to them.

Whiteley tried opening the conversation on a non-confrontational note, hoping not to spook her. "Mary, we're here because of the Gary Hinman killing," he said.

But Mary surprised them with her candor. "Yes, I know, I've been expecting you," she said. "I knew that sooner or later you would want to talk to me. I've been trying to straighten myself out. I have a job and I've been trying to care for my baby. My mind is very confused. I don't know whether I am thinking my thoughts or Charlie's thoughts. I just don't know what happened."

"We're only interested in the facts," Whiteley said.

"Bobby and Sadie and I went to the house to get some money," she said. "We didn't mean to kill him. He was a nice man. We wanted the money to go out to the desert and live. We didn't always live like this, only after those motorcycle bums showed up."

She seemed genuinely torn as she described how she'd taken care of Gary that weekend. "I don't know why we killed him. I don't know why this had to happen. I guess it was just his time to go."

Trying to put her at ease, the detectives suggested they have dinner, then head down to the sheriff's office to record her statement. At that point Brown left to prepare.

As Mary and the two LASD detectives talked informally, she ordered two Manhattans, but didn't finish the second one. The detectives saw no indication that she felt intimidated or threatened into speaking to them. Nor did she seem drunk or high on drugs as she volunteered information even when they weren't asking questions. In fact they urged her to eat something before they got into the meat of her story.

"Let's wait until we get down to the police station," Whiteley said.

But she seemed remorseful, as if she wanted to get something off her chest. "I want to talk about this," she told them. "This whole thing has been very weird. I don't know why we had to kill him. We just did and it doesn't make any sense."

Mary testified later, however, that she only talked to the detectives because she feared they would arrest her and take her two-year-old son away from her permanently. For the moment, Michael, whom she called Bear, short for Pooh Bear, was staying with her mother in a foster care arrangement 185 miles away from Mary's job, so she only saw him on weekends.

Mary said she also felt intimidated by Sergeant Whiteley, who had been doing most of the talking. Guenther was able to play on her emotions while Whiteley was in the bathroom, she said, because she was tipsy and emotional from the Manhattans.

She said Whiteley told her that her fingerprints had been found at Gary's house, that witnesses had placed her in a stolen car, and that Bobby and Sadie had both blamed her, in large part, for the murder. If she talked she could get her probation dropped and also regain custody of her son.

Mary voiced concerns about the possible ramifications of word getting out that she was cooperating with law enforcement. "I don't want any publicity for my family," she said.

"Well, we haven't come here to talk to the newspapers," Whiteley said. "Okay, that's good."

At that point, they moved the conversation into the restaurant next door, where Mary ordered a salad for dinner.

"Tell me what's going to happen to me," she said a few minutes later. "Am I going to be separated from my baby? Am I going to have to go to jail?"

Once they got to the station, the detectives turned up the heat and asked her more probing questions. All told, they talked for a grueling seven hours that night.

Until then, Mary had only implicated herself, Bobby, and Sadie. It wasn't until Whiteley reassured her that the DA was prepared to offer her immunity that she finally conceded that Charlie Manson and Bruce Davis had also been involved in the events at Gary Hinman's house. All she had to do was assist in the investigation by providing valuable information and then testify about it in court.

That night, Mary became one of the first longtime Family members to agree to help build the case against the brothers and sisters she loved, a decision with which she struggled for years to come.

———

At the same time Mary was being questioned, two LASD detectives—Deputy Bill Gleason from auto theft and a detective from homicide—were interviewing seventeen-year-old Stephanie Schram about Charlie and the Family.

"How can you convict him?" she asked. "I mean he instigated—he had so much control over everybody—but they all did [it]."

Expressing a mix of optimism and frustration, Gleason said they still didn't have enough evidence to file homicide charges against Manson, at least in the Hinman case. But they were also hearing rumors that Shorty Shea had been murdered.

"We're right on the edge," he said, "but we just can't get it."

Stephanie also asked them about news reports concerning another murder victim, a seventeen-year-old Jane Doe, whom she said could have been a Family member trying to escape. "If you left the group, Charlie would kill you," she said.

Gleason said they hadn't been able to identify the girl because she'd never been arrested, so they didn't have her fingerprints on file.

He then spoke to her sympathetically. "I'm glad you got away from it when you did," he said. "It got pretty bad."

Stephanie's mother said she wondered how Manson kept getting released from jail after being repeatedly arrested if he was still on parole.

"We couldn't get his parole officer off the dime to violate him when we arrested him in August," Gleason replied.

Questions concerning why that didn't happen still linger to this day.

———

Meanwhile, the prosecution team had gathered enough evidence to seek indictments against Manson and four others in the Tate-LaBianca case.

On December 8, the grand jury issued indictments charging Charles Manson, Charles "Tex" Watson, Patricia "Katie" Krenwinkel, Susan "Sadie" Atkins, and Linda Kasabian with seven counts of murder each and one count of conspiracy to commit murder. Leslie Van Houten was indicted on two counts of murder and one count of conspiracy to murder.

That same day, Susan Atkins gave permission to her attorneys to sign agreements with writer Lawrence Schiller and Twenty Pimlico, Inc. to write a first-person story of her life, before and after the murders, based on jailhouse interviews.

Titled *The Killing of Sharon Tate*, the book was published by a Times-Mirror Corporation subsidiary months before the trial started; excerpts also appeared in the *Los Angeles Times*.

This raised a number of ethical and legal issues, yet the DA never objected publicly, perhaps because he believed that it would help his biggest case ever.

Sadie's former cellmate Virginia Graham waited to relay her version of the jailhouse stories until she arrived at the women's prison in Corona, where she confided in a psychologist. But by the time the therapist conveyed the details to the LAPD, they had already been in the news. Still, Graham and Sadie's other cellmate, Ronnie Howard, would both be important witnesses for the prosecution.

———

With the indictments in hand, the LAPD wasted no time before sending two sergeants to pick up Charlie Manson from the Independence jail on December 9 and bring him back to LA to be arraigned on the murder charges.

After collecting him from the tiny cell he shared with six other prisoners, they placed him in an isolated cell at Parker Center, the LAPD's headquarters downtown, away from the other inmates.

"Keep your distance!" the sergeants yelled at the nearly three dozen reporters who wanted to catch a glimpse of the scruffy, bearded, long-haired Manson as he was led silently in handcuffs through the hallway to the elevator. Wearing his leather pants, moccasins, and long-sleeved, fringed buckskin shirt, Manson, for once, looked straight ahead with no expression.

Two days later, he was taken to the courthouse to be arraigned before Judge William Keene, whose courtroom gallery was packed to capacity with reporters and curious observers.

———

The LASD had been looking for Shorty Shea's wife, Magdalene, for a month before she contacted them on December 9, freshly released from jail.

Three days later, after her burglary charges were mysteriously dropped, she filed a missing person's report for Shorty. Saying she'd last seen her husband and his white Mercury in Hollywood in the wee hours of August 16, she recounted their conversation about Charlie throwing a knife at him at Spahn Ranch.

Around the same time, Sergeant Whiteley followed up on the Mary Brunner interview and went to the Family's former Gresham Street address, where he found Shorty's Mercury parked in front of the house. Judging by the heavy grime and rain spots, it had been there for quite some time.

Dusting it for prints, a technician lifted one from a foot locker in the trunk that matched up with Bruce Davis's palm print, adding one more important piece of physical evidence linking the Family to Shorty's disappearance.

With enough evidence to go to the grand jury, prosecutor Burton Katz called more than forty witnesses to testify about Shorty's murder, which resulted in additional murder and conspiracy indictments for Manson and the first charges against Bruce Davis in mid-December.

Later that month, the grand jury also indicted Manson, Atkins, and Davis for murder and conspiracy to rob and murder Gary Hinman.

Whiteley and Guenther tried to turn Steve "Clem" Grogan during questioning a few days after the Shorty Shea indictments, but he was unfazed. Without a body, he seemed smugly confident that they couldn't prove Shorty had even been murdered.

Grogan claimed he didn't know Shorty well, saying the last time he'd seen him he was on his way to San Francisco to work in a talcum or salt mine.

Told that the grand jury had already indicted Manson and Davis based on testimony from dozens of witnesses—many of whom relayed Grogan's boasts about cutting off Shorty's head—Grogan smiled widely.

"People will say anything and you haven't found where his body is," he said.

The detectives countered that Gypsy had admitted to following

Manson's orders to drive Shorty's car to Gresham Street and abandon it there. But Grogan shrugged that off as well.

"Gypsy told me she talked with you about the car," he replied, saying he knew they'd threatened her with the gas chamber if she didn't.

Asked if he'd ever seen Shorty's pearl-handled revolvers, Grogan said truthfully that he'd seen Danny DeCarlo with a couple of .45s fitting that description.

Getting nowhere, the detectives took Grogan to jail, where he was booked for murder. Like Manson, Grogan and Davis asked to represent themselves, but their requests were summarily denied.

Meanwhile, Shorty's friends did their own investigation. Dawn Quant, who had witnessed Manson throwing the knife at him at the ranch, went with Ruby Pearl to confront Manson in jail.

"Where's Shorty's body, Charlie?" Pearl asked. "We want to bury him properly."

"Ask the Black Panthers," he retorted.

"You know there haven't been any Black Panthers around the ranch," she said.

With that, Manson said he didn't want to answer any more of their questions.

———

Shortly after seventeen-year-old Barbara Hoyt gave several statements to the prosecution team in early December, she began receiving death threats by phone from two familiar female voices: Lynette Fromme and Sandy Good.

Although Barbara knew her interviews were available to the defense, she tried to pretend she was cooperating with authorities only under duress and agreed to go to Hawaii with a couple Family members to avoid testifying.

But Barbara soon learned that it was a trap. She was finishing a hamburger with her Family "sister" Ouisch in the Honolulu airport when Barbara realized she was in trouble. Lethal trouble.

"Just imagine if there were ten tabs of acid in that [hamburger]," Ouisch said.

Barbara ran to the bathroom and stuck her finger down her throat until she vomited, but she'd already absorbed enough of the drug to feel its effects. Telling a passerby that she was sick and to call prosecutor Vincent Bugliosi right away, she was rushed to the hospital, where she was hooked up to an intravenous line of Valium. She survived.

Ouisch, who was very pregnant at the time, reached a deal with prosecutors to plead no contest to one count of conspiracy to dissuade a witness from testifying. Clem, Lynette, and Gypsy were also charged in the scheme.

Ouisch, however, ended up getting off completely. She was allowed to have her baby before she was to start her ninety days in jail, then never showed up for her sentencing hearing. Her codefendants, on the other hand, had to complete their entire three-month terms.

CHAPTER 25

THE FIRST DEATH
SENTENCE

Because of the unprecedented high-profile nature of the Tate-LaBianca murders and the extensive national media attention they had garnered, the judge presiding over the case issued a sweeping gag order on December 10, 1969.

Judge William Keene's order, issued the day after Charles Manson was arrested on murder and conspiracy charges, prohibited all attorneys, elected officials, grand jurors, subpoenaed witnesses—or any other parties who had received information about the case—from speaking or releasing any related documents outside of court, other than the basic facts. The same parties were also prohibited from expressing opinions on the defendants' guilt or innocence.

———

Once Bobby Beausoleil's ties to the Manson Family came to light, his second trial was moved to Judge Keene's downtown courtroom.

Bobby's attorney attempted to have the case retried under the same sentencing guidelines as before—"other than a death penalty case"—but Keene denied the motion. The DA was going all the way with this one.

Although Vincent Bugliosi had been appointed to take over the case after the mistrial, he, too, had to be replaced because of scheduling conflicts with the Tate-LaBianca trial, so Burton Katz took the helm.

After Katz presented his opening statement on April 3, 1970, the proceedings went quickly.

———

The DA's office flew Mary Brunner out from Wisconsin on April 8, the day before she was to testify before the grand jury as prosecutors sought indictments against Manson, Atkins, and Davis in the Hinman murder case. Mary was also slated to be the prosecution's primary witness in Bobby's trial.

The night she arrived, Mary and her attorney met with the prosecution team to go over her testimony and immunity agreement, which required her to admit being part of a conspiracy to rob, torture, and murder Gary Hinman. As this story was told multiple times by Mary and others, Hinman's alleged inheritance sum varied from three thousand to thirty thousand dollars.

It was a long night. After the initial discussion, everyone left except for Deputy District Attorney Aaron Stovitz, who stayed behind so he could review some questions in more detail with Mary.

Knowing that Family members Lynette Fromme and Brenda McCann, whose real name was Nancy Pitman, had visited Mary in Wisconsin the week before, Stovitz urged Mary to try to rest up at the hotel and ignore any pressure from the Family. He also asked why she'd never reported Gary's murder to police.

"'Cause I was an outlaw then," she said.

"I see," Stovitz said. "You do feel it's wrong to murder, right?"

"I feel that either all was wrong or all was right and there's no 'sometimes it isn't,'" she said.

After Mary finished her grand jury testimony, Stovitz said, he wanted her to hear Bobby's anticipated testimony that Charlie was the one who had killed Gary Hinman.

"I just want you to know what—how—these people do things, that they say anything they can to save themselves. And I don't think it's right," Stovitz said. ". . . We don't want any harm to come to you."

The prosecutor was right to be concerned. When Mary took the stand the next morning she announced that she couldn't testify.

"I can't do it, man," she said. "They're my brothers."

"Who are your brothers?" Stovitz asked.

"Everybody. I can't use my life, you know, I can't use their life to buy mine, man."

Stovitz reminded her that she saw her friend Gary die at the hands of these "brothers."

"Do you think that the people who are responsible for his death should continue walking and being free and living their normal lives even though they are responsible for Gary Hinman's death?"

"The people that did it, you know, they're going to get it anyway, and if you got to give it to me too, okay," she said. "But I can't testify against them to save myself, because they're me too."

Mary claimed that Lynette and Nancy's visit had nothing to do with her decision.

"You are asking for the death penalty on Bobby, man, and you want me to help you," she said. "Killing is wrong any way you do it and I'm not going to help you."

Reminded that she would go to jail if she didn't testify, and that she would also likely be indicted for murder, Mary conferred briefly with her attorney, then reluctantly returned to the stand.

———

After recounting the story she told during Bobby's trial, that he had stabbed Gary Hinman, Mary stayed in court to hear Bobby's contradictory testimony, which went just as Stovitz had predicted.

The jury believed Mary and found Bobby guilty of first-degree murder. Within three days, the jury had also voted to send him to the gas chamber.

As is typical in such cases, Bobby's defense attorney filed a motion for a new trial and to reduce the death penalty punishment. But the Manson Family trials never fit the norm.

Manson was determined to represent himself in the Family's "united" strategy, and his codefendants all followed suit, including Bobby. During his weeklong motion hearing, Bobby represented himself as his two ex-girlfriends, Gypsy and Kitty, sat watching in the courtroom with Sandy Good.

When Bobby recalled Mary to the stand, he knew that she had just submitted a signed affidavit disclaiming her previous testimony, and claiming that she'd "been coerced, lied to, and tricked into making statements" out of fear that she would "lose [her] baby." He then tried to lead Mary through new testimony that would support his claim that Charlie had killed Gary.

"Bobby didn't kill Gary," Mary said.

"Who killed Gary?" Judge Keene said, jumping in.

"I don't have to answer that."

"Yes, you do have to answer that," Keene said.

But Mary still wouldn't budge, citing the Fifth Amendment against self-incrimination. When she still refused to answer, Keene cited her for contempt, had her taken into custody, and told her again she could be arrested for murder.

In the prosecution's view, her affidavit and false testimony nullified her immunity agreement. In fact, prosecutors later contended that she never had full immunity, which became a matter of debate.

Mary's brief break outside the courtroom, away from the Family's watchful stare, gave her a chance to reconsider. When she returned, she was on the verge of tears as she retook the stand. Her voice shaking, she returned to her original story, admitting that she'd simply been trying to help Bobby get a retrial and save his life.

"Bobby got the gas chamber, and . . . you're doing the same thing to him as he did to Gary, and you've made me a part of [that]," she said.

Three days later, Judge Keene denied Bobby's requests for a new trial and reduced sentence. Before sending him to death row, Keene posed one last question.

"Is there any other legal cause why sentence in this matter should not now be imposed, other than what you have already stated for the record?"

Brash and indignant as always, Bobby did not hold back.

"I just would like to say that you are right when you say that I have no remorse," he said. "I have read the definition of remorse and the definition of remorse is a strong feeling of guilt . . . I have none of those feelings."

Keene said Bobby would be sent to San Quentin State Prison within ten days. But Bobby was determined to have the final word.

"I only have one last thing to say," he said.

"There is nothing further to say, Mr. Beausoleil," Keene replied. "You are now excused."

"You can't judge me."

"Take Mr. Beausoleil out of the courtroom," the judge ordered.

"Only God can judge me and God is on my side!"

———

Deputy Public Defender Paul Fitzgerald was appointed to represent Manson the day of his arraignment. But as Manson stubbornly argued that it was his constitutional right to represent himself, Fitzgerald was relieved eleven days later.

Judge Keene asked Manson to consult with Joseph Ball, a well-respected local attorney, whom he hoped would talk some sense into the defendant.

After doing so, Ball reported back that he found Manson to be "an able, intelligent young man, quiet-spoken and mild-mannered" with a good understanding of the law and a high IQ.

"Mr. Manson is a man with a fine brain, good intellect," Ball said, recounting that Manson didn't believe he could get a fair trial in California because he'd already been tried and condemned in the press.

"I must sympathize with him in that attitude, because I don't think that there has ever been a case that has received worse publicity than that which Mr. Manson has received," Ball said. "I did tell him, however, that I thought that in the hands of an able, experienced lawyer that perhaps he would set the pattern and that he would have a chance to show his quiet, benign personality to a jury through his lawyer."

Ball said he'd advised Manson against representing himself, but he was unable to change the defendant's mind. Manson insisted that he still wanted to go it alone, albeit with the help of two attorneys to assist him.

Judge Keene reluctantly agreed that day, Christmas Eve, to allow Manson to proceed.

———

It took six weeks before Manson agreed to enter a "not guilty" plea on the charges against him, which started a sixty-day clock for his right to a "speedy trial" to run its course.

At a hearing on February 9, Manson politely posed several requests to the judge, including a change of venue, access to contact information for a number of prosecution witnesses he wanted to question as defense witnesses, and, of course, a dismissal.

"Today was supposed to be my trial date," he said. "Everything that has been denied, the district attorney always says I am stalling for time, but now that it's time, somebody else seems to be stalling for time."

After correcting Manson's miscalculations based on the "speedy trial" provisions, Keene set the trial date for Monday, March 30. The judge denied him access to the witness contact information, but said he would allow Manson to argue for a change of venue at a hearing on February 16.

———

Susan Atkins had been cooperating with the prosecution team, including the investigators who were pursuing every possible lead to try to locate Shorty Shea's body.

In January, Sergeant Whiteley obtained a court order to take Atkins from jail to an area along Santa Susana Pass Road, where she claimed that Charlie had taken her in the middle of the night, pointed to some bushes down a ravine, and told her to clean up Shorty's blood. Atkins tried to lead Whiteley to the spot, but they couldn't find any trace of Shorty's allegedly dismembered body.

By February, however, Atkins had changed her tune. She disclaimed her grand jury testimony and refused to testify for the prosecution, which nullified her arrangement with the DA.

Stovitz and Bugliosi were actually relieved. They met with Linda Kasabian and offered her full immunity if she testified truthfully. The deal wouldn't become official, however, until after she'd proven her worth on the stand. She had now moved into the top slot for most important prosecution witness.

They also granted immunity to Family member Ella Jo Bailey, who, in exchange for her testimony, would win dismissal of the pending first-degree forgery charges against her in Washington State.

———

Judge Malcolm Lucas filled in for Keene at Manson's change of venue hearing, where Manson showed that he could conduct himself quite rationally and respectfully when he so chose.

Manson argued that the trial should be moved out of California due to the sweeping negative publicity that he and the case had received, but he didn't see how a fair trial could be held anywhere in the nation.

"You know there has been more publicity on this, even more than the guy that killed the president of the United States," Manson said. "I think it's not like anything we have ever done in this country."

To support his argument, Manson submitted a sampling of articles from national publications such as *LIFE* magazine, as well as a prescient *Sacramento Union* editorial that described the state of "communication in our society" as "disturbing."

"The claim by defendant Charles Manson that news media have already tried and convicted him in the Sharon Tate murder case has a familiar and disturbing ring," the editorial stated. "It is familiar because hardly any criminal case of special notoriety reaches the courtroom these days without the issue of pre-trial publicity being raised to argue that the defendant's right to a fair trial has been abridged."

Manson also maintained that the DA and some judges were unfairly giving statements to the media, despite the gag order.

"The media is used by the district attorney to try a man before trial," he said. "But I got a side . . . to my story [too]. You know, like, they say I am a vicious demon overnight, and actually I am not."

Prosecutor Aaron Stovitz argued that the trial should remain in LA, where the county's vast population could provide a "wider base of jurors to draw from" than anywhere else in California. He also disagreed that Manson had already been "condemned or tried in the newspapers."

Judge Lucas denied Manson's motion, noting that given the nation-wide media coverage, it wouldn't help to move the trial elsewhere. But he said the court would continue to safeguard the defendant's right to a fair trial, "even against his own perhaps ill-advised actions." Manson's phone privileges had been temporarily revoked, he said, because he was giving out "unauthorized telephone interviews, possibly to his own detriment."

The trial, he decreed, would stay in LA.

CHAPTER 26

"MOCKERY OF JUSTICE"

By March, Judge Keene had decided that the tenuous basis for Manson's self-representation had run its course. Based on his "outlandish" conduct, Manson had proven that he wasn't capable of acting as his own attorney.

At a hearing on March 6, Keene recited a litany of bizarre filings with several different judges, which had generally wasted the court's time.

"You filed a motion to associate fellow prisoners," he said, referring to Manson's request for a hearing in an eight-page motion, filed on behalf of a group of fellow inmates known as the Family of Infinite Soul Inc.—only to contend later that he'd never asked for it.

"You filed a writ of habeas corpus in which you put into that writ an aka, and, that is, you are also known as Jesus Christ."

Finally, Keene said, "You came into this court and you demanded that we go to trial on that date of February ninth," seven weeks early.

He also noted that Manson had claimed to be incapable of following the jail's most fundamental rules, such as eating and taking a shower, and had brashly suggested that an evidentiary hearing should be held in court any time an inmate broke such a rule, thereby encouraging the prisoners to rebel.

The judge said he'd given Manson a chance to exercise his constitutional right, but he'd concluded that allowing him to continue "would be a fundamental, absolute denial of due process."

"You're going to conclude before I get to say anything?" Manson asked. "You gave me three weeks. Very gracious. You give me three weeks to become an attorney. Now, nobody else will help me."

All decorum dissipated as the judge tried to keep order and Manson tried to control the courtroom.

"Mr. Manson—" the judge said.

"I didn't interrupt you."

"Mr. Manson—"

"Let me finish . . . I have a voice. Do you hear it?"

Clearly irritated, Keene tried to educate Manson on matters of respect and protocol. When a judge speaks, he said, "you're to remain silent and you're not to tell the judge to wait for a minute . . . I'm not going to engage with you, at this time, any type of debating contest . . . Mr. Manson, your status, at this time, of acting as your own attorney is now vacated."

Keene proceeded to appoint Charles Hollopeter as the defendant's new attorney, but Manson wouldn't accept him.

"You can kill me, but you can't give me an attorney. I won't take one."

The judge told Manson he could substitute a different attorney, but he could no longer represent himself.

"There is no love in your courtroom," Manson said, signaling to the four Family members sitting in the gallery to jump up.

"Your status as a pro per—" the judge began.

"You are a mockery of justice," interrupted Sandy Good.

"—is now revoked."

"You are a mockery of justice," Gypsy called out. "You're a joke."

As Mark Ross, Gypsy, and Sandy stood laughing and calling out antagonistic remarks to the judge, the scene was reminiscent of the Marx Brothers movie *Duck Soup*.

"I certainly am in contempt of this court," Ross said.

"May I say your conduct has been most outlandish," Sandy said.

Keene was not amused. Holding them in contempt, he sentenced the hecklers to five days in jail. Because Catherine "Cappy" Gillies stood with the group but did not make catcalls, the judge let her leave as a free woman.

Patricia Krenwinkel and her attorney, Paul Fitzgerald, tried their own change of venue motion five weeks after Manson's. After being dismissed as Manson's attorney, Fitzgerald had quit his public defender's job, hoping to build a new private practice by representing Krenwinkel, virtually pro bono. He ultimately became head of the defense team.

After Manson's objection to Charles Hollopeter as his attorney, the judge appointed Ronald Hughes, a new lawyer who had never tried a case before. Hughes said Manson wanted to join in Krenwinkel's motion.

Fitzgerald reminded the court of Judge Keene's initial rationale for issuing the gag order, that it was necessary to ensure the defendants got a fair trial in light of the "excessive" publicity so far.

Arguing that recent coverage had already irreparably tainted the jury pool, he threw out several tabloidish headlines that had implicated the defendants not only in the murders for which they were charged, but in a number of unsolved murders as well:

"Hidden Cave May Have Secret Cult Bodies"

"Murders Multiply, Total to Date 12"

"Cult Killings May Reach 14"

"Hinman Girl Killers"

"Tate Suspect Described As Messiah of Sex and Sadism"

"Mystic Cult Blamed for Tate Murders"

Accompanied by photos of bulldozers digging for bodies that were never found, he said these stories "have linked Mr. Manson and his group of followers—and I am adopting their language—to every unsolved murder in California. They have accused him of mounting machine guns on dune buggies and of trying to precipitate a race war. They have taken from every aspect of our society the worst possible aspects of any human beings in our society and combined them into one man."

And yet not a single article, he said, pointed out that Manson, or any of his codefendants, was "presumed to be innocent . . . until his guilt is proven beyond a reasonable doubt."

Fitzgerald pointed out that Susan Atkins's story, which had already been published in the *Los Angeles Times* and as a book, illustrated that she had a problem differentiating between fact and fantasy. Yet, her codefendants, who were implicated in the tale, had been unable to cross-examine her on its details.

Prosecutor Vincent Bugliosi argued against the change of venue motion, with his hyperbole and sarcasm in full force. "I believe that my good friend Paul Fitzgerald got so carried away with himself that for a moment I thought he was going to ask . . . to have the court in sympathy with Mr. Manson and let him walk out of the court right now and join his Family," he said. "In fact, I looked around to my left and right and I wanted to see if anyone was weeping."

Bugliosi acknowledged that the case had received widespread coverage reaching Europe and the Far East, and that foreign media had already reserved seats for the trial. "I don't think there is any question that this particular trial has received as much or more publicity as any trial within memory, or perhaps in the United States' history," he said.

But the press has the right under the First Amendment to cover the murders, he said, which are "among the most savage, nightmarish murders in the recorded annals of this community," as well as any others that remain unsolved.

The cost of relocating a complicated trial with so many defendants and such great security and personnel needs would be prohibitive, he said, adding that he was quite confident they could find a jury that would "fairly and impartially try this case."

Judge Lucas noted that a case of such magnitude could only be tried in one of the state's eight largest counties. But after examining all the evidence submitted, he stood by his previous ruling, that a change of venue, even to one of the other large counties, would be "ineffectual," as the publicity seemed quite evenly distributed throughout the state.

———

The succession of attorney-switching by Manson and his codefendants was only one in a constant stream of disruptive antics during the pre-trial proceedings that created a circus atmosphere at the courthouse. Generating even more publicity for his case, Manson choreographed these antics to perpetuate the chaos, then disseminated them to his codefendants in side-room meetings every morning that continued throughout the trial.

His daily directives also spilled onto the streets, where Lynette Fromme led a contingent of female Family members in protests by day and sidewalk sleepovers by night. With Sandy Good at her side, Lynette orchestrated these attention-grabbing theatrics for the media on Manson's behalf, even as she denied that role and insisted they were all independent thinkers. Charlie had programmed his followers to believe that they were acting on their own.

"They said I was a lieutenant, we weren't lieutenants," Lynette told a TV reporter. "We didn't have orders, we didn't have badges. We weren't appointed anything. We did what we wanted to do. We each one of us picked up what we could carry and we did it because we wanted to. If we did it because we thought it would make Charlie happy, then we must have loved him or something like that."

Although Lynette wasn't at either murder scene, she said, killing those people "was a very difficult thing to imagine doing."

"I still believe that they were right because they felt right," she said. "They felt that despite the ugliness of it, it was the right thing to do."

Always the true believer, Sandy piped up: "There's a revolution coming very soon."

———

Susan Atkins, Leslie Van Houten, and Patricia Krenwinkel were led through the courthouse halls, wearing matching themed outfits in satiny lavender, sky and navy blue, a fashion blend of Renaissance-period dress and French maid costumes.

Holding hands, dancing, singing, and giggling like little girls on the playground, they appeared carefree, joyful, and completely indifferent to the horrors they were accused of committing.

Such performances continued throughout the trial. The defendants spent many days sitting in cells adjoining the courtroom, listening to the proceedings via piped-in speakers, after being removed for misbehaving. The disrespect they showed to the judicial system, law enforcement, the victims' families, and society in general was shocking—and Manson's goal all along.

Meanwhile, Manson told the girls in private that everything was going to be all right.

"He was saying that time was going to stop and we were all going to walk out, and we believed that," Krenwinkel said later. "He thought for certain that we were going to take it all, and he would walk free."

They were also still feeling the effects of their intense, long-term use of psychedelics, which Van Houten's father said he witnessed when he visited his daughter in jail. "She said she didn't know whether to cut holes in the back of her blouse or to sew little pockets for her wings," he said. "She thought she was an angel," with her wings "nubbing out" of her shoulder blades.

"How am I going to hide my wings?" she asked her codefendants.

———

Attorney Ronald Hughes lasted two and a half months before he, too, upset Manson. On June 1, Irving Kanarek replaced him as Manson's attorney, just two weeks before jury selection began on June 15. Then, right before opening statements, Leslie Van Houten asked that Hughes be appointed to replace her previous attorney.

Kanarek had a reputation for repeatedly interrupting court proceedings with wildly irrelevant or inflammatory questions and objections. He would do that and more in the coming months, annoying not only the judge and other attorneys but his client as well. He did, however, manage to win some points in the process.

After Manson filed an affidavit of prejudice against Judge Keene, the judge disqualified himself and the case was assigned to Judge Charles H. Older.

Manson told Older that he didn't want any attorney to represent him, but Kanarek was "the worst man in town I could pick," Manson said, "and you are pushing him on me."

Told once again that he couldn't represent himself in such a complicated case, Manson grudgingly accepted Kanarek. But he warned the judge that he was going to cause "as much trouble as possible" going forward.

Manson kept his word and was no less disrespectful to Judge Older than he had been to Keene. He carried out his threat to be outrageously difficult by sitting with his back to the bench on June 9. As usual, the girls followed his lead.

"The court has shown me no respect," Manson explained, "so I'm going to show the court the same thing."

Older ordered all four codefendants to be removed from the courtroom. After the lunch break, the girls were allowed to return, but they were taken out again after pulling the same stunt.

The next day in court, Manson shoved his arms out dramatically into a crucifixion pose, a rare public showing of the Jesus Christ reenactment he used to perform for the Family.

———

As Kanarek prepared for trial, he set out to discredit Linda Kasabian, whom he knew would be the prosecution's star witness. He deposed Gypsy, who asserted that Linda referred to herself as Yana the Witch and claimed to have supernatural powers. In a written affidavit, Gypsy stated that Linda had admitted to taking LSD three hundred times—and as many as two hits, or one thousand micrograms, of "orange sunshine" LSD at a time in the several weeks before the murders. Gypsy also claimed that Linda had used speed and ingested peyote hundreds of times. During this same period, Gypsy said, Linda made bizarre statements that illustrated her difficulty differentiating between reality and fantasy.

"Nothing is real," she told Gypsy. "I don't know who I am. I am not here."

Whether or not any of this would undermine Linda's credibility as a witness remained to be seen.

CHAPTER 27

THE TRIAL OF THE
CENTURY

The public began lining up for courtroom seats at 6:00 a.m. on July 24 to hear the opening statements. Promising even more heightened drama than an episode of *Perry Mason*, the Manson Family story was stranger than fiction.

Never one to miss the opportunity to stand in the spotlight, Charles Manson strode into the courtroom with an "X" carved into his forehead, just above the bridge of his nose. The girls made the same marks over the weekend, using hot bobby pins and needles to dig grooves into their skin.

Still lacking any evidence that Manson had ever stabbed or shot any of the homicide victims, Aaron Stovitz had wanted to prosecute the Tate-LaBianca case as a "robbery gone wrong," just as the police had first suspected.

But Vincent Bugliosi managed to persuade his co-counsel to use a combination of conspiracy law—the Family's messages in blood left at the crime scenes, which he argued were "tantamount to finding Manson's fingerprints" there—and the "Helter Skelter" theory he proposed.

The theory was supported by witness interviews and a couple pieces of physical evidence—Juan Flynn's cabinet door and the glass jug at Spahn Ranch that sported the "Helter Skelter" slogan. The detectives had collected the door but didn't think it was relevant enough to enter into evidence until an irritated Bugliosi happened to find it a month before the trial started.

Also, through interviews and a stack of magazine articles about Adolf Hitler that Bugliosi had found in the Family's bus near Barker Ranch, the prosecutor was able to connect Manson with Hitler—another leader who ordered mass murders but never killed anyone himself.

As Bugliosi delivered his opening statement, he began what would turn into a nine-month relationship with the jury of seven men and five women, who were sequestered in the Ambassador Hotel as soon as they were sworn in.

"What kind of a diabolical mind would contemplate or conceive of these seven murders?" Bugliosi asked rhetorically. "What kind of mind would want to have seven human beings brutally murdered? We expect the evidence at this trial to answer that question and show that defendant Charles Manson owned that diabolical mind. Charles Manson, who, the evidence will show, at times has had the infinite humility, as it were, to refer to himself as Jesus Christ."

Bugliosi went on to describe Manson in more earthbound terms, as "a vagrant wanderer, a frustrated singer-guitarist, a pseudo philosopher," but most of all, "a killer who cleverly masqueraded behind the common image of a hippie, that of being peace loving," but who was in truth "a megalomaniac who coupled his insatiable thirst for power—"

Kanarek interrupted at this point, beginning his persistent pattern of obstructionist objections, and insisted on approaching the bench. Bugliosi proceeded to chastise the defense attorney for his "gross discourtesy," which Kanarek later characterized as one of the prosecution's many prejudicial statements. The judge, however, overruled Kanarek's objection and allowed Bugliosi to finish his sentence.

"—with an intense obsession for violent death."

The prosecution would show, Bugliosi continued, that although Charles Manson didn't personally kill any of the seven victims, he was still the leader of the conspiracy to commit those murders, so under the law that made him "equally responsible and equally guilty."

Although the prosecution had the burden of proof, Bugliosi pointed out, it didn't have to offer "one single, solitary speck of evidence as to the motives these defendants had for committing these murders," only that they did, in fact, commit them. He said, however, that he believed there was more than one motive, and the primary one was "as bizarre, or perhaps even more bizarre, than the murders themselves."

Couching it as "admittedly far out," he described that motive as Manson's "fanatical obsession with Helter Skelter," a revolution he hoped to ignite with a race war sparked by murders of the white establishment. "Pigs," he called them, the same word written on Sharon Tate's front door.

The evidence would show that "these seven incredible murders were perhaps the most bizarre, savage, nightmarish murders in the recorded annals of crime, of course, excluding wartime atrocities," he said.

After Bugliosi finished his opening, all the defense attorneys joined in Kanarek's motion for a mistrial. Paul Fitzgerald pointed out that Bugliosi said Sharon Tate's thirty-eight-week-old "fetus child" was murdered, knowing full well that the Supreme Court of California had recently ruled that a fetus didn't have the legal status of a human being, and therefore could not be "murdered" under state law.

The judge denied the motion, saying he saw nothing improper in the statements.

As was their right, the defense attorneys said they wanted to wait to make their opening statements until the prosecution had rested its case. But the jury would never hear them.

———

As Linda Kasabian was about to begin her testimony on July 27, Kanarek, armed with Gypsy's affidavit, stood up and objected.

"This witness is not competent and she is insane!" he shouted.

Judge Older rebuked Kanarek for making such a defamatory statement in front of the jury, then allowed Linda to proceed.

Kanarek moved for a mistrial and objected countless more times that day. As punishment, he and attorney Ronald Hughes, who had cursed in the courtroom, both spent the night in jail for contempt. Not playing favorites, Older also found Bugliosi in contempt in late September, offering him a choice of a five-hundred-dollar fine or a night in jail. He paid the fine.

When Linda began speaking, she sobbed as she described what she'd witnessed and heard at the Tate house. The victims' screams, she said, seemed to go on forever.

"It was horrible!" she said, a response to which Kanarek objected and Older told the jury to discount.

Linda said she tried to intervene. "Sadie, make it stop, I hear people coming!" she said she yelled at Atkins.

"It's too late," Atkins replied.

When Bugliosi asked if Linda had really heard people coming, she said no, "I just wanted them [the killings] to stop."

———

The irony of the prosecution's argument that Manson had not been "condemned or tried in the newspapers" played right into his hands on August 3, in the middle of Linda's testimony.

Manson smiled as he stood up at the defense table that afternoon and raised a copy of the *Los Angeles Times* for everyone in the courtroom, including the jurors, to see:

"MANSON GUILTY, NIXON DECLARES," the tabloid-sized headline read, a violation of the judge's gag order by the nation's most powerful elected official.

"Here is a man who was guilty, directly or indirectly, of eight murders without reason," Nixon was quoted as saying during an impromptu campaign stop at a law enforcement conference in Denver.

The president also criticized the media for its efforts "to glorify and to make heroes out of those who engage in criminal activities," which made Manson seem like "rather a glamorous figure."

The defense wasted no time in moving for a mistrial. Although the jurors were sequestered and had been ordered not to read news accounts,

Kanarek said he was worried they might learn of the president's comments during the allowed weekend family visits.

After news of the courtroom mishap broke, the Nixon camp issued a "clarification," alleging that the president wasn't purposely trying to interfere with the criminal justice system; he'd simply "failed to use the word 'alleged' in his comments."

Alarmed by the situation, Judge Older questioned all twelve jurors and six alternates independently to see if they could remain impartial. Satisfied that they could proceed, he ordered Susan Atkins's attorney, Daye Shinn, to spend three days in jail for putting the newspaper close enough for Manson to grab it and make another mockery of Older's courtroom.

Linda was on the stand for a tedious nineteen days, prolonged by Kanarek's interruptions. At one point, Manson made a slicing motion across his throat, a silent threat to kill Linda for betraying him and violating the "no snitching" oath of loyalty to the Family.

Linda had to earn her immunity deal. To ensure she testified truthfully, the prosecution left the murder indictment hanging over her like a hammer until she completed the prosecution's questioning under direct examination. Only then was the paperwork filed granting her protection as "a necessary witness."

——

The prosecution had other challenges as well. Earlier in the year, prosecutor Aaron Stovitz had put his career in jeopardy by giving a pretrial interview to two writers for *Rolling Stone* magazine. As he set the ground rules for an interview that he knew violated the gag order, he said, "Let's do it this way. I will answer all of your questions, if you give me one definite promise: that you don't quote me."

"Can we use your words but not your name?" one reporter asked.

"My words will be the words used by other people," Stovitz replied cryptically. With the promise of cover, he then went on to blame the police for the gag order.

"If more law enforcement officers had made responsible comments, the court order would not have been necessary," he said. "But some police officers were shooting off their mouths and . . . used some words recklessly. And the defendants might not get a fair trial."

Eventually, Stovitz's interview as well as comments he later made to a reporter about Susan Atkins caught up with him. Facing a defense contempt motion for violating the gag order, he was removed from the case in early September.

From then on, Vincent Bugliosi served as lead prosecutor, with a couple of younger deputies assigned to help him behind the scenes—Donald Musich and Stephen Kay, the latter of whom went on to represent the DA's office at parole hearings in the years to come.

———

Manson continued to act out, his behavior growing increasingly volatile as the prosecution called dozens of witnesses, ranging from detectives to forensic technicians, pathologists, Family members, and others who testified about the physical evidence and gave crucial explanations for Manson's philosophy and the Family's inner workings.

The judge, in turn, attempted to remain calm and continued to remove Manson and his codefendants when they got out of hand.

Manson's behavior reached a climax on October 5, when he started speaking quietly from the defense table. As his voice rose, it became clear that he was threatening the judge.

"Are you going to use this courtroom to kill me?" Manson asked.

Older, who had allowed Manson back into the courtroom after sending him out for yelling and singing the day before, instructed him to stop talking.

"The minute you find me guilty, you know what I'm going to do to you, don't you?" Manson taunted.

"What are you going to do?" the judge asked, daring him to go on.

"You know."

"I'll have you removed if you don't stop," Older said.

"I'll have you removed if you don't stop," Manson mocked. "I have a little system of my own. You think I'm kidding?"

With that, Manson jumped up from his seat, a pencil in hand like a courtroom shiv, and pounced on the defense table. From there, he flung himself ten feet over the table and onto the floor, leaving just ten feet between him and Older on the bench.

One of the bailiffs immediately dove on top of Manson to prevent him from getting any closer. Two other bailiffs piled onto the heap of bodies to subdue Manson and pry the pencil from his grip.

"Remove the defendant from the courtroom!" the judge ordered.

"In the name of Christian justice, someone should cut your head off!" Manson yelled as the bailiffs dragged him out, still struggling.

Susan Atkins, Patricia Krenwinkel, and Leslie Van Houten began to chant the same Buddhist phrase that Gary Hinman repeated to himself before he died: "Nam-myoho-renge-kyo."

Older told them to be quiet, and when they wouldn't stop, he had the bailiffs remove them as well.

Voicing concern about the judge's emotional state and ability to remain impartial after such a melee, attorney Paul Fitzgerald moved for a mistrial, but the judge denied it.

"If he had taken one more step, I would have done something to defend myself," Older told the attorneys in a sidebar, raising questions of what methods he would have used. "They aren't going to profit from their own wrong."

Although the attorneys may not have known the judge's history, Older was a WWII "double ace" fighter pilot who had flown a P-40B Tomahawk in China and Burma with the Hell's Angels squadron of the Flying Tigers. He later flew with the Army Air Forces in Shanghai. Those who did know his history surely had an even greater respect for a man so able to keep his cool.

———

But Manson wasn't the only one misbehaving.

Judge Older was not pleased when the gag order didn't stop three sources, including two attorneys on the case, from quietly releasing Virginia Graham's police interview to William Farr, a *Los Angeles Herald Examiner* reporter.

Farr's exclusive story ran on the *Examiner*'s front page on October 9 with this sensationalistic lede: "Susan Atkins talked to cellmate Virginia Graham about killing Liz Taylor, Richard Burton, Frank Sinatra, Tom Jones and Steve McQueen as part of a murder master plan for Charles Manson's hippie 'family.'"

When Older questioned Farr, he wouldn't reveal his sources. The judge let it go, but made it an issue again seven months later. Farr chose to spend forty-six days in jail for contempt—and many days in court—rather than disclose the parties who gave Graham's statement to him.

Presumably, the trade was worth the "exclusive," which also elicited a historically significant discussion over the media's First Amendment rights to publish such information.

Once his court battle was over, Farr went to work as press secretary for the DA's office.

———

The prosecution rested on November 16. Three days later, as the courtroom and the public eagerly awaited what possible explanations the attorneys would offer in response to the prosecution's case, Older asked the defense to call its first witness.

Speaking for all four defense attorneys, Paul Fitzgerald said they had none. "The defense rests," he said.

Clearly upset, the three female defendants burst out shouting that they wanted to testify, so Older called all the attorneys into chambers to resolve the dispute.

The defense attorneys explained that they'd had a disagreement with their clients. The women said they wanted to take responsibility for planning and carrying out the murders, and testify that Manson had nothing to do with them. The attorneys understandably opposed this move, but Older replied that the defendants should be allowed to exercise their right to testify.

Back in the courtroom, Atkins took the witness stand and gave her attorney a list of questions to ask her, but he refused, saying he believed they would incriminate her.

"I have a certain obligation to my client," Shinn said.

Calling another bench conference, Fitzgerald argued that it would be like "aiding and abetting a suicide" to let the girls testify to what would amount to a confession.

———

The disruptions continued the next day, as Manson announced that he wanted to make a statement. Older allowed it, but only in the absence of the jury.

Taking the stand, Manson spoke for nearly two hours, saying he "killed no one and ordered no one to be killed."

He began by recounting how he'd grown up in institutions, alone, uneducated, poor, and unwanted, just like the "children" he'd taken in at Spahn Ranch. "Most of the people at the ranch that you call 'the Family' were just people that you did not want," he said. "I took them up on my garbage dump and I told them this, that in love there is no wrong . . . I'm only what lives inside each and every one of you . . . You want to kill me? Ha! I'm already dead. I have been all my life."

He said "the children" were listening to the music and it told them what to do. "It's not my conspiracy, it's not my music . . . It says 'Rise,' it says 'Kill.' Why blame it on me? I didn't write the music."

Bugliosi briefly cross-examined him, then the judge asked Manson if he was ready to testify. But he declined after all.

"I have relieved all the pressure I had," Manson said, stepping down from the stand.

Turning to the girls, he added, "You don't have to testify now."

CHAPTER 28

RONALD HUGHES
DISAPPEARS

When the trial resumed after the Thanksgiving break, everyone had taken his place in court but Leslie Van Houten's attorney, Ronald Hughes. Both sides had rested, but the jury instructions had yet to be finalized and closing arguments were still to come.

Because Hughes had been previously scolded for showing up late to court, no one seemed too concerned by his absence, other than annoyance at the delay. But as Older quizzed the other defense attorneys, none of them knew where he was. Paul Fitzgerald said Hughes had sounded fine when they'd last talked over the holiday.

Hughes was a thirty-five-year-old, 250-pound balding single man with a long, scruffy beard. He'd only just passed the bar—on his fourth try—in June 1969, right before the trial began. An odd bird who had known the Manson Family before the trial, he slept on the floor of a friend's garage, where he proudly hung his bar certificate on the wall. He often spent weekends camping at the Sespe Hot Springs near the mountain community of Ojai, in Ventura County.

The next day, they learned that Hughes had, in fact, driven up to the hot springs on the Friday of Thanksgiving weekend with two teenagers, James Forsher and Lauren Elder, in Elder's Volkswagen.

When police questioned the teens, they said it had started to rain so they decided to come back to LA, but Hughes wanted to stay until Sunday. There was such a downpour that their vehicle got caught in some mud, forcing them to leave it there and hike their way to safety.

Ventura County sheriff's deputies had to wait two days for the bad weather to pass before they could safely search the area by helicopter. During that time, some in LA's legal community speculated that Hughes had purposely gone into hiding to sabotage the trial. But Bugliosi knew that wasn't true as soon as he read the news story describing the law degree hanging in Hughes's messy garage.

On December 2, after the court received a number of reported Hughes sightings—in Mexico, in Reno, and on the freeway somewhere—the judge wanted to get the trial moving so he offered Leslie another attorney. But she declined.

When Lauren Elder's Volkswagen was finally found, investigators retrieved some of Hughes's court transcripts. However, other paperwork, including a psych report on his client, was suspiciously missing.

—

Also on December 2, after evading capture for nearly a year, Bruce Davis turned himself in to authorities.

As reporters surrounded him on a street corner and peppered him with questions about why he'd come back and what he hoped to accomplish, he laughed nervously as he stood with an "X" carved into his forehead.

"It's time," he said. "We're just going to say what's true."

"Have any deals been made, and if so what are they?" a reporter asked.

"Well, some people were supposed to be cut loose," Bruce said.

"Who?"

"Mary Brunner, for one," he replied.

"You know that you'll be facing murder charges?"

Bruce laughed again. "Is that all?"

"You do know that?"

"They're putting murder charges on everybody," he said.

"Are you guilty of murder?" a reporter asked.

"Are *you* guilty of murder?"

In the end, the reporters failed to get a straight answer about his motives. "You'll just have to watch," he said.

———

The next day, Judge Older ignored Van Houten's—and Manson's—objections and appointed attorney Maxwell Keith to represent her.

Older also denied Keith's motion to sever his client from the trial as well as a joint defense motion for a mistrial. Instead, the judge delayed closing arguments to give Keith more time to prepare his statement.

Vincent Bugliosi led off with the People's closing argument on December 21, with the codefendants absent from the courtroom. Older said he wouldn't stand for any more disruptions, so he condemned the codefendants to their adjoining cells for the remainder of the trial's guilt phase.

After recounting the testimony of his eighty-four witnesses, Bugliosi concluded his three-day argument a week later. As he slowly read aloud the names of all seven victims, he said they "are not here in this courtroom, but from their graves they cry out for justice, and justice can only be done by coming back to this courtroom with a verdict of guilty."

Paul Fitzgerald began the defense's closing arguments by noting that even Linda Kasabian, the state's most important witness, admitted that she was unaware of any conspiracy to murder anyone.

"Linda Kasabian said eleven times that there was no conspiracy," he said. "How can you join a conspiracy and not know what it is?"

He pointed out that she said she'd seen only one of the seven victims being murdered—Steve Parent—and that was by Tex Watson, who wasn't even on trial yet.

"How can you convict these defendants?" Fitzgerald asked. "We don't know who killed who."

Taking over, Irving Kanarek stretched out his closing argument for seven days, complaining when the DA's office interrupted his statement to arraign Manson in another courtroom on the reissued indictment against him in a consolidation of the Hinman and Shea murder cases.

"This is deliberate," Kanarek said. "Is this Russia or is this the United States?"

Kanarek summed up the proceedings as a political campaign against alternative ideas and lifestyle choices that were antagonistic to the status quo, such as the communal way in which Manson and his friends were living.

"The District Attorney of Los Angeles County, as we have said, is a political office and this is a political trial," he said. "No matter how we look at it."

Manson's attorney spent the better part of a day attacking the credibility of Linda Kasabian, painting *her* as "the manipulator," rather than his client, noting that she'd gotten herself granted immunity even after being labeled as an accomplice to the murder of seven people. He also pointed out conspiratorially that Bugliosi kept referring to her intimately by her first name instead of Mrs. Kasabian.

Going through the exhibits one by one, Kanarek pointed out that the prosecution had showed the jury no physical evidence or crime scene photos that tied Manson in any scientific way to the murder scenes or to any criminal wrongdoing. He cited the leather thongs as an example.

"It doesn't connect Mr. Manson with this any more than any one of us who may have leather on his or her person."

"Manson is a very small part [of this case]—he is a person who is merely a symbol" of those antagonistic ideas, he said. Hearkening back to six-year-old Charlie's argument to his aunt and uncle, Kanarek said Manson had the right to share his opinions with others and should not be held accountable if they acted on those opinions.

———

The case went to the jury at 3:20 p.m. on January 15, 1971. The jury returned ten days later, after a week of deliberations, with the verdict that Bugliosi had requested: guilty on all counts.

About two weeks later, on the eve of the death penalty phase of the trial, a *Los Angeles Times* reporter managed to track down Charles Manson's chain-smoking, emphysema-ridden mother, Kathleen, who did her best to paint a sympathetic portrait of her son.

"I still believe that if those jurors would just talk to Charles for fifteen minutes, they could see he's mentally ill. He needs treatment, has for years," she said.

Kathleen said she thought the girls in the Family were taken in by Charlie's personality and the LSD they took, not any special power of hypnosis.

"He always had a way with people," she said. "Even later, when he was in prison, he was able to get special treatment."

Kathleen died two years later in Spokane, Washington, married for a third time and leaving behind an eleven-year-old daughter from her second marriage.

———

To mark the start of the next phase, on January 28, 1971, Manson shaved his head. The girls, of course, all followed his lead.

Before the jury was brought in that morning, attorney Paul Fitzgerald tried to enter a new plea of not guilty by reason of insanity for his client, Patricia Krenwinkel.

Prosecutor Vincent Bugliosi argued that by waiting until the second phase of the trial to do so, it was "much too far after the bell has already been rung." Judge Older agreed, saying Fitzgerald should have done this during the guilt phase.

But Fitzgerald described this as a tactical decision, contending that doing so earlier would have been admitting guilt. At the very least, he said, the court should appoint psychiatrists to determine whether Krenwinkel was sane so the jury could consider that before deciding if she deserved a death sentence.

The judge countered that he saw no grounds for making the public pay to appoint private clinicians. "There is nothing on the record, nothing that the court has seen, that would indicate that any of these defendants has any mental illness, any diminished capacity, any insanity is now present or was present at the time of the crime," Older said.

That point would be debated—in and out of court—for years to come. Tex Watson would make the same insanity claim during his trial, Leslie Van Houten would argue a "diminished capacity" defense at a retrial, and Charles Manson would subsequently be classified as a mentally ill inmate.

Older rejected the insanity plea as well as Fitzgerald's argument that the death penalty was unconstitutional, amounting to cruel and unusual punishment in violation of the Eighth Amendment. From there, the proceedings moved once again into the realm of the bizarre. Manson asked Older one more time to relieve him of Kanarek so he could represent himself.

"I don't have any more money," Manson said. "You see, he has been working seven months now, and I haven't got any more money to pay him. That is one good reason. Another good reason is that I have personal knowledge of the people involved, and could probably put on a very sensible penalty phase if the judge would let me do this."

Older noted that this same request had been considered half a dozen times by at least four different judges, including him. "I see no reason to change my mind that you are competent to represent yourself," the judge said.

When Older suggested that Manson could still assist his attorney in his own defense, Manson pointed out that Kanarek, like the rest of his team, had still yet to put forth a defense.

"The attorneys wouldn't understand the defense if it was put on in front of them," Manson said. ". . . We wanted to put on a defense from the minute I was arrested. I knew that nothing could come between us . . . There is no way I can speak through any of these people and there is no way any of these people can speak through me . . . What good is a court-room if it is only one-sided?"

"Sit down, Mr. Manson."

"Now, am I supposed to sit here like a dummy? . . . There is no justice here, Older. Dammit man, look at it!"

"All right, I am going to have you removed, Mr. Manson, and you will not be present during the penalty phase of your trial."

"It doesn't mean anything. I am already removed from the first day."

Older tried to sideline Manson by calling on Kanarek to make a motion he'd been trying to make, to no avail.

"He ain't got no guts. He's a woman," Manson said. "You can't face me in this courtroom. If you let me go in here, I'd tear that little boy apart," he said, referring to Bugliosi. "You know it too."

"You already called me a genius, Charlie," Bugliosi said.

"That will be enough, Mr. Bugliosi, let's proceed," Older said.

Kanarek used the break in the drama to try to get one of the female jurors dismissed, alleging that she'd "taken to alcohol" during the sequestration, but Older ignored him, too, and called the prosecution's first witness, Bernard Crowe, to the stand. Before seeing him in the courthouse that day, Manson had thought he'd killed Crowe in Rosina's Hollywood apartment.

Manson, however, would not be upstaged. Before Bugliosi could ask Crowe a question, Manson began to strike his attorney at the defense table, hitting him several times in a karate chop to the chest and side as they faced the jury box, which was about twenty feet away.

"I can't get nothing from this man," Manson said. "I can't even communicate with him."

Older ordered the bailiffs to take Manson out of the courtroom, and at Kanarek's request, told the jury to disregard the incident.

———

Bugliosi still had no physical proof that Manson had killed anyone himself, only witnesses who claimed that he'd ordered the killings in a conspiracy. He'd wanted Crowe to have the bullet removed from his gut to show the jury direct physical evidence that Charlie had shot him with the intention to kill.

But when Crowe took the stand he still had the slug in his body. The doctors had advised him that it was too risky to remove, because the lead could leach into his blood stream.

As Crowe recounted the night of Tex's drug burn for the jury, he described the scene in Rosina's apartment, when Manson denied having anything to do with Tex's activities. "Then he backed up a little bit, and he pulled a revolver out of his belt and started pulling the trigger," he said.

After Manson shot him in the stomach, he added, "I played possum and held my breath" until Manson left, wearing Crowe's friend Steve's suede shirt.

—

On Saturday, March 27, 1971, after the jury had begun its deliberations, two fishermen found Ronald Hughes's naked body in Alder Creek, eight miles below the Sespe Hot Springs. His head was lodged, face down, under some rocks.

Because his remains were badly decomposed, the medical examiner ruled the cause of death as "undetermined." Authorities said it looked like a drowning accident, suggesting that he got swept up in the swollen creek and hit his head as he was sent downstream, until his body got caught between the rocks.

Before Hughes's body was discovered, an anonymous caller to the LAPD had reported that the attorney had been murdered by the Manson Family and buried out near Barker Ranch.

Shortly before he disappeared, Hughes had a run-in with Manson in the courtroom. Pointing directly at Hughes, Manson said, "Attorney, I don't ever want to see you in this courtroom again."

"And we never saw him again," prosecutor Stephen Kay recalled later.

Based on the evidence, Bugliosi suspected that Hughes had been killed to win a mistrial for Manson and his codefendants, to delay the outcome, or to scare the whole defense team.

On Monday, March 29, the jury voted to give the death penalty to Manson, Atkins, Van Houten, and Krenwinkel.

Judge Older sentenced all four defendants to death row. Because the state had only one prison for female inmates at the time, the California Institution for Women (CIW) in Corona, the three women were placed in a special isolation unit there. Manson was sent to San Quentin State Prison on April 22.

CHAPTER 29

FOLIE À DEUX

The DA's office was successful in obtaining indictments consolidating the Hinman and Shea murders into one case, but it failed in the attempt to jointly prosecute Charles Manson, Bruce Davis, and Steve "Clem" Grogan as codefendants in one trial. After Davis was able to get his trial severed from the others, each man was tried independently.

Grogan's first trial for Shorty's murder ended in mistrial in late August 1970—before the jury even began its deliberations.

Judge Joseph Call, who had been on the bench for more than thirty years, had been receiving death threats, as had Grogan's attorney. As the pressure escalated, Judge Call got more spooked during a meeting with Grogan and the lawyers in chambers when the defendant abruptly kneeled in front of him, smiled innocently, and touched his knee.

Call's face went pale at the inappropriate gesture. "Steve doesn't mean anything by it," he said, hopefully.

"It's okay, Joe," Grogan said gently, again testing propriety by using the judge's first name. "I know you're just trying to be fair. You'll do the right thing."

Prosecutor Burton Katz sensed that the judge was trying to convince himself that the gesture was not an implicit threat of violence. But considering the testimony that the seemingly harmless Grogan had taken a machete to Shorty's head and chopped him into nine pieces, Call was understandably anxious about the defendant's conduct in chambers.

Tensions escalated further when a group of Family members robbed the Western Surplus Store, a gun shop in Hawthorne, in late August. In a scheme to break Charlie out of jail, the group planned to use the stolen weapons to hijack a 747 airplane and kill hostages, one at a time, until Manson was released.

But they never made it that far. While they were grabbing up 141 guns in the store, an employee triggered a silent alarm. The group ran outside with the weapons and jumped in a white van.

After the police showed up, a long shootout ensued, with more than fifty rounds of ammunition exchanged, wounding Family members Gypsy and Mary Brunner, whose immunity deal had left her free to keep testifying as a prosecution witness. The police found a bloody bra in the Family's van, which had apparently been shot off Gypsy's body during the firestorm.

Back in the courtroom, Judge Call ordered a mistrial on the grounds that the jury had been highly prejudiced by inflammatory questions and prosecutorial error. Call then declined to preside over the second trial.

———

Charles "Tex" Watson lost his extradition fight in September 1970 after a Texas judge ruled that he didn't see any evidence preventing Watson from receiving a fair trial in California.

Although many news articles had identified Tex as the actual killer in the Tate-LaBianca murders, the judge said the sensational publicity surrounding the case was not due to an irresponsible media, but rather that "sensational events involving weird personalities cannot be accurately presented in prosaic terms." So he ordered Watson to be sent back to California to await trial.

Within a short time of Watson's arrival at the LA county jail, he began to lose weight and refused to eat many foods, claiming they made him sick. He spat up or wouldn't eat meat, fried chicken, anything oily, sweet, fatty, or white, including potatoes and bread.

Although Watson claimed he hadn't done any hard drugs since leaving the Family in the desert, he suggested his dietary problems could be a delayed result of repeatedly eating belladonna root at the ranch. He also said they could be a vestige of consuming a mostly vegetarian diet with the Family.

Whatever the cause, he fell into a catatonic state, unable to talk, move, or take care of his bodily functions, and had to be tube fed. Declared incompetent and unable to stand trial, he was sent to Atascadero State Hospital for emergency treatment on October 30, where he recovered over the next several months. After doctors there determined that he had no mental disorders, he was sent back to the LA county jail.

In May 1971, he pleaded not guilty by reason of insanity to all charges, meaning that at the time of the crimes he was mentally incapable of premeditation or forming intent or malice and could not differentiate between right and wrong.

Meanwhile, his odd behaviors and avoidance of many foods resumed. His weight fell to 112 pounds, 48 pounds lighter than his healthiest weight as an athlete.

Several of the doctors who examined him concluded that the effects of his previously heavy and prolonged daily use of psychedelics and hallucinogens had taken their toll, causing classic symptoms of organic brain disease, even eighteen months after he'd stopped using them.

One doctor diagnosed him with a condition known as "*folie à deux*," meaning that Manson's dominant personality had taken over his, fusing with Watson's weaker personality to carry out the stronger, dangerous, and delusional ideology.

Dr. Ira Frank, of the UCLA Neuropsychiatric Institute, said Watson's mood seemed flat at times, and his thinking and speech were "often slowed, vague, concrete and at times illogical. Reality was freely mixed with material derived from his hallucinations and psychedelic experiences, which at times appeared delusional. Memory, concentration and judgment seemed impaired and concepts seemed difficult to grasp. . . . He seemed unable to comprehend the complexity and the enormity of his present situation."

Based on Watson's description of the murders, Dr. Frank concluded that his actions were mechanical, stemming from a "drug-induced psychotic state," and rendered him dissociated from emotion and "without rational motive." Frank thought it "extremely unlikely" that Watson would be dangerous again, saying his condition resulted from a "unique combination of drugs, Manson and the family." Resolving his mental issues would require a long hospitalization.

By July, Watson still weighed only 114 pounds. He complained that other inmates were harassing and choking him, and that he still couldn't eat jailhouse food.

The court granted the defense permission for two psychiatrists to interview Watson after administering sodium pentothal or sodium amytal, more commonly known as truth serums. He was also examined by a series of clinicians to evaluate his brain functioning and legal competency to stand trial in light of his insanity claim.

The psychiatrists' conclusions ran the gamut. Several said he was legally insane during the crimes and still had not regained his sanity. Others said he was insane then but was sane now and able to face trial, and although Watson's behavior was not "normal," he had always known that it was wrong to kill. At the other end of the spectrum, one doctor said Watson was legally sane before and he was faking his symptoms now for "personal gain."

All of this only delayed the inevitable outcome for Tex Watson, the man who had stabbed, shot, and brutally mutilated seven innocent victims at the Tate and LaBianca homes.

After the guilt phase of his trial began on August 2, prison staff had to inject him with Thorazine, a tranquilizer used to calm difficult-to-control prisoners, after he tried to harm himself by sticking his hands into the workings of the cell gate, and ramming his head and body against the wall. But on October 12, a jury of six men and six women found him guilty nonetheless.

A subsequent "sanity" phase began next, during which a sampling of his psychiatric evaluations was presented to the jury. The panel found him to be legally sane at the time of the murders.

During a short penalty trial, the same jury deliberated for only five hours before voting on October 21 to send him to the gas chamber.

The DA never charged Watson in the Shorty Shea murder because he was already serving a death sentence for the seven others.

———

On October 23, 1971, Kenneth Como, one of the crew who stole guns from the surplus store to break Manson out of jail, was arraigned on felony charges for his sixth jailbreak in seventeen years.

He'd sawed his way out of his cell on the thirteenth floor of the Hall of Justice, dropped down the side of the building by using a rope made from strips of mattress cover, then kicked through an eighth-floor window to walk out unnoticed.

After waiting for him in a van below, Sandy Good sideswiped a car on their way to a safe house. Como was hiding in a shed behind the house when authorities captured him six hours later and returned him to jail.

Good, who was arrested for aiding and abetting Como's escape, was arraigned at the same time. In typical Family style, Como shouted at the judge in Good's defense: "You should give her a medal for performing a community service!"

———

Steve Grogan's second trial proceeded quickly in a new judge's courtroom, that of Judge James Kolts.

A successful prosecution of a "no-body" case is rare, but this time the jury believed the testimony presented by witnesses who recounted the claims by Grogan and others that they had fatally stabbed, decapitated, dismembered, and buried Shorty somewhere at Spahn Ranch.

The jury deliberated only eight hours before convicting the twenty-year-old of murder. Grogan showed no emotion as the clerk read the verdict, though he smiled a little as the jurors were polled individually.

A week later, on November 8, the same jury of eight men and four women deliberated twice as long before voting to send him to death row.

———

Manson's trial for the murders of Shorty Shea and Gary Hinman had been under way in another courtroom at the same time as Grogan's.

On November 2, after forty-three hours over nine days of deliberations, the jury found Manson guilty of murdering both men, as well as conspiracy to rob and murder Hinman.

After the clerk read the verdict, Manson smiled as if on cue, then began to shout at reporters and people in the gallery. "You're from the United States of cowards! You're afraid to face me. All you have is muscle. You don't have any mind."

Still screaming, Manson refused to walk out of the courtroom on his own, so the bailiffs had to carry him.

When the penalty phase began the next day, Manson was immediately removed to the same type of holding cell where he'd spent most of his trials.

He was allowed back into the courtroom, but continued to cause problems as he called out to Leslie Van Houten, who was about to testify in his defense.

"Leslie, this is not my defense," he said. "They got nothing to do with me out there."

Still under his powerful influence, she told Manson's lawyer that she'd changed her mind. "Mr. Kanarek, I've decided I don't want to testify," she said, citing her right under the Fifth Amendment.

Although Manson faced the death penalty on all three counts, he ended up with a life sentence in this case, which even the DA's office has since admitted was weak.

Nevertheless, he was sent back to death row at San Quentin on December 13, 1971.

———

Even before the Hawthorne gun store shooting, the DA had obtained an indictment against Mary Brunner for Gary Hinman's murder in light of her disruptive behavior at Bobby Beausoleil's trial. But the prosecutors didn't press forward to trial, presumably because they still needed her to testify in other proceedings.

Mary had gone on to testify truthfully for the prosecution during the penalty phase of the Tate-LaBianca trial, acknowledging that Susan Atkins told many different versions of how Hinman was murdered. But she lied on the stand again during Manson's trial for the Hinman-Shea murders, saying she wasn't there for Hinman's murder, nor had she seen Atkins hold a gun on him. She then abruptly stopped testifying and refused to answer any more questions, citing the Fifth Amendment.

After that, the DA's office decided to try Mary for murder *and* four counts of perjury, arguing that she'd lost her immunity deal by lying and refusing to cooperate.

But the murder charge didn't stick. During a hearing in March 1972, Judge George Dell supported the defense's claim that Mary had been offered immunity seven times since December 1969, and ruled that the offer still stood.

Mary had given enough testimony for Bobby Beausoleil to be sentenced to death, the judge said, and for Manson to be convicted as well. The People have gotten "virtually everything they bargained for," and Mary had "delivered to the People everything they had a right to expect."

"It is rather obvious that friends of Mr. Manson and hers contacted her and she changed her story," Dell said, though in light of her false testimony, he conceded that she should stand trial for perjury.

Her commitment to the Family still deeply ingrained, Mary admitted that she still loved Charlie and Bobby.

"Did you love Bruce Davis?" her attorney asked.

"We were all the same, man," she replied.

"In other words, you loved everybody, right?"

"The whole Family."

"And you still love everybody, is that correct?"

"That's right."

———

It took several years, but Leslie Van Houten and Patricia Krenwinkel realized on the same day in March 1973 that they'd finally broken free of the Family.

Still in the isolation unit at Corona, they and Susan Atkins were joined by Mary Brunner and Catherine "Gypsy" Share, who had been convicted of armed robbery at the surplus store.

Talking the same old Manson jargon, Mary and Gypsy told the three women that Charlie had lost them in a card game to another Family member.

"You now belong to Kenneth Como, we're all going to escape, and we have the blades to do it," they said, explaining that they had smuggled in hacksaw blades by hiding them in their private areas.

Van Houten and Krenwinkel independently had the same reaction. They were finished with Manson, the Family, and the subjugation that had put them in prison.

"No, I'm not," Krenwinkel said, realizing that she now had the emotional distance and fortitude to leave the Family for good. "I'm not going with you. You do whatever you want to do. I'm done."

Van Houten echoed that sentiment as well. "I've changed," she said.

After several years in isolation, Van Houten was finally feeling the guilt of what she'd done and had decided to find a way to live with what she'd become. And that mind-set didn't include bowing to Charlie Manson any longer.

It took Atkins another year or so before she felt that Manson had left her brain and that he could no longer control her thoughts.

———

Mary Brunner was sentenced to life, but was released in July 1978, after serving only five years and four months of her sentence. With her immunity deal still in place, she'd gotten off completely for the murder of Gary Hinman. Catherine Share was discharged in April 1977.

Once Mary was paroled, she changed her name, dropped out of public view, and went to live in the Midwest. Meanwhile, Michael Brunner, her son with Manson, was raised by her parents in Wisconsin, thinking for years that his mother was his older sister.

CHAPTER 30

DEATH PENALTY
OVERTURNED

In 1972, the death penalty was ruled unconstitutional by both the Supreme Court of California and the US Supreme Court. As a result, the death sentences for Manson and his codefendants were commuted to life with possible parole.

Bruce Davis, who was convicted of two counts of murder and of conspiracy to commit murder and robbery two months after the California ruling, was sentenced to life in prison.

Four years later, Leslie Van Houten's conviction was thrown out by the Second District Court of Appeal of California, which ordered a retrial.

Van Houten had successfully argued in her appeal that she'd been denied effective assistance of counsel when Maxwell Keith was appointed to replace Ronald Hughes, with only a week to prepare his closing argument after also missing the entire guilt phase of the trial.

During her retrial, which began in March 1977, Keith presented a defense of diminished capacity based on mental illness induced by Manson, the peculiar Family communal organization, and Van Houten's chronic, prolonged hallucinogenic drug use.

But after deliberating for twenty-five days, the jury announced it was hopelessly deadlocked. The judge declared a mistrial on August 6.

Van Houten was allowed to be released on bail until she could be tried again. Taking the LaBianca family's feelings into account, she asked to stay in prison until after the Christmas holidays so as not to cause them any more suffering. Released on December 27, she remained free for seven and a half months.

In the end, Van Houten's third trial resulted in the same guilty verdicts as the first. Ordering the counts of murder and conspiracy to run concurrently, the judge sentenced her to life, with eight years credit for time served. She was returned to prison on August 17, 1978.

———

Steve "Clem" Grogan was labeled by many as mentally challenged. The day that Judge Kolts reduced his sentence to life for the murder of Shorty Shea, he called Grogan "too stupid and hopped up on drugs to know what his role was other than to carry out his assignments."

But Grogan was smart enough to contact authorities and tell them where Shorty's remains were buried as his parole eligibility date approached. As such, he is the only Manson murder codefendant to be granted parole *and* actually released from prison.

His change of heart came slowly, as time passed and he befriended Lieutenant Cecil Chandler, a watch commander at the Deuel Vocational Institution in Tracy.

Grogan had been in prison for a couple of years when a teenage girl started writing to him. Once she turned eighteen she came in person, and after eighteen months of visits they got engaged. Grogan had come to trust Chandler enough to invite him to the ceremony in December 1975.

It wasn't long before Grogan's wife began getting threatening calls from Lynette Fromme and Sandy Good in Sacramento, saying she wasn't good enough for him and they were going to kill her.

After Grogan was stabbed by another inmate in 1976, he asked Lieutenant Chandler for a heart-to-heart. "I've been thinking about my crime," he said. "I would like to talk to you about it."

Chandler got clearance to develop a personal relationship with Grogan, and after a few conversations, the inmate admitted responsibility in Shorty's murder. He confessed specifics in a conference call with his wife and father, then Chandler contacted the LASD, the LAPD, and the DA's office on Grogan's behalf, offering to help locate Shorty's body.

Grogan spent all night drawing a map from memory for the search team, which Chandler flew down to assist. But after a hectic day of digging in sand piles, flying over the area with a helicopter, and taking photos and video to show Grogan, the effort proved unsuccessful.

Still unsure if Grogan was making up the story to escape or get a nice field trip, the search team asked Chandler if they should risk releasing Grogan to help them find the body.

"Are you willing to take a chance?" they asked.

"I'll take a chance for Grogan," Chandler replied.

So, in December 1977, they transported the inmate more than three hundred miles to Spahn Ranch so he could point them to the right spot. Over the years, however, the landscape had changed due to rainstorms and mudslides. When they still couldn't find the remains, they put him in jail overnight to try again the next day.

Grogan made one final attempt on December 15, and this time the team unearthed Shorty's skeletal remains at the side of an embankment, 150 feet off Santa Susana Pass Road and one mile west of Topanga Boulevard.

Contrary to the killers' exaggerated boasts, Shorty's skeleton was intact except for a missing left hand, which was likely caused by an animal post-mortem. That said, his skull had been crushed, as if he'd been hit in the back of the head, and his chest bones and ribs showed evidence of multiple stab and chop wounds, as Grogan had described.

To keep Grogan safe in prison and also to protect his family, who lived near the burial site, the authorities simply told the media that they'd found the body with the help of an "informant."

———

By Grogan's first parole hearing in 1978, he'd already helped the authorities find Shorty's remains, and he was looking at the Manson Family in hindsight.

Grogan was twenty when he'd entered the prison system in December 1971. Although he and Manson were at the state prison system's mental health facility in Vacaville at the same time, Grogan had tried to keep his distance from his former guru.

"I was young then, stupid, and I've really got no cleanup for what I did. It was wrong," he told the board. ". . . I've learned. Experience is the best teacher. There's nothing that I can see that would ever coerce me or persuade me to do anything that I don't want to do."

Prison psychiatrists had initially diagnosed Grogan with aspects of schizophrenia, but those diagnoses receded as he recovered from the drug damage. By 1976, most doctors reported seeing no identifiable "personality problems" and a below-average potential for violence.

Still, the board denied his first parole request, noting that it had taken him nine years to volunteer to help find Shorty's remains. They also cited one doctor's persistent and troubling diagnosis of "schizophrenia, chronic undifferentiated type."

At his hearing three years later, Grogan reassured the board that he wouldn't decompensate, get hooked up with another charismatic figure, or slip back into distorted thinking and values.

"I've seen Manson for what he really is," he said. "The romanticism is out of the game. I'm not sixteen years old anymore, and I can see what— I've seen the whole scope of all the charismatic people that have and I—that's not going to happen again."

This time the commissioners agreed, deciding that Grogan had matured enough to deserve parole.

After two progress hearings in 1984 and 1985, the board approved his plan to work as a sign painter and graphic artist, with side jobs as a musician and house painter, and he was released to the San Fernando Valley in the middle of the night on November 18, 1985.

As a parole condition, the thirty-four-year-old father of two was forbidden to have contact with Family members. He must have complied because he was discharged from parole on April 13, 1988.

Today, Grogan sometimes goes by the alias Adam Gabriel—his two sons' first names. He apparently divorced his first wife, because he has gotten remarried to a psychologist who evaluates criminal defendants for legal sanity and competency to stand trial. Still a musician, he has played in various bands in Contra Costa County.

———

In the years after the murder trials, Lynette "Squeaky" Fromme and Sandy Good remained close, and both kept in regular contact with Charles Manson.

Focusing more now on protecting the environment from evil corporate overlords, Manson came up with a religious construct for his remaining followers. He called it the Order of the Rainbow.

Charlie had given each woman in his inner circle a name corresponding to a color while they were all still active and loyal Family members, but this was the first time they became public. He called Lynette "Red" for her red hair and her task, to protect the redwoods. Sandy was "Blue" for her blue eyes and her assignment, to fight for clean air, water, and the ocean in particular. Katie had been yellow, Leslie green, Sadie violet, Brenda gold, and Cappy silver.

Red and Blue, two of the few longtime Family members who weren't in prison, were directed to continue Charlie's militant eco-terrorist philosophy and activities, like the tractor-loader fire in Death Valley.

The duo lived in an attic apartment in Sacramento and were often photographed together, Sandy in a blue head-covering robe, tied at the waist, and Lynette in a red hooded poncho with jeans. They told the media they were celibate nuns, waiting for their lord, Charles Manson.

"He expects people to be cleaning the Earth," Red said when they were photographed on July 8, 1975.

The two women were also photographed chained together, holding up one forefinger to communicate Charlie's message, "One, us, me," which Blue said also signified "an alternative to anarchy" or "a broken peace sign."

But they were largely on their own, because most of the other Family members had distanced themselves from Charlie, the Family, and them too. They did, however, manage to recruit a third roommate to join their crusade: Susan Murphy, who also wore a hooded robe and described herself as a "sister of Manson's church."

———

On September 5, 1975, Lynette Fromme took action to further the Manson cause by strapping to her leg a Colt .45-caliber automatic that she pointed at President Gerald Ford in Slate Capital Park in Sacramento. The Secret Service agents who wrestled her to the ground before she could fire it later learned that the magazine was loaded, but had no shell in the chamber.

She never intended to kill the president, she said, claiming to have purposely ejected the bullet onto her apartment floor before leaving for the park. She said she simply wanted to make a statement and relay a message from Manson about saving the redwood trees.

Allowed to represent herself at trial, Fromme was found guilty of attempting to assassinate the president. During her sentencing hearing on December 18, she pulled out an apple, hidden in her sleeve, and threw it. Although she hit the prosecutor above the right eye, she said the judge had been her intended target. Sentenced to life in prison, she was dragged from the courtroom, screaming. She would be eligible for parole in fifteen years.

———

With her partner in crime behind bars, Sandy Good was one of the—if not *the* only—remaining core Family members on the outside who continued working, at least publicly, on Manson's behalf.

In March 1976, Good was sentenced to fifteen years in federal prison for conspiracy to mail death threats to 171 corporate executives she'd accused of polluting the environment. She was convicted of threatening to harm them and their wives in the name of the International People's Court of Retribution as well as making telephone threats to a newspaper and four radio stations.

At trial, Good refused to put up a defense, saying she wanted to go straight to prison to be with Fromme and the other Family members.

"I cannot bear to be outside [in] your society," she told Judge MacBride at her sentencing. "I want to be inside with my family."

Susan Murphy, also convicted of sending death threats to corporate executives, received a five-year sentence.

In mid-August, Murphy and inmate Diane Ellis, who was serving eight years for bank robbery, escaped from Terminal Island in LA by overpowering a female guard and taking off in her car. They were captured nine days later in Portland, Oregon.

———

Good began her sentence at Terminal Island, where Manson had spent his first federal term. She was supposed to be released ten years into her sentence, in March 1985, but she refused to accept the parole conditions that she stay away from Manson and other Family members. Good said she also didn't want to be freed while other members were still in prison, nor did she want to be released to a halfway house in New Jersey, which she described as "a toxic dump."

Instead, she was released that December to Vermont, where she lived under an assumed name until her true identity was revealed.

Lynette Fromme started her time at the federal prison in San Diego, but was transferred to a facility in Alderson, West Virginia, after hitting an inmate with a hammer. She was on good behavior there for eight and a half years, although she skipped her parole hearing in 1985, figuring they wouldn't let her out so soon.

Two years later, she escaped from a medium security area and made her way into the rugged, snowy mountains, in the height of winter.

Prison officials knew that she'd been communicating with Manson by mail, but they couldn't determine whether she'd had outside help. She was captured on foot two miles from the prison a day and a half later, wearing a thick jacket, a cap, and two pairs of soaking wet pants.

From there, she was transferred to facilities in Kentucky and Florida before landing in a maximum-security unit in the Federal Medical Facility in Carswell, Texas. She was released in August 2009, after serving thirty-four years behind bars.

———

As soon as Sandy Good was off parole, she returned to California. Even though she wasn't allowed to visit Manson, she still wanted to be close to him. By then he'd been moved to Corcoran, so she settled in Hanford, about twenty-three miles away.

Good picked up her environmental activism where she'd left off, but now did it online. In 1996, she created a website aimed at freeing Manson, changing his image, and disseminating his ideas. It was called Access Manson or ATWA—an acronym for Air, Trees, Water, Animals—and represented Manson's mantra for protecting the environment: "ATWA is your survival on earth. It's a revolution against pollution. ATWA is ATWAR with pollution."

Archived today as a "historical document" on mansonblog.com, the website stated it was dedicated "to begin to lift the shroud of lies and distortions that have been used for thirty years by self serving individuals, the mass media, and certain California state departments and offices to cover the reality that is Charles Manson."

In 1997, Good's life partner, George Stimson, established ATWA in Hanford as a non-profit corporation. It was suspended several years later.

CHAPTER 31

MANSON COMES UP
FOR PAROLE

When he first entered the prison system, Charles Manson was transferred back and forth between San Quentin and Folsom prisons and the Vacaville psychiatric facility.

In 1976, officials decided to keep him at Vacaville, where he repeatedly threatened to hurt or kill correctional officers, and also hatched a failed escape attempt in 1982.

At Manson's first parole hearing in 1978, he acted as his own attorney, denying his guilt and launching objections to the prosecution's case.

Not surprisingly, Manson disputed the "Helter Skelter" scenario presented at trial as the primary motive for the killings.

"This was the district attorney's motive. It has nothing to do with me," Manson said. "He put all of this together to win the case ... He didn't care what he put on paper—race wars, Jesus. He's got the devil in it, he's got Christ, God—he's got everything he could think of, and every little bit of information he could collect from every phone in town to grant him immunity for some crazy thing, and then call it motive, and then he calls it Helter Skelter."

The commissioners discussed Manson's psychiatric evaluations, which had found him to be friendly and cooperative, but said he had gone in and out of mental disorders, including aspects of schizophrenia, that produced antisocial, paranoid, and delusional behaviors, "nonsense statements with reference to bizarre things" and the more serious "sporadic psychotic episodes requiring hospitalization."

Also diagnosed with drug dependence, Charlie likely inherited genetic predispositions for substance abuse and mental illness as well. His mother spent most of her life trying to stop drinking, his father died at forty-four from cirrhosis of the liver, and his grandfather died in an "asylum" in his forties.

Doctors also noted that Manson tended to get anxious and frustrated when he was in a restrictive closed ward, and had asked to be transferred to a more general population setting. But his requests were denied for fear that other inmates would try to injure him to boost their reputations.

———

Manson had a parole hearing every year until 1981. Showing his usual lack of respect for the judicial process, he attended his hearing that year wearing a black T-shirt with a skull on it. He started his usual verbal antics the minute he sat down, immediately asking if he could deliver his remarks standing up.

"Hey, Kay, how you doing, man?" he asked the prosecutor, Stephen Kay. "You still doing what the teacher tells you?"

Manson was honest about his obstructionist intentions, joking about what a waste of time the hearings were. He knew very well the board wasn't going to release him. "You'll do as fair as you can, which won't be fair. I accept that. I accepted that before," he said. "I just came over here to play. I wanted to see all you guys again."

As the chairman tried to proceed, Manson interrupted, pretending he didn't understand what was going on. "I've been in solitary confinement for ten years. I've been in the S Wing, nut ward, for almost eight years. I ain't got no mind. It's gone, man."

The commissioners noted, however, that he had been cogent enough in 1976 to tell a doctor that he didn't want to discuss his case because it was still under appeal, that he didn't "command or program followers to kill anyone," and that there was "no such thing as the Manson Family."

"I told you I didn't break the law in 1967 [sic]," Manson said. "God knows that. I know that."

The board allowed Manson's attorney, Glen DeRonde, to ask him a series of questions about issues he was never able to address in court. In an exchange that encapsulated his views on the case, he gave them a dose of quintessential Manson-speak, a circular flow of past experiences and counterculture philosophy, in which some saw signs of schizophrenia and others viewed as magical mysticism.

"Let me ask you this, Charlie. Did you have Sharon Tate killed?" DeRonde asked.

"No."

"Did you have any people killed?"

"I don't have people killed. Who's got the right to have people killed?"

"Did you tell them to go kill Rosemary and Leno LaBianca?"

"I told them the same thing I tell any of you. You do what you feel is right. You have confidence in your own ability. Stand up and be your own person. Norman Vincent Peale, that's all I said. I read the book. I went to Dale Carnegie. I went through all the things that you teach me in jail, and I was your son. But, when I come home, you hit me in the eye and the guy wants to fight. I said, I don't want to fight, man, I'm antiviolent."

"Why are you here?"

"I'm here because I'm a product of you guys. I'm your refuge. I'm the bum or hobo. I shoot dice, and I run in the alley. I do little gangster things, and I steal bicycles. I go to people's houses and eat when they're not home. I'm not a harmful mouse, but I live like an animal. I'm a jail bird."

"Do you think you are society's scapegoat for this thing?"

"I don't care about society or their scapegoats. I've quit that thought in '54. I was a teddy bear in '54. The Pope and I went through that on the basketball court down on McNeil Island . . . I don't want to know what's happening, but I know everything that's happening . . . unless the devil knows something that the rest of us don't."

Unsure how to respond to what one commissioner described as

Manson's "philosophical dissertation," they moved on to the Hinman murder, which Manson blamed on "the kid," Bobby Beausoleil. He said Bobby asked him for help, then killed Hinman on his own.

Manson said he'd only come over to the house, got Hinman to give back the gun, then cut his ear. But as soon as Hinman said he wouldn't call Manson's probation officer, he was satisfied and left.

Asked if he tied up Leno and Rosemary LaBianca, Manson said no. "My work isn't that sloppy. If anybody looked at the knots, they'd see I'm a professional."

"Did you ever go in that house?"

"Yeah, I had been in it four or five times, a lot of times. It used to be a party house."

Manson said he didn't know Sharon Tate, but he'd seen her once. "It was a party down by the beach in Malibu. Doris Day's pad," he said, referring to the house where her son Terry Melcher was staying, for which Manson reportedly never knew the address.

He said people were confused when they said he wanted to start a race war—he was actually talking about the activities the Black Muslims were already doing.

"There's been a race war since day one," he said.

Noting that he wasn't taking any psychotropic medication, he said he wanted out of the psychiatric ward. "If you put me with insanity, then I'm going to reflect insanity. If I'm going to be put with rational, I might get rational. You can't put a guy in a nut ward ten or fifteen years and then have him come back out and be the guy he was. I'm doing the d****dest I can in the balance of all these people."

He also said he wasn't scared that other inmates would hurt him if he were placed in the general population. "Everybody respects me in jail . . . If you want me to walk in the mainline, I won't have no trouble because there ain't one swing in this whole planet that don't know what I can do."

He claimed he could handle anyone who tried to do him harm. "If they come up to me with a knife, I generally take it away from them and then I give it back and ask, 'What did you want to do that for? Do you want me to teach you something else today?'"

Manson got back on point with this question to the board: "If I say I hypnotized those kids, why don't you let the kids go?"

He got no response.

Knowing that he had no reasonable chance for parole, Manson typically rebuffed questions about what "release" plan he'd come up with to "fit into society."

"I don't fit into your society," he said.

"Not unless you all do what I tell you . . . By the time I get out, I'll parole to space . . . I don't particularly want to go out on parole, not until I can be left alone."

Kay pointed to Manson's fashion choice of the skull T-shirt and his bizarre commentary as proof that he was unsuitable for parole. "He is the same old Charlie—volatile, unpredictable, crazy. The enormity and cruelty of his commitment offenses almost defies—"

"—the second world war," Manson interjected.

"—description," Kay finished, linking Manson's comment to his state of mind, his admiration for Adolf Hitler, and the swastika on his forehead.

"He says he doesn't care to get out on parole. So that's fine," Kay added. "We should give him his wish and keep him in forever."

With that, the commissioners decided not to allow Manson another hearing for eleven years, ironically to give him time to work on the parole plan and the "programming" that the prison had to offer, such as self-help groups and education courses.

———

On the morning of September 25, 1984, Manson was still at Vacaville when a fellow psychiatric inmate came up behind him in the arts and crafts room, poured a cup of paint thinner over his head, and lit him on fire with a match.

Manson could feel the cold liquid being poured on him, but didn't realize exactly what was happening because the liquid stung his eyes and blurred his vision. As the flames spread, singeing his face, hair, and beard, he tried to put his jacket over his head to squelch the flames.

"My face is burned!" he screamed.

The fire scorched his scalp, hands, and face, partially obfuscating the swastika tattoo, and causing second- and third-degree burns over 18 percent of his body. Sent to the infirmary in serious condition, he eventually recovered. His facial hair apparently prevented more serious scarring.

His assailant, thirty-six-year-old Jan Holmstrom, was serving a life sentence for firing four fatal shots at his father in 1974. Similar to Manson, he'd been diagnosed with paranoid schizophrenia and had a history of drug abuse, including LSD.

Holmstrom told prison officials that the burning incident came in response to Manson's chiding him—or threatening him, depending on the account—for chanting Hare Krishna phrases.

Assault charges against Holmstrom were dismissed because prosecutors determined that given Manson's past attacks on guards and other inmates, his assailant probably acted in self-defense, so a conviction was unlikely. Holmstrom was later released to San Francisco, where he stabbed a Hare Krishna member seven times at a temple in 1990. He was found guilty by reason of insanity, and was sentenced to a "high security mental facility" for up to twenty-five years.

At Manson's next hearing in 1992, he made reference to the Vacaville immolation incident: "It's okay if I have to spend my life in prison . . . just to hold me, because I've shown you some strong strength and I haven't surrendered to this by copping out to you or telling tales on someone else or playing weak. You've medicated me, you've burnt me, you've beat me, you've stabbed me, you've done everything you can do to me and I'm still here," he said. "And you're still going to have to face the truth about this case sooner or later. If not here—in the street."

———

Manson was finally allowed to leave Vacaville in 1985, when he was shipped back to San Quentin, arriving there with a hacksaw blade in his shoe. Inmates often make or carry makeshift weapons for self-protection, knowing full well that doing so is a rules violation, for which Manson was cited.

He stayed at San Quentin until 1989, when he was moved to Corcoran and its Protective Housing Unit (PHU). This unit typically has fewer than two dozen inmates who are placed there for their own safety because they are too high-profile to be in the general population, where they are likely to be harmed as "trophies" by other inmates. Prisoners have a hierarchy among themselves, with child molesters and child killers at the bottom.

PHU inmates have included sex offenders Phillip Garrido, who kidnapped and raped eleven-year-old Jaycee Dugard, and John Gardner, who raped and killed teenagers Chelsea King and Amber Dubois. Other high-profile inmates include Sirhan Sirhan, Robert F. Kennedy's assassin.

For a while Gardner was one of the inmates Manson chose to read his enormous stacks of mail to him. Gardner also helped sign and answer some of Manson's letters—until they had a falling out.

———

Manson's last parole hearing was in 2012, but he didn't appear. In fact, he hadn't attended any hearings since March 1997.

Officially classified as a mentally ill inmate without severe symptoms, Manson was known to have poor hygiene and let his nails grow long. He purposely knocked out the front tooth of his dentures, and he sometimes showered with his clothes on.

When he turned up with two black eyes, stories circulated that he'd been beaten up by another inmate. John Gardner was subsequently moved to Mule Creek Prison.

"He won't talk about it," said John Michael Jones, Manson's friend of nearly twenty years. "He told me he fell [off his bunk], but I don't believe that. If you fall, how do you get two raccoon eyes? Charlie lives by this code, 'you don't snitch.'"

But like other convicted killers, including Gardner, Manson claimed to be a victim of the system, complaining that it beat him down—literally.

"You got me being everything's bad. I'm only five foot tall. I was five-seven, then I went to five-six, now I'm down to five-two," he said, referring to the height Bugliosi ascribed to him. "I figure about another twenty years, I'll be about four feet tall, because everybody's just constantly pushing it over on me, like they got permission to get away with doing anything they want to do to me, because I don't have no parents, because I don't have no money, because I don't have no education."

Sheriff's booking records from the 1960s do list Manson as five feet seven inches tall. The CDCR lists Manson's most recent height measurement as five feet three inches.

———

As of 2012, Manson had still done nothing to satisfy the parole board's suggestions that he participate in self-help, drug-recovery, vocational, or other programs. He had never completed his GED, had no parole release plan, still presented a high risk for violence compared with other male inmates, and was still being caught with weapons.

"He has no indication of remorse, no insight into the causative factors of the crimes, lacks understanding of the magnitude of the crimes and has an exceptional, callous disregard for human suffering," CDCR spokeswoman Terry Thornton said in 2016.

By that time, he'd chalked up more than 113 rules violations that sent him to the Security Housing Unit for a year at a time. He was cited for threatening peace officers, harassing female officers with sexual references, and possessing contraband cell phones in 2009 and 2011.

He subsequently accrued several more violations for refusing to provide a urine sample, threatening staff, possessing another weapon, and attempting to punch a certified nurse assistant.

It didn't help that in one of his last psychiatric evaluations, he said, "I am special. I am not the average inmate. I have put five people in the grave. I have been in prison most of my life. I am a dangerous man."

The 2012 parole hearing lasted only eighty minutes, a contrast to the nine- and ten-hour hearings for his codefendants, who truly wanted to get out of prison.

Not surprisingly, the board denied him parole and set the next hearing for the latest date allowed—fifteen years out, in 2027.

As Sharon Tate's sister, Debra, said at the end of the hearing, "he clearly does not want to be released into the public."

Manson said as much himself many times.

CHAPTER 32

ALTERNATIVE SCENARIOS

Charles Manson often complained that he never had a chance to tell the real story in court of how the Tate-LaBianca murders went down and why, but he did share details with friends.

They, in turn, have spread alternate scenarios to Manson case researchers and supporters, many of whom have found one another on social media. Some believe that he was wrongly convicted, while others say that though he wasn't innocent, he was still overcharged.

"We feel like we haven't been told the truth," said Bruce Fox, who has cultivated relationships online and in person with some of the original Family members and many others who reject the prosecution's argument that the "Helter Skelter" race war was the primary motive behind the murders. Fox, like many others, believes the motives were drug- and money-related.

Elements of such alternative scenarios find support in evidence collected by the LAPD detectives as they investigated their original theory of a drug-burn-robbery motive. Others are bolstered by evidence from FBI investigations as well as research conducted for this book.

John Michael Jones first contacted Manson in 1999 and they stayed in regular phone touch until Manson died. Jones heard Manson's story firsthand, became a confidante, and also went through Manson's mail for several months at his request while he was in "the hole."

According to Jones and other friends, the following is Manson's perspective on what happened in the summer of 1969, though, of course, one must ask why this account should be more credible than anything else Manson has claimed.

The call to the ranch from Tex's girlfriend, Rosina, during which Bernard Crowe threatened to kill everyone at the ranch, started "the ball rolling." Manson felt he had to respond to the threat against his people, which prompted him to shoot Crowe.

Manson said it was Tex and Linda Kasabian's idea to rob yet another set of dealers—Voytek Frykowski and Jay Sebring—of drugs and money at the Cielo house. Manson knew Tex had been to the house before, when Terry Melcher had lived there; Melcher had loaned Tex his credit card and Jaguar XKE for a trip to a friend's court hearing in Ukiah.

Tex's plan was to tie up Jay and take him back to his house to clean out his stash of money and drugs. Only Tex didn't realize that Jay knew karate and that he and Voytek would fight back so hard. Things got out of hand, causing Tex and the girls to panic.

They also didn't know that Sharon Tate was going to be home, because her car was in the shop and not in the driveway, so she and Abigail Folger ended up being killed as collateral damage.

When Tex, Sadie, and the crew returned to Spahn Ranch that night, Charlie was not happy to hear what a bloody mess they'd made of it. He'd thought it was going to be a simple robbery and drug burn.

"We did it for you," Sadie told Charlie.

"No, you just sent me back to prison for the rest of my life," he replied.

"Did you at least wipe the place down?" Charlie asked Tex, who said no. "Well, now I got to go back."

Manson claims he took a Family member with him to assess the mess, clean it up to deflect blame from the Family, and throw off investigators. They wiped down the house for fingerprints, moved the bodies around, planted a pair of glasses, and placed a towel over Jay Sebring's face.

Author Ed Sanders wrote about this return trip in his book *The Family*, saying that Manson admitted as much to an attorney at trial.

"I went back to see what my children did," Manson said. "My only concern was whether it resembled the Hinman killing. Would the police now have reason to believe that Bobby was not the slayer of Hinman?"

This scenario would explain why the neighbors and private security officers heard gunshots and arguing at 3:30 and 4:00 a.m., people screaming, and dogs barking long after midnight. Taken in concert with the odd blood patterns, it also supports the detectives' conclusion that Sharon's body had been moved.

"Why wasn't that brought up in court?" Jones asked Manson.

"I wasn't allowed to present a defense," he replied.

Over time, Jones came to believe Manson's story. Jones has dismissed testimony by witnesses like Linda Kasabian, saying they were coached to support the prosecution's Helter Skelter theory. He also noted that prosecutors made deals with and threats against key witnesses if they didn't agree to testify against Manson, which is also not uncommon or illegal.

"I'm not pro-Manson. I love him, he's a friend, but he's made a lot of mistakes in this life," Jones said in 2017, before Manson died. "He's not innocent, but he's not a hippie cult leader. He knows how to manipulate. He knows when to act crazy and when to act normal. Manson is guilty for going back to the scene, for helping to cover it up, and he admits it. But he did not orchestrate these murders."

———

Drug dealers working within a certain geographical area often know one another, or at least *know of* one another. Some also know where their competitors keep their drugs and money, so it's not uncommon for them to steal one another's stashes, knowing such thefts are unlikely to be reported to police.

In this case, Tex, who often interacted with his and the Family's drug suppliers, had a proven history of stealing from other dealers, including Crowe and even his own girlfriend, Rosina.

Jay Sebring and Voytek Frykowski were both described by witnesses interviewed by LAPD detectives as heavy recreational users and also as buyers of drugs, apparently for sale—a claim backed by the cocaine,

MDA, pot, and other pills found in the Tate house and Jay's car, and from their recent drug buys.

On the day of the murder Voytek met with a drug trafficker at the Tate house to discuss dealing MDA. According to Jay's receptionist, Karlene Ann McCaffrey, Jay had already been the victim of a drug burn earlier in the week, when he purchased the two thousand dollars in bad cocaine.

Police learned that Jay and Voytek had also purchased cocaine and mescaline that same day from McCaffrey's ex-boyfriend, Joel Rostau, who was a known drug dealer and had been a victim of a drug burn himself.

Just four months earlier, on April 13 at 6:00 a.m., Rostau and McCaffrey had called sheriff's deputies, claiming that two armed men had broken in, tied them up in Rostau's apartment, and shot him in the foot. The deputies found enough pot, cocaine, and hashish in the apartment to arrest Rostau for possession of narcotics for sale. The LAPD's Tate homicide team questioned Rostau and McCaffrey about this incident; Jones believes Tex was one of the armed robbers who shot Rostau.

The FBI arrested Rostau a few months after the Tate murders for trying to sell stolen securities in Switzerland to pay off $225,000 in debts to underworld figures. He was ultimately found murdered in the trunk of a rental Cadillac at JFK airport in May 1970.

The FBI and New York police suspected that Rostau was killed by one of his associates, convicted felon Gino Massaro. During an unrelated arrest, cops in LA found Rostau's .38-caliber revolver with a second gun, equipped with a silencer, under a cushion at Massaro's apartment.

Described by the FBI as "armed and dangerous" and apparently tied to organized crime, Massaro was under federal surveillance and investigation for years, and was suspected of crimes including selling cocaine, loan sharking, and running prostitutes on the Hollywood Strip. In 1969, he was awaiting trial on kidnapping, burglary, and conspiracy charges in an LA murder case, and was eventually acquitted on a retrial.

Massaro appears to have been a likely drug supplier to Tex and the Family, because Tex mentioned a dealer who sounds like Massaro in his book: "I'd arranged to buy a kilo of grass from the dealer who'd been supplying the Family—he fronted the dope with a vending-machine company and people said he was with the Mafia."

Tex's description is supported by Massaro's FBI file, which says that as vice president of Disc-O-Mat Inc., Massaro was "allegedly . . . in the business of producing and placing vending machines that dispense the top ten records on sale in any particular week."

Tex didn't name Massaro by name in his book, but he specifically mentioned the Family's drug supplier as one of the dealers he considered burning in the Crowe deal, along with Rosina: "Since grass was particularly scarce at the time, I called [Rosina] back on July 1 and said that the Family had a hundred dollars and wanted to buy a kilo of grass, but our Mafia vending-machine connection would only sell twenty-five kilos at a throw, for a cool $2,500."

This suggests Tex targeted the Tate house on Cielo Drive for another drug burn on August 8, just a week after the Crowe incident and at a time when Manson was pushing the Family to come up with money to prepare for their move to the desert.

It also makes sense to explain why Manson would have gone back to Cielo Drive in the wee hours as he now claims, to clean up another one of his "children's" messes, to keep them all out of prison. Counting Bobby's mess at Gary Hinman's house, this would be the third such mess in about ten days of failed looting that ended in murder by Manson Family members.

After working for two years to find Manson a new lawyer and get him a new trial based on this information, Jones said he managed to persuade Gerry Spence, a big-name defense attorney, to agree. Spence did not respond to a request for comment.

But then Manson surprised Jones by refusing to sign the necessary paperwork. "I don't want out. I'm afraid of your world," Manson told Jones, who was understandably upset after his efforts. "Do you know what it feels like to look over your shoulder and not know whether it's going to be your last day? At least in here I'm protected."

Jones said he also believes Manson's claim that the choice to murder the LaBiancas was not any more random than the Tate killings, and that it didn't stem from frustrations about not becoming a rock star or a desire to send a message to Terry Melcher. Rather, Jones said, it could have been some kind of arranged hit, as LAPD detectives and others suspected.

The LaBianca homicide team initially pursued a theory that the couple was murdered in a hired hit by Mafia mobsters or loan sharks because Leno, a chronic gambler with a five-hundred-dollars-a-day race-track habit, had taken out numerous loans and also had misappropriated at least $123,000 from the family company since 1964. And yet, while Rosemary's estate was surprisingly probated with assets worth $2.4 million, police said the couple was "extensively mortgaged" and living beyond their means.

If the Mafia didn't issue the hit, Jones and others wonder if Rosemary's daughter, Suzan LaBerge, could have played a role. Before the LaBiancas were murdered, Rosemary had expressed disapproval of her daughter's relationship with Joe Dorgan, Suzan's fiancé, who was reportedly a member of the Straight Satans and had been convicted of grand theft auto and arrested for drug possession.

After Rosemary's death, Suzan applied to become an executor of Rosemary's estate, and was appointed as such by a judge. Independent case researchers have since claimed that in the year before the murders Suzan and Tex lived in Hollywood apartments near each other, which would add a possible access to means—Tex, a drug dealer who robbed other dealers—to her potential motive.

To further support this claim, Jones points to the unusual efforts Suzan made to secure the release of her parents' killer, even testifying at his parole hearings. While Suzan claimed her support for Tex arose from their common "born-again" experience and a desire to forgive, Jones does not accept this explanation, noting that Tex had been running a spree of drug-dealer robberies an entire year before the murders. Sharon Tate's mother, Doris, who also attended parole hearings while she was still alive, didn't buy it either.

"I couldn't put my finger on it, but there was more going on than mere forgiveness," Doris wrote in her journal after one hearing, noting that she saw Tex looking at Suzan "like a proud parent" as Suzan testified on his behalf.

Jones summed it up like this: "Drugs and money. That's it. Murder was secondary. Murder came after."

———

Regardless of whether people believe Charles Manson was rightly or wrongly convicted, some people today still believe his claim that Helter Skelter was never the real motive behind the killings. Arguing that other factors played more of a role, they note that just because a prosecution theory results in a guilty verdict doesn't mean that the theory provides the whole truth.

"Court is not a search for truth," Dr. David Smith said, "so the trial is not the truth." But, he added, "If you try to analyze this [case], people say you're being sympathetic."

Certain events or motives also may turn up during homicide investigations but are never presented in court by either side. For example, Dr. Smith said he was frustrated that he wasn't asked to testify at trial about how the use of psychedelic drugs played into the Family's violent acts, because neither side thought that would help its case. The prosecution saw this information as "mitigating circumstances," he said, and Manson's attorney only seemed interested in arguing that his client wasn't guilty of murder because he wasn't physically there to stab or shoot anyone.

In the end, court cases are about winning, achieving justice for the victims, and ensuring defendants receive a fair trial. As a result, many important human details like the ones Dr. Smith mentioned are often deemed tangential, confusing, or not as powerful to a jury.

Jeff Guinn, author of the biography *Manson: The Life and Times of Charles Manson*, is one of those skeptics who believes other motives were involved.

"To me, the whole Helter Skelter thing was maybe 10 percent of it," Guinn said in an interview with *The Oklahoman*. "The real reason was to cover up a murder. Bobby Beausoleil killed musician Gary Hinman in 1969, and they killed these other people to try to cover it up."

Guinn said he debated this issue extensively with Bugliosi before he died in June 2015, but the retired prosecutor wouldn't budge.

"You couldn't tell Vince that. He would argue for hours, and I mean hours. He never backed down and wouldn't consider anything else."

Beausoleil has also always argued that the Family's motive for killing was not an impending race war any more than it was Manson mind control—claims that many Manson supporters still believe to be true today.

"They killed out of desperation during a time when many people felt frustrated. They felt their backs were to the wall, and the only place they could go was the desert," Beausoleil said in 1981. "This wasn't mere discontent. This was lunacy."

"At least in their minds . . . they couldn't travel any more together without a caravan of law enforcement people behind them. . . . They were at the end of the edge of the world and they were scared to death of being pushed off the edge. The desert is death. They wound up in Death Valley trying to live off the bugs."

But as California's Second District Court of Appeal pointed out, it doesn't really matter if the Helter Skelter scenario was a real motive in Manson's mind or just a "fanatical fantasy. . . . The gist of the conspiracy was the comprehended common design, however bizarre and fanciful. It is not necessary that the object of the conspiracy be carried out or completed."

To date, there is no indication that the LAPD is pursuing any of these alternative theories.

CHAPTER 33

THE FIGHT
AGAINST PAROLE

A long table filled the width of the small room at Mule Creek State Prison, where participants crowded in for the third of four parole hearings for Manson-related defendants in 2016.

Seventy-year-old Charles "Tex" Watson sat on one side with his attorney; the two parole commissioners sat on the other. Deputy District Attorney Donna Lebowitz sat at the other end, guards were posted at both doors, and Lis Wiehl, then a legal commentator for FOX News and the only media representative present that day, sat just a foot and a half from Watson. The victims' family members and representatives sat in several rows behind the prosecutor, ready to once again face the man who had killed their loved ones.

The room fell silent as Watson, his Texas twang still strong, matter-of-factly recounted his version of the events that had occurred forty-seven years earlier.

By all appearances, this tall, athletic-looking inmate with angular cheekbones, who had gotten married and had four kids while in prison, looked like the kind of man a woman of a certain age would set up with a single friend. Well groomed, the nails on his long, lean hands were neatly trimmed, his hair was nicely cropped, and his white leather tennis shoes were scrubbed clean.

As he told his story, his voice rang clear, with few lingering signs of the brain damage recorded by psychiatrists so many years ago. He claimed to be a man of God. A good Christian.

But as the victims' representatives sat listening with their arms crossed, their distaste for him hung in the air. They uttered no gasps or sighs during his soliloquy, in which he intended to show his remorse, insight, and accountability for his crimes—until he started making comments they couldn't stomach.

"I have a real good identity," he said. "I sit here forgiven, I believe. And I really feel good about myself."

As John Peck, the presiding commissioner, began to ask questions, the exchanges became heated as he shouted and pointed at Watson.

"Why would a churchgoing country boy from Texas, that was going to school, that was doing all the right things in his life . . . come to California and then be involved in one of the most horrible crimes in the history of this state?" he asked.

Watson responded calmly with a well-practiced mantra, an academic mix of religion and the psychology of group dynamics, saying that he'd had "no significant goals" in his life back then. He'd become radicalized. He had anger in his heart.

When the commissioner grew frustrated and told Watson to stop lecturing him like a teacher, Watson didn't seem to know how to use other language. He said he lacked core values and a core identity. He was emotionally unstable, was fearful of failure and judgment, and constantly sought acceptance by trying to perform well.

Clearly frustrated, Peck quipped, "So why not join a chess club then?"

Asked whether he believed Manson's ideology, and if he, too, was a racist, Watson replied, "No, I wasn't a racist. His views were not racism at all. He thought the blacks were going to be on his side to destroy society."

Although Watson said he was "deeply sorry for the pain" he'd caused the victims' friends and families, the board countered that he wasn't helping his own cause by continuing to associate himself with Manson. Commissioners pointed out that he was still selling the book *Manson's Right-Hand Man Speaks Out* on his Abounding Love Ministries website.

Watson tried to minimize the title, saying it was just a "catchy" way to hook readers, but he did acknowledge that he was Manson's "go-to" guy for the Tate-LaBianca murders.

Growing flustered, he contradicted himself and said he didn't know why he gave certain answers, all of which fueled the commissioners' conclusion that he lacked insight into why he'd committed his crimes.

The victims' families weren't allowed to address Watson directly, but that didn't lessen the passion of their remarks now that it was their turn to talk.

After seeing one another through dozens of these traumatic hearings over the years, they had become a close-knit group, sharing in the trauma as their wounds of grief were re-opened with each grueling session.

Some of them couldn't handle coming in person to all four hearings in 2016, but most made a point to be present that day to face the man who gave the orders to carry out the seven highest-profile murders. Debra Tate, Sharon Tate's sister, and Anthony DiMaria, Jay Sebring's nephew, sat alongside Gary Hinman's cousin, Kay Martley, while Steve Parent's sister and two members of the extended LaBianca family—Leno's nephew, Lou Smaldino, and Leno's grandson, Tony LaMontagne—sent representatives.

Before going through security, the group had hugged one another in the lobby, their faces tight with nerves. Once they were inside, no one could leave until the meeting ended, which, in this case, was ten hours later.

Noting that she'd been attending these hearings since 1998, Debra Tate told the board that she'd also helped her mother, Doris, prepare for them for many years before that.

She questioned Watson's claims of remorse, pointing out that he still had to read his victims' names from a piece of paper, even after all this time. He'd also never reached out to her, she said, so she offered to sit down with him and tell him about the sister he'd killed.

"Let's see what kind of Christian he is and what kind of Christian his counsel is," she said. "Let me see. Let me understand."

DiMaria, who was three when his uncle Jay was killed, noted that this was his sixteenth hearing and expressed his "profound sorrow" for everyone involved, including Watson.

Reading his prepared statement, DiMaria began to cry, going off script as he tried to hold his emotions in check. But he finished with a strong statement: "I urge the board to recommend parole for inmate Watson when you can parole his victims from their graves."

After taking a recess to confer, the commissioners took a hard line and denied Watson parole for five more years, during which time they suggested he "get some more understanding" into why he committed his crimes.

"Without that understanding there certainly is a nexus to current dangerousness," Peck said.

"The sad fact is that forty-seven years later you're still the boogie man in the American psyche," Commissioner Kathleen Newman said.

Exhausted after a long day, the families hugged again and expressed their mutual feelings of relief. Then they immediately began planning for the next hearing.

Watson has since been moved to the Richard J. Donovan Correctional Facility in San Diego County.

Susan Atkins found God and married twice in prison. Although the first marriage lasted only a short time, her second—to James Whitehouse, an attorney who advises female inmates—lasted for nearly twenty-two years.

Whitehouse was by her side at her very last parole hearing, on September 2, 2009. Asleep in a gurney for most of it, Atkins's cancer-ravaged brain rendered her unable to speak or hear what was being said.

Her request for compassionate release in July 2008 had been denied, despite the support of her prison warden and prosecutor Vincent Bugliosi, who wrote in an e-mail that it was wrong to assume that just because she "showed no mercy to her victims, we therefore are duty-bound to follow her inhumanity and show no mercy to her."

Before developing cancer, Atkins had earned a paralegal certificate and worked as a teacher's aide, receiving "exceptional" reports from her supervisor. After her diagnosis, her left leg had to be amputated, she had to quit work, and she was confined to a bed. By her final hearing, she was 85 percent paralyzed, including her remaining leg, which left her unable to sit up in bed or feed herself.

She'd come a long way from being Sadie Mae Glutz, who sought love and attention from Manson and just about everyone else. In her last years, she tried to steer young girls *away* from Manson.

The mother of a seventeen-year-old girl named Ashley wrote to Atkins in 1998, saying that her daughter "was going to move away from home so she could be near Charles Manson."

When Atkins responded, dissuading the teenager, the girl's mother wrote back to thank her. "Ashley did read your letter. She looked at it for more than an hour and then put it in her special drawer. With your kind words, I think she's coming around."

After Atkins's last psych evaluation in February 2009, the doctor noted that she was "non-ambulatory and appeared frail and markedly older than her chronological age"; appeared nervous, confused, and disoriented; and struggled to answer questions and recall events. Still, she was able to state "that she had no regrets about the life she had lived thus far."

Although the board had received 258 letters supporting her release, citing her turnaround over the years, her church work, and her education and training, it also had received a stack of letters in opposition that stood an inch and a half thick. One of them was from former Family member Barbara Hoyt.

"Even on her deathbed, about to meet her maker, she still isn't telling the truth," Hoyt wrote, begging the board not to release Atkins because she could never take back her part in the savage slayings. "Murder isn't something you get over and the victims don't get to rise from their graves. The families don't get the gaping hole in their hearts where their loved ones belong repaired."

When Atkins died in prison three weeks later on September 24, her last word was "Amen."

Bobby Beausoleil had his eighteenth parole hearing in 2016 when he was sixty-eight, and was denied once again. Although he has changed his story about Gary Hinman's murder a number of times over the years, he has consistently maintained since his first hearing in 1978 that he went to Gary's to collect one thousand dollars for a bad batch of mescaline— one thousand tabs that Gary had sold to him for the Straight Satans. The tabs turned out to be strychnine, and the bikers were after him to get their money back. Bobby said Gary was not a big-time dealer, but that he mostly sold pot to friends. Beausoleil also claimed that Charlie didn't tell him to kill anyone; rather, he killed Gary to prevent him from going to the police after Charlie cut his ear.

Gary's cousin, Kay Hinman Martley, doesn't believe the drug story: "They murdered him because they'd already just caused such a ruckus and they just wanted to finish it off."

Beausoleil is the only codefendant to spend part of his sentence out of California. In 1994, he was transferred to a prison in Oregon after marrying a woman who lived there. After his wife died, he was returned to California in 2015 and housed at the California Medical Facility in Vacaville.

While in prison, Beausoleil has had a number of disciplinary violations for various infractions such as fighting, tattooing himself, disobeying orders, and smoking marijuana. At one time, he was able to set up a recording studio in his cell, where he composed a soundtrack for Kenneth Anger's film *Lucifer Rising*. In Oregon he was allowed to sell online his music, art, and graphic design, but California frowned upon that commerce. He has also worked as a videographer and in hospice, taught music to other inmates, and stayed in touch with his three biological children. His next parole hearing is slated for 2019.

After Steve Grogan was released, Bruce Davis was the next Family member to receive the parole board's nod—for the first time in 2010, and four more times through 2017. But each time, the sitting California governor—first Arnold Schwarzenegger and then Jerry Brown—overturned the board's decision, with Brown saying he still believes that Davis "poses an unreasonable danger to society."

Brown has expressed concerns over Davis's psychiatric diagnoses over the years, noting that one evaluator still recognized signs of an "unspecified personality disorder with anti-social and narcissistic features." He also cited Davis's "conformist tendencies and failure to address his self-esteem issues and lack of assertiveness," noting that Davis had associated with American Nazi Party inmates at Folsom Prison.

Like Bobby Beausoleil, Davis politely declined to be interviewed for this book, the only two codefendants who responded to such requests.

After his conviction in 1972, Davis entered the prison system at Folsom. Eight years later he was moved to the California Men's Colony (CMC) in San Luis Obispo, where he remains today.

A woman named Beth started writing and visiting him at CMC in 1984. They were married about a year later, and eventually had a daughter.

Davis generated controversy by running a prison ministry with Tex Watson, and again when one of them acted as the other's best man at his prison wedding. But their close association ended in 1993 when Watson was transferred to Mule Creek.

Going on to earn a PhD in religion, Davis said he was forced to reexamine his past actions while reading a *Los Angeles Magazine* "oral history" account of the murders in 2009.

"I noticed the photos of the victims in the Tate home, how young they were, and then realized their chances to grow old had been snuffed by the Manson cult that I had once been a part of," he said. ". . . I had done dreadful things, but I also influenced others to participate in horrible crimes . . . I felt the pain of what I had done to these innocent people . . . I should have loved them, but instead of that, I did the worst thing I could have done to them. I murdered them. I felt guilty, dirty and condemned. Secondly, I felt aching, loss, and hopeless sorrow for Gary [Hinman] and Don's [Shea] family and friends, because I had killed a part of them too."

He has admitted he deserves the death penalty for his crimes. But because he's been given a life sentence, he wants to keep helping others, as he's done for the past twenty years.

———

In the years since the trials and sentencings in this case, California has adopted new laws that have increased the codefendants' chances for parole, prompting concern among the victims' families.

In February 2014, an elderly offender program was instituted in response to a class-action lawsuit purporting the unconstitutionality of overcrowded prisons. The parole board must now consider whether inmates over sixty have served at least twenty-five years of their sentences.

In October 2015, Governor Brown signed a youthful offender measure, which forces the board to also consider whether an inmate committed a crime before reaching the age of twenty-three.

Davis and Watson (and also Manson before his death) qualify under the elderly offender program, while Beausoleil, Van Houten, and Krenwinkel, who is California's longest-serving female prisoner, qualify under both programs.

But these measures have only deepened the commitment of the victims' families to keep any and all Family members behind bars. Debra Tate and Anthony DiMaria have historically underscored the persistent peril of letting Manson and his codefendants out of prison, fearing that they could face similar triggers as before and also exert powerful, lasting copycat influences on others.

A case in point: Jason Sweeney, a teenager from the Philadelphia area, was brutally murdered in 2003 by four drug-abusing teenagers he knew— three boys, sixteen and seventeen years old, and a fifteen-year-old girl, who lured Jason to a remote area with the promise of sex.

The boys psyched themselves up by listening to the Beatles' song "Helter Skelter" forty times before bashing Jason in the face and head with a hatchet and hammer, then pounding him with a boulder as he begged for his life. Afterward, they spent his five-hundred-dollar paycheck to celebrate the slaughter.

"It is a powerful legacy," DiMaria said. "For these teens . . . [the] murder rampage was exciting." The threat to society of releasing Watson or any of his codefendants—"whether immediate, symbolic or repercussive—is real and it's current."

Before Manson died, Tate said she'd been told by prison security teams that the Family members still "link up with each other . . . Charlie is getting caught with cell phones . . . Leslie Van Houten is getting letters from Charlie. Everyone is hooked up with Squeaky on the outside . . . This is a dangerous situation for society and I have full intentions of doing everything I can to keep this travesty from happening."

———

The parole board granted parole to Leslie Van Houten for the first time in April 2016 and again in September 2017, but Governor Brown overturned both decisions.

Hoping to find new evidence that could help free their client, her attorneys attempted to force the release of a 326-page transcript of conversations between Tex Watson and his attorney in 1971, which were recorded before he was extradited from Texas to California for trial. Van Houten's attorneys and others believe these so-called Tex tapes, seized by the LAPD in 2013, may "minimize the involvement" of the women's role in the murders.

But the DA's office, LA City Attorney's Office, and LAPD jointly refused to release the tapes to Van Houten's attorneys, saying they have no right to discover information post-conviction, and that the tapes contain no new information anyway.

The DA's office also denied a public records request made in the research for this book, providing another reason also given to Van Houten's attorneys—the tapes are part of an ongoing investigation into "unsolved crimes Manson Family members are suspected of committing," and releasing them "could endanger the investigation."

Other investigators and journalists who have fought for the tapes' release say these two reasons are in obvious conflict. They suspect the real concern is that releasing the tapes could hamper the state's efforts to keep the former Manson Family members behind bars.

If the tapes truly do minimize the women's involvement or offer new details about unsolved murders committed by the Family, that could certainly change the historical narrative of what happened all those years ago and provide incentive to dig deeper for bodies some Family members bragged about burying in the desert.

CHAPTER 34

JASON FREEMAN:
"CHARLES MANSON III"

The families of the murder victims are not the only ones whose daily lives have been shaped by the crimes committed that summer in 1969. Charles Milles Manson Jr., Charlie's firstborn son with Rosalie, lived a life of heartbreak and tragedy, worsened by the name he carried and his failed attempts to form a relationship with his birth father.

After Rosalie married and had two sons with her truck driver boyfriend, Jack White, they moved to Cadiz, Ohio. Rosalie thought it made sense for Charles Jr. to take his stepfather's last name, with a new first name of Jay so his initials matched his brothers', Jesse and Jed. However, Rosalie never changed his legal name through the courts. So, although he went by Jay White around town and got a new social security card bearing that name, he still had to keep the original card reflecting his birth name.

The identity of Jay's birth father wasn't a big deal growing up. He wasn't around, and Jay didn't know much about him. But that all changed when the Manson Family was arrested for murder. Charlie's name and face were everywhere, and the highly publicized trials kept on coming.

"When all that happened, people who knew who his father was—family members, close friends—probably said, 'Well, that's your dad and he's a murderer,'" said Shawn (Freeman) Moreland, who started dating Jay when he was seventeen. "Being a . . . young man, that was a lot on him . . . His mom probably tried to shield him somewhat, but that was a big deal back then."

Like Charlie's mother, Rosalie often put her boyfriends and husbands before her son. By this point, she had moved on to a third husband. Jay claimed his stepfather beat him and his mother didn't care, so he left.

When he met Shawn at a party in Uhrichsville, Ohio, a town of about five thousand people, he was living on the street. Shawn was sixteen and pregnant with another man's baby, but Jay didn't mind. He had his own cross to bear. He confessed that his father was Charles Manson, but he didn't want to talk about him.

Jay was an outgoing, fun-loving kid. "He was a really funny guy, easygoing. We had a lot of friends," recalled Shawn, now a home health-care worker in Ohio. "There wasn't a mean bone in his body."

Shawn brought Jay home to live with her mother, grandmother, and younger brother, and he stuck around after Shawn's baby was born.

His troubles started when he applied for a job at the local coal mine, because he had to show his original social security card. By that time, Charles Manson was a household name and word spread quickly that Jay White was actually Charles Milles Manson Jr., the son of the most notorious murderer in US history.

Even though Jay hadn't had any contact with his father since he was a baby, "everybody wanted to kill him because his last name was Manson," Shawn's brother Bill recalled. "But he wasn't no criminal."

It didn't help that Jay had inherited some of the same features and personality traits as the infamous man who smiled mischievously at the news cameras.

Diagnosed with a learning disability, Jay had inherited his father's poor reading skills as well. When he took the test for his driver's license, they had to read the questions to him. He also enjoyed playing guitar, and Bill said he wasn't "too bad" at singing either.

But it was tough for him to live in such a small town, especially one with so many bars, because other patrons kept picking fights with him.

"He never actually started the fights," Bill said. "He had a couple buddies stick up for him, tried to protect him."

One night, with no provocation, a bartender hit Jay over the head with a whiskey bottle. The next night, when Jay, Bill, and another friend went back for revenge, armed with clubs and canes, ten law enforcement officers were there ahead of them, to head off the attack. They took Jay to the police station, but they didn't book him, the bartender, or anyone else who had instigated fights with Jay.

"They just let that [stuff] go," Bill said.

Jay was angry about the double standard, but he couldn't do much about it. And he still didn't want to talk about his father.

When he and Bill watched the television movie *Helter Skelter* in 1976, Jay didn't seem upset. He sat quietly for most of the three-hour film, breaking the silence only once.

"That ain't my dad, it's an actor," Jay said, referring to Steve Railsback, who played the starring role.

Like his father and grandmother, Jay liked to party. But over time his lifestyle wore on Shawn, who was trying to make a nice home for her infant son.

The beginning of the end of their relationship came when Jay missed the boy's birthday party, because he was in jail on drug charges.

Shawn argued with her mother, who called him "worthless," and tensions escalated further when Shawn got pregnant again, this time with Jay's baby.

"He wanted me to get rid of him and I wasn't going to do that," she said.

Over the holidays, the police came by to tell Shawn that Jay was in jail again for being under the influence, and they had impounded his car. And that was that. She didn't want to have anything more to do with him.

Shawn still loved Jay, but she knew she'd never find a new man if she stuck by him.

———

When Jason was born in September 1976, Shawn gave him her maiden name, Freeman.

Just like Charlie's mother, she had to go to court to force her son's birth father to pay child support. Jay eventually signed papers admitting he was the boy's natural father, but he still denied it to his family. Shawn didn't know about Jay's denials until years later.

Later on, Jay wrote and called to talk to his son, recalling regretfully that he'd never had a real father figure in his own life. He also wrote to Manson in prison, asking if he could visit. When Jay got no response it tore him up inside.

Shawn urged him to shake it off. "Why would you even want to do that, when that man don't care about you at all?" she asked.

But Jay wouldn't listen. He just became increasingly obsessed with getting his father to acknowledge him.

———

Shawn hadn't planned to tell Jason about his infamous grandfather, hoping to shield her boy from the stigma and pain, especially after witnessing the effects on Jay.

Her resolve lasted until Jason was in junior high school, when her nephew Dewey's mother spilled the secret, then Dewey spread it around school. When Jason came home upset that day, Shawn sat him down and admitted that the gossip was true. Charles Manson was indeed his grandfather. Then she advised him how to handle it.

"Just say 'Yeah, he was my grandfather,' because no one is going to believe it, so little Dewey is going to look like an idiot."

The knowledge hit home for Jason in eighth-grade history class when the teacher talked about the notorious killer. As Jason exchanged winks and covert smiles with his best friend, he looked around to see if any classmates were staring at him. But no one sent him a stray glance and the teacher didn't call him out either.

"It was a topic that I was forbidden to bring up," Jason recalled recently. "I know my mom said that my father suffered a lot through his childhood, seeing who his father was, and they wanted to keep that so far away from me to protect my innocence as a child . . . The only thing I really knew was that he was a bad character and that people visualized him as the boogie man."

Jay eventually joined Rosalie in Las Vegas, where he ran his own house-painting business. But Shawn wouldn't let Jason spend even a summer with him.

"I don't want [you] filling his head with a bunch of [stuff] about Charles Manson," Shawn told him. "If Rosie wants to come and take him, she can, and she can be the one to be with him most."

Jason never saw his father again.

Jay married a woman named Elisabeth and they had a son, Paul. After Elisabeth earned a civil engineering degree, they split up, in part because of the discrepancy in their education. Three weeks after their divorce was finalized on June 9, 1993, Jay shot himself in the head on the side of the highway in Burlington, Colorado.

——

Knowing that Charles Manson was his grandfather caused Jason to question what he was really made of. "Seeing that things run in the family genes, I didn't want to ever be in the same shoes," he said.

Yet, by the time he was eleven years old, he was already on probation for breaking a window with a baseball.

Like his dad, and probably his grandfather, too, Jason's learning disability made schoolwork tough. He was popular as the class clown, played football, and excelled on the wrestling team, but he kept getting into scuffles.

"I was either fighting for standing up to somebody or . . . I got picked on," he said. "I stutter. I couldn't read that well. I'd ball up and sweat. I really didn't like people who picked on other people."

He also fell in with the wrong crowd, started smoking pot, and got in trouble with the law. In and out of jails and prison, he remained on probation until he was twenty-seven, for charges ranging from vandalism to breaking and entering, fighting, and selling and receiving marijuana through the mail.

"It was a consistent, constant battle in self-mutilation," he said. "I still had to go through it so I could speak about it . . . I want the world to see that you can pick yourself back up and you can overcome your past."

Did he think about his grandfather while he was locked up? "More about my father, but I guess I thought about them both." And after realizing that he "was either going to be dead or in prison" if he didn't change his mind-set, he set out to do just that.

"I fight for my kids now and I work every day for myself to help my family and see that you can have anything you want in life."

———

When Rosalie died of lung cancer in Tucson, Arizona, in 2009, she'd been married at least four times, and all three of her sons had died tragically many years before her: Jed by accidental shooting, Jesse by drug overdose, and Jay by suicide.

Still, in an echo to her unwanted legacy as Charles Manson's first wife, Rosalie Handley's obituary didn't list Jason as a surviving grandchild. It did list a "loving companion," however, who called to tell Jason that his father had finally succeeded in communicating with Manson fairly close to the time that Jay shot himself in 1993.

"It makes me wonder if it all just became too much for him at that point," Jason wrote on his blog. "Who truly knows of the demons he had been running from all of his life. [Maybe he] just got tired of running."

———

Jason turned his life around by becoming a professional boxer and mixed martial arts fighter. He won a championship title in 2009, using the moniker "Charles Manson III."

Proud of his victory, he wrote his grandfather in prison, enclosing a news article and photo of himself. "I felt like I achieved something," he said. "I wanted him to acknowledge that. He hadn't acknowledged my father. I wanted him to see that I accomplished something—that I was rising above."

But just like his dad, Jason got no response from Corcoran prison.

After his last professional fight in 2011, Jason moved his family to Florida, where he worked nights on an oil rig and started his own construction business.

Jason tried contacting his grandfather again, and this time Manson responded by writing on Jason's letter and sending it back to him.

In 2012, soon after Jason published a book, titled *Knocking Out the Devil*, Manson reached out to him by phone.

"You can't knock the devil out, kid," Manson said, assuming the book title referred to him. Jason explained that he was talking about his struggle to break free of the mind-set that kept putting him behind bars.

"I was working for the devil," Jason said.

Finally, after all the years of wondering, he was able to ask his grandfather this nagging question: "Why didn't you acknowledge your firstborn son and give him some of your time?"

Manson replied that "everyone in the world" was trying to contact him, so he thought it best not to talk to Jay—for his own safety. Also, after years of looking for help to tell his story, he grew tired of people who came into his life, grabbed what they needed, and left.

For the next couple of years Jason spoke with his grandfather weekly or monthly. The calls tapered off by the third year, but then Manson, who was having health issues, invited him to California.

"If you're worried about taking care of your family, your kin, all the money in the world you would need is sitting here for you," Manson told him. "I've got fifty thousand dollars in an account that can get you out here and establish you . . . I've got some people you can work with."

When Jason said he didn't want anything from his grandfather, Manson didn't seem to understand his motives.

"What *do* you want?" he asked.

"I just want to get to know who my grandfather is," Jason said, explaining he wanted to do this by talking with him, not from reading books about him. "I don't know how to be a grandfather," Manson responded. "I don't know how to be a father. The fathers I know are the police and the correctional officers. They tell me what to do. That's all I know."

Jason started recording their calls. During these brief conversations, he offered to help his grandfather in any way he could. They were family, after all, *real* family—by blood. But Manson told him not to bother.

"I ain't nothin' but another tramp on the road," he said. "Be sensible . . . You've got to be yourself . . . I'll take care of this guy."

Every so often, though, the old man seemed to hear Jason's pleas for connection, and repeated his standard story—that he'd always felt alone, born without a real father and abandoned by a mother who kept sending him away to reform schools.

When Jason didn't hear from him for a while, he thought Manson had given up on him. But Manson always called again, knowing what to say to keep the loyalty strong.

"Aw, man. How the f*** could I do that? You're my blood, man," Manson told him. "I'm always with you, forever—"

"—I know, you're in my heart," Jason replied.

"You realize? You know that, don't you?"

But mostly, he and his grandfather seemed to be on different planes. Sometimes Manson responded to Jason's emotional overtures with a joke or a story, like the time he stole a car and sold it to an Italian Mafioso in Cleveland, who paid him with three hundred dollars, some triggerless guns, a few Frank Sinatra albums, and the promise of more money.

"He didn't send the money so I went and stole the car back" and drove it to Fort Lauderdale, he said.

Or he launched into song, singing and playing the guitar into the phone. "Did you get that?" Manson asked afterward. "We could cut a couple albums."

That led to another story, or maybe it was a joke. It was hard to tell with Manson. "Used to be in reform school I used to fight with my fist.

Then I found out what a knife was. Then I found out what a gun was," Manson said, going into his "teaching" mode.

During the presidential election in 2016, Manson said he didn't like either candidate. "Any way you go you'll still be d**ned," he said.

But Manson always seemed to circle back to his favorite topic: the power of the sun and how the "mobsters"—big cities like New York, Paris, and London—were destroying the planet.

"I love the sun," he said. "I know the sun has all the power in the world. I try to be in harmony with the day and the sun and motions, my oceans. Every day is a good day."

The end of the calls sometimes came abruptly when the allotted fifteen minutes ran out, leaving a question or comment from Jason lingering in the air. Jason would sigh and hang up, waiting to try again next time.

CHAPTER 35

MANSON'S LEGACY

A new generation of followers has been exposed to Manson ideology through the work of his closest associates outside prison, whom he called Star Manson and Gray Wolf.

Star, aka Afton Elaine Burton, grew up in Bunker Hill, Illinois, a rural white community of 1.25 square miles and seventeen hundred residents. An idealistic animal advocate who grew up playing in the woods with her brother, Star was so inspired by Manson's environmental philosophy that she began writing him. It took only one letter for him to write her back.

Next thing her parents knew, their eighteen-year-old daughter had moved to California in 2006 to be near a convicted mass murderer who had given her a new name.

Star acknowledged "it might sound strange" that it took such a short time for her to decide she wanted to be with Manson. "He never asked me to come here, I just did it," Star said in a radio interview in 2015. "I just knew that's what I was going to do."

For the next decade, she seemed to have helped inspire Manson to reinvent himself and his image, disseminating his ideas about saving the planet in new ways via interlinked websites and social media.

Even though Star carved an "X" into her forehead like her predecessors, her well-coordinated multimedia approach was much more benign, and a marked contrast to the fire and blood of Manson's old-school "activism."

Under her watch, the blog *Release Charles Manson Now* was launched, with a letter-writing plea for advocates who believed in his innocence, along with the websites Atwaearth.com and the more political Mansondirect. com. After a decade of lying fallow, ATWA was also resurrected as a non-profit, tax-exempt corporation by Star and Craig Hammond, a decades-old friend of Manson's who went by the name Gray Wolf.

Over the years, Manson had invented a device dubbed the Savior, an unpatented seed gun, similar to a paintball launcher, that uses "seed balls" made from clay, compost, and seeds to help renew and restore public and private lands. The goal of Manson's larger mission, perversely titled the Savior Project, was to sprout trees and "beneficial native plant species" in California areas "that have been degraded by logging, erosion, fire, drought and other natural and industrial processes," according to the ATWA website.

A Manson warning from 2011 is also posted on the site, cautioning that people who used chemical products such as toothpaste, soap, mouthwash, bleach, and hair dye were enemies of planet Earth: "Everything I touch is polluting. The birth of life on the planet has got to be green, it's got to come through the bushes, got to come through the trees, it has got to come through the seaweeds and the fish, the birds, the bees. Your bumble bees are dying. Your trees are being warred upon."

Manson isn't mentioned anywhere in ATWA's organizational paperwork on file with the state attorney general's office, however, which states that the group is raising money to carry out these same educational programs.

In 2012, ATWA projected it would raise $73,000 over the next three years. But by 2015, it had collected only $8,986, with a mere $86 coming in that year. ATWA isn't required to disclose funding sources because it collects less than $50,000 a year.

"I have to be always above board, because I know that people want to catch me doing something, so I don't do anything, and the same goes for Charlie," Star said in 2015, adding that the interest in ATWA hadn't been as strong as they'd hoped. "I'm not using this [money] to buy candy."

Curiously, though, after Gray Wolf was booked into the Kings County

Jail in March 2013 for bringing a phone into Corcoran before a planned visit with Manson—possession of an illegal communication device, and conspiracy to commit a crime—he was able to cover the thirty-thousand-dollar bail and get out of jail within just four hours.

———

On November 7, 2014, Star created a national media furor when she walked into the Kings County Clerk-Recorder's Office and obtained a license to marry Manson in a prison wedding.

Star had already told *Rolling Stone* a year earlier of their plans to marry. "When that will be, we don't know," she'd said. "But I take it very seriously. Charlie is my husband. Charlie told me to tell you this. We haven't told anybody about that." If she and Manson had been allowed conjugal visits, she added, they would have tied the knot already.

"It's what I was born for, you know," she said.

Manson confused matters by dismissing the marriage idea in the same *Rolling Stone* article. "'Oh that,' he said. 'That's a bunch of garbage. You know that, man. That's trash. We're just playing that for public consumption.'"

Not long after they got the marriage license, Manson had a routine checkup and was immediately sent to a community hospital. He'd been taking nitroglycerin for heart problems since at least 2010, and had long suffered from chronic obstructive pulmonary disease, or COPD. After some kind of operation, possibly to place stents to enhance blood flow to his heart, he was moved into Corcoran's hospital unit.

There, he still had a single cell, but he slept in a hospital bed instead of a pad on a slab. His phone access also became more limited, and he wasn't allowed visitors for several months.

Manson told friends that prison staff had also started requiring him to be shackled while walking from that unit, through his old digs in the PHU, to the visiting room, so he stopped accepting most visitors.

The marriage license expired after ninety days on February 5, 2015. Three days later, the *New York Post* ran a story headlined "Charles Manson's Fiancée Wanted to Marry Him for His Corpse: Source."

Manson's friend John Michael Jones said the article was based at least partially in fact: Star had told someone, who told the media, that she and Gray Wolf were planning to display Manson's corpse in a glass case and charge admission.

Once the story went public, Star said it had nothing to do with the wedding delay. "We got blindsided, because when he went to the hospital—I don't want to accuse anyone [at the prison]—but they took that as their chance and I didn't hear from him for like a month . . . I wasn't able to see him for ninety days," she said. "So, yes, that was the reason, not because I wanted to [display] his dead body."

Four months later, a videographer saw Star and Gray Wolf acting chummy at a gem show an hour's drive from Corcoran. When the videographer asked Star about her wedding plans, Gray Wolf reportedly put him in a chokehold. The result was a *National Enquirer* story headlined "Charles Manson Lover Two-Times Him With Cult Disciple 'Gray Wolf.'"

Manson had asked Star to let Gray Wolf sleep on her couch, but he ultimately had to acknowledge that the man, who was also many years older than Star, had become more intimate with Charlie's girlfriend than he'd expected. Feeling betrayed by Gray Wolf, Manson started referring to him as "Dead Rat."

Manson's grandson, Jason Freeman, had gotten to know Star well enough by phone to jokingly call her Grandma. When he asked her about the marriage delay, she said she couldn't get Manson to sign paperwork that would give her a say over his estate and belongings.

"Charlie's so hard to speak with sometimes, he moves so slow," she told him.

———

By 2016, Manson's longtime friend Ben Gurecki said Charlie had never been serious about the wedding, and that Star had since moved to Malibu to be with a guy closer to her age.

A year later, Jones confirmed that Manson knew all about Star's new man: a Hollywood actor in his midfifties named Vincent Gallo, who sought out Star, did in fact live in Malibu, and, because of his physical resemblance to Charlie, had been asked to play him in a movie. Could this all be part of his method-acting prep?

Manson's friends on the outside contend that other inmates had been stealing his mail and belongings for years to sell them on the Internet. Recently, Manson told Jones that personal items such as his dentures and reading glasses had been found in the cells of inmates who worked in the prison hospital.

But what most infuriated Jones and Gurecki was that Star and her new boyfriend convinced Manson in 2017 to ship them his beloved guitar, a hand-made instrument crafted out of Bulgarian rosewood and cedar, with the promise that they would send him a "better" one. Jones and Gurecki had split the cost of that guitar and sent it as a gift to Manson years ago.

Jones said he was also upset that Star had left the town of Corcoran for LA with a bunch of Charlie's artwork and other items, which Jones valued at twenty thousand dollars.

Nonetheless, Jones said, "I think he's still in love with her."

———

Even in his final days, Manson still wouldn't comment on other murders that he and other Family members had boasted they committed fifty years ago.

When asked, he said, "I'm not a snitch, and the last person I'll snitch on is me."

Based on ranch hand Juan Flynn's statement that Manson had bragged about killing thirty-five people, prosecutor Vincent Bugliosi said he believed the number of victims could "be very close to, and may even exceed, Manson's estimate," which would leave at least twenty-six unsolved murders. Leslie Van Houten, Susan Atkins, and Ruth Ann "Ouisch" Moorehouse have all said there were eleven murders, still two more than the official total.

As such, the LAPD continues to deny public record requests for information on this case, citing open investigations into "unsolved crimes Manson Family members are suspected of committing."

When details of the known murders hit the news in 1969, authorities up and down California looked for possible connections to unsolved homicides in areas where Family members had stayed or been arrested.

These included the deaths of two teenagers who were each stabbed more than fifty times, their right eyes removed, and the girl left naked near Scientology communes in LA; an antique store owner and her granddaughter in Ukiah; and a nineteen-year-old Swedish-born girl from Canada whose body was found on Mulholland Drive not far from Spahn Ranch. After the Canadian visitor was finally identified in 2016, LAPD detectives traveled to Corcoran to interview Manson, but got no useful information from him.

The list of potential victims also includes Charlie's paternal uncle Darwin Scott, who was found stabbed nineteen times in his apartment in Ashland, Kentucky, by either a kitchen knife or a bayonet, both weapons used in the Tate and LaBianca slayings. Due to the "overkill" nature of the crime and its timing—on May 18, 1969, three months before the others—some believe this could have been a revenge killing in retaliation for Darwin's brother Colonel abandoning Charlie and his mother.

Ronald Hughes was another whose death Vincent Bugliosi and others attributed to the Family. Bugliosi said as much in *Helter Skelter*: "One thing is now known, however. If an admission by one of Manson's most hard-core followers is correct, Ronald Hughes was murdered by the Manson Family."

James Forsher, one of the teens who drove Hughes to the Sespe Hot Springs, subsequently sued Bugliosi. Forsher, who accused the author of libel, invasion of privacy, and obliquely linking him to Hughes's suspicious end in *Helter Skelter*, lost his lawsuit.

Similarly, Bugliosi saw a connection between the Family and the murder of a young marine whose car was parked outside a house where his young wife's body was found buried in fresh dirt in the basement. Family members Nancy Pitman and Priscilla Cooper were arrested there—with Xs on their foreheads—along with two men with "AB," short for Aryan

Brotherhood, tattoos. Police also arrested Lynette Fromme after she called the house to ask for a ride there.

Cooper claimed that the dead marine's wife had killed herself playing Russian roulette, just like Zero. But Bugliosi believed that the couple, who had been associated with the Family for a year, had been murdered because they knew too much and were about to report the Family's crimes, including Hughes's murder, to police.

Other Manson Family victims were thought to have been killed in Death Valley, where Atkins and other members said "two boys and a girl [were] buried about eight feet deep behind the Barker Ranch." More specifically, members said a girl went for a walk toward Myers Ranch with Charlie and Tex but never returned, and a teenage hiker suspiciously "disappeared" from Barker, leaving his backpack behind. Investigators tried searching at the time, but never uncovered any graves.

Paul Dostie, a retired Mammoth Lakes Police Department sergeant, has been on a mission to unearth these bodies in the desert for more than a decade. Dostie has made numerous trips to Barker and Myer Ranches, where his trained cadaver dog, a Labrador named Buster, "alerted" at more than five sites. The sites have since been reconfirmed multiple times by Dostie's colleagues, forensic anthropologists Arpad Vass and Marc Wise, using devices designed to detect chemicals specific to the decomposition of human remains.

Dostie, Vass, and Wise have attempted to persuade authorities, ranging from Inyo County law enforcement to the federal Office of Inspector General and US senator Dianne Feinstein, that local officers have never dug deep enough to find the remains.

Previous digs have gone no deeper than four feet at all but one of the sites, even after Dostie relayed this comment from Manson, who attributed the tip to his Mafia mentors at Terminal Island: "You always bury bodies eight feet deep because the cops won't dig past six. If you can go twelve, go twelve."

But after officials found no remains, they refused to dig again, insisting it was fruitless and costly, and that their conclusion was based in science.

Vass strongly disagreed. "We were in the right spot, I'm sure of that," he said recently. "There's absolutely no question there are bodies out there. We knew the bodies were going to be deep. Even Manson was freaked out that we were digging out there."

Vass was referring to a remark Manson made after reading news reports about Buster's "alerts" in the desert. "I'm having nightmares about that dog," Manson told John Michael Jones. "That dog is trying to get me the death penalty."

Dostie blames the roadblocks on Inyo County politics and fear of revealing the incompetence of past investigations. "The reason why they refuse to do any further investigating and ignore proven science and additional investigative leads that we have developed is because they don't want to expose the poor job that they have done investigating the Manson Family's activities in their county for over forty years," he said.

Dostie said he personally interviewed Manson 170 times by phone, but was never able to obtain any admissions. However, he is still convinced that the remains of at least five missing people are waiting to be discovered in the desert where the Manson Family was arrested in October 1969, and that the victims' families should have justice and closure.

"Those families deserve to know what happened to their loved ones," he said.

CHAPTER 36

"I'M DYING."

Nearly half a century after the murders that made him infamous, Charles Manson is still *everywhere*, woven into the fabric of our culture.

Manson often pointed out that people have and will continue to profit from the Tate-LaBianca murders by portraying him as the height and definition of *evil*. He and his fans still believe this was the case with Vincent Bugliosi, who sold a reported seven million copies of *Helter Skelter*. Dozens of other books have been published since then, including multiple titles by Family members Susan Atkins and Tex Watson, one by Dianne Lake, and even one by Manson himself, recounting their own versions of events.

Manson remains to this day Internet click-bait and fodder for TV and film projects: *Aquarius*, a two-season NBC series starring David Duchovny, was inspired by real events in the case. In 2017, Jason Freeman announced that he was going to be filmed attempting to visit his grandfather in prison for the first time, but that effort proved unsuccessful. He also said he was going to star in a reality TV show focusing on the children of different killers. ABC ran a two-hour documentary, boasting "unaired footage" from Diane Sawyer interviews at least twenty years old. Even director Quentin Tarantino announced plans for a new feature film.

The name Charles Manson still holds power and makes news, partly due to the fear of what his cohorts might do if set free once again.

"They built whole penitentiaries in the fear that they generated off of this case," Manson said in 1992. "So the public can feel safe against this monster, we're going to charge you two hundred million dollars to build another set of penitentiaries. So, people living in my life, they don't care whether I broke the law or not. They'll make up a lot of things and sell a lot of books, fifty-eight of them to be exact, and billions of dollars has been made."

Even his own Family was out to make a buck off his infamy. Once music producer Phil Kaufman realized Manson was guilty, he was forced underground to hide from the members who came after him for the rights to distribute the album he'd tried to sell to help cover Manson's legal fees.

"They have attempted to kill me three or four times," Kaufman said at one point. "They wanted to get the rights back. The music never made a nickel, it's always been bootlegged."

Manson's music was not meant purely to produce joy, Kaufman said, but rather to convey his philosophy. "At first it's intriguing, but then when you get to it, there's always that bottom line message."

But other than for the potential profit, Kaufman said he didn't understand why people still found interest in Manson's music all these years later. "It wasn't very good music to begin with," he said.

Nonetheless, artists such as Trent Reznor, Axl Rose, and Marilyn Manson, whose stage name came from combining Marilyn Monroe with Charles Manson, have been inspired by it.

Rudi Altobelli, the owner of the Cielo Drive house, profited as well. He paid less than $150,000 for his house in 1963, then sold it for $1.2 million in 1989.

The new owner built a mansion on the site, gave it a new name, Villa Bella, and a new address: 10066 Cielo Drive. Although all physical traces of the historic house have been erased, tour guides still regularly bring visitors to the property to describe its storied past. And yet, the story continues to unfold as these killers repeatedly come up for parole and disclose new details about the murders. At some point, one of them might actually get an unexpected release.

———

At her parole hearing on December 29, 2016, Patricia Krenwinkel and her attorney, Keith Wattley, created a sensation by alleging that she had been a victim of "intimate partner battery" by Manson at the time of the murders. Similar to battered woman syndrome (BWS), this form of post-traumatic stress disorder is often used as a legal defense by women who kill their husbands.

Krenwinkel said her view of Manson had completely changed over the past five decades. "He's the epitome of everything that is ugly to me. I mean, he's a pedophile. He slept with girls that were twelve years old at the ranch," she said. "He is a man who uses every single thing that comes in his way for power and control. He's violent, abusive . . . He's a horrid, petty, mean, ugly man."

Wattley then made the formal allegation during his closing statement at the nine-hour hearing. After taking a two-hour recess to deliberate, the commissioners determined that the allegation warranted an investigation, and delayed its finding until the probe was concluded.

Although some saw it as too late to cite this rationale forty-seven years after the crimes, BWS was not yet an accepted legal defense when Krenwinkel went to trial—as a codefendant with her abuser—in 1970.

It wasn't accepted until the late 1970s, when Dr. Lenore Walker wrote *The Battered Woman*, a book based on a study of women who exhibited physical, sexual, and psychological symptoms, including learned helplessness and a cycle of violence, stemming from abuse by a man with whom they were intimately involved.

Krenwinkel's change of heart and words of contrition have done nothing to sway the victims' families. Calling the investigation a "colossal waste of tax dollars," Debra Tate dismissed Krenwinkel's new defense.

"She totally minimized her actions and blamed everything on other people the whole hearing," Tate said after the meeting. "We all have to be accountable for our actions . . . She was there because she wanted to be there. Nobody held a gun to her head."

Lou Smaldino, Leno LaBianca's nephew, called Krenwinkel a serial killer who should "already be dead for her part in these vicious and unprovoked slayings. I believe society has been most merciful by allowing her to live with all her needs cared for."

In June 2017, the commissioners conceded that Krenwinkel had been abused, but said it wasn't enough to warrant her release and denied her parole for the fourteenth time.

———

On January 3, 2017, just days after the Krenwinkel development, reports spread that Manson was "temporarily out of prison" after being rushed to the ER with "gastrointestinal issues."

Charlie Manson became a trending media celeb once again.

The debate raged on social media over whether he should still be in prison: his fans advocated for his release, arguing that he'd never actually pulled the trigger or killed any of the victims, while his opponents complained that taxpayers shouldn't have to pay for a mass murderer's expensive health-care costs, contending that he should have been executed long ago and never had his death sentence commuted.

Five days later, Manson was transported sixty miles from Corcoran prison to Mercy Hospital in Bakersfield, where he was "signed in as 'Joe Doe.'" Manson's body had been failing him, little by little, and now he was bleeding through lesions in his colon. Speculation surged that he was on his deathbed.

Although the hospital spokeswoman told reporters she had "no information" on any patient named Manson, the media remained camped outside, alongside several prison vans. When prisoners are taken to a community hospital, correctional officers must stand guard around the clock for everyone's safety.

After four days at Mercy, a hospital source reported that the nurses had shaved Manson's face and trimmed his hair. His handcuffs were taken off and a priest came to his room, possibly to give him his last rites.

"He and the priest had a long talk and the priest said that he believes that he washed away all of his sins," Jack Cook, who communicated with Manson for years, announced to one of the larger Facebook groups that discuss the case.

When Jason Freeman had talked to his grandfather two weeks earlier, the aging prisoner had seemed in good spirits. His mind was still sharp as ever, in between his typical off-beat riffs. But after hearing the news that his grandfather had been hospitalized, Jason quickly tried to gather paperwork to prove he was Manson's grandson so he could meet the man personally for the first time before he passed.

"I guess he is not facing his situation," Jason wrote in an e-mail. "Not accepting it . . . Hoping to fly out in the next couple days with all my proper court documentation."

Jason explained that he didn't want to show up "with no proof that we are related" like Matthew Roberts, a man who claims that his birth mother told him—while she was in a mental health facility—that he'd been conceived during an orgy with Manson in the late 1960s.

At the hospital, Manson, who was known not to trust anyone, initially refused surgery to remove the bleeding lesions, thinking the doctors were trying to kill him. By the time he came around, the surgeons decided he was too weak to undergo the operation so he was transported back to Corcoran.

The next day, Manson called his friend Ben Gurecki, who posted the recorded call on his YouTube channel. Manson could be heard slurring his words, a marked contrast to his clear voice on calls Jason had recorded a few months earlier.

Manson didn't know which hospital he'd been taken to, but complained that his belongings—his spider dolls and other artwork, along with the vitamins from his "quarterly package"—had been taken in the move.

"It shows you that you've got no friends, when it gets down, nobody is going to stand up for you," he said.

Gurecki countered that this wasn't true, noting that many people on the outside were concerned about Manson.

Asked why he was hospitalized, Manson said, "It was bleeding—rectal bleeding. I had some blood in the stool."

"Like a polyp or something like that?" Gurecki asked.

"Yeah, like a tumor," Manson said, adding that it wasn't considered critical. "No, no, it's small. If I want to do the procedure. They make it big 'cause, 'cause they want me to go under the knife."

Gurecki said he planned to open a museum of Manson "murderabilia," including fifteen years of their recorded calls, but was waiting until after Manson passed. He also said he had already spent more than thirty thousand dollars to print two thousand albums of music Manson recorded years ago.

Manson was coherent enough to ask how his record was selling on Gurecki's website, then seemed confused to hear that six hundred copies were still left.

After his hospital stay, Manson called his friend John Michael Jones far more than usual, as many as five fifteen-minute calls per day. Although he'd been saying, "I don't have much time left" for the past decade, he was obviously feeling his mortality even more now.

"I'm dying," Manson told Jones in March 2017.

With the COPD and heart problems, Jones said, Manson had difficulty breathing and walking on his own, so the staff would no longer let him walk the "hallways of always," as he called them. He also didn't have much upper body strength to get himself around much in a wheelchair either.

"He's very frail," Jones said.

———

On Sunday, November 12, Manson was again taken to Mercy Hospital in Bakersfield. The prognosis was grim. For the next week, he was wheeled on a gurney, escorted by five guards, from one treatment to another, his skin extremely pale. The following Sunday, at 8:13 p.m., he died.

Manson's death made worldwide news, with reactions ranging from exultation to mourning. Within days, battles erupted among several parties claiming to be entitled to Manson's body, along with the rights to his estate, including the use of his image, artwork, belongings, and music.

Manson's friend Ben Gurecki maintained that he possessed a will dated January 11, 2017, that disclaimed all relatives and previous wills and that named as Manson's beneficiary Matthew Roberts, who still claimed he could be Manson's son. (CNN sponsored a test comparing Roberts's DNA to Jason Freeman's and found no match.)

In addition, Michael Channels—a longtime pen-pal who posted items about Manson's life on his website devoted to "murderabilia," collectibles related to violent homicides—filed claims with the Kern County court. He, too, claimed to have a will signed by Manson, one dating from 2002 and witnessed by a fellow inmate, that disclaimed all relatives and named Channels as the sole beneficiary.

The assertions by Gurecki and Channels were quickly challenged. Manson's friend John Michael Jones said Manson had told him shortly before his death that he didn't want a will. Meanwhile, Jason Freeman began steps to assume control of his grandfather's remains and affairs. Freeman hired an attorney and filed claims with the Kern County coroner and in Los Angeles County Superior Court. He hoped to have Manson's body cremated in California, spreading some of the ashes in Death Valley and taking the remainder to his home in Florida.

Jones set up a GoFundMe account to help Freeman pay for expenses, but the online service shut down the account as soon as it drew media coverage. Jones switched the campaign to PayPal, then to Facebook, with the same results. Eventually, anonymous parties stepped forward to cover the costs.

Manson's death certificate indicated he died of cardiac arrest, with respiratory failure and metastatic colon cancer as underlying causes. "He had cancer. We knew that last year, it's just not something we shared with people," Freeman said.

As the fight over the right to Manson's remains and to his estate moved into the courts, officials remained silent about the location of the body. Looking for answers, Freeman and Jones went to the Kern County morgue with a documentary film crew.

"Yeah, he's here," a morgue employee admitted to Freeman and Jones. She then leaned forward and said, "You guys are six feet from him right now."

At that, Freeman and Jones both choked up. "I lost it," Jones said. "Jason lost it."

By February 2018, Manson's body was still on ice in Kern County, as the disputes over his remains and his estate were divided into separate battles in different jurisdictions. Ultimately, Michael Brunner, Manson's son with Mary Brunner, staked a legal claim as well.

The fight over Manson's remains was finally resolved in mid-March, when a Kern County Superior Court commissioner awarded the body to Freeman—over Brunner and Channels—as the "surviving competent adult next of kin of the decedent" to do with as he saw fit. Roberts ultimately had folded to support Brunner's claim to the body.

The estate portion of the battle appeared poised to continue for months, if not longer, in the court system of Los Angeles County, Manson's last place of residence.

Such uncertainty notwithstanding, murderabilia vendors, moviemakers, podcasters, and others flooded the marketplace and airwaves with products and projects, hoping to make money from whatever remained of Charles Manson, whose infamy lives on, even in death.

EPILOGUE

Despite Manson's claims that all the fear this case has generated is unfounded, the Family's crimes set a historic standard that persists today, creating an everlasting mythology and intrigue around the man convicted of ordering them, even as he continued to deny doing so for the remainder of his life.

Dr. David Smith, the Haight-Ashbury clinic founder, said it is still important to analyze the Manson case in the context of current events. He disagrees with the naysayers who believe that crimes perpetrated by Manson and his cult were a product of their time and will never be repeated, even if his codefendants, now in their seventies, are released.

Back in the 1960s when the Manson Family was formed, Smith said, kids were smoking marijuana with only 2 to 3 percent of the active chemical compound THC, short for tetrahydrocannabinol. Today's pot, which is more accessible because of new medical- and recreational-use laws, has been cultivated to a much higher grade. It also has been refined into concentrated hash oil, which is upward of 70 to 90 percent THC.

"It's like the difference between beer and pure grain alcohol," Smith said.

The conduit for the oil is a long, thin butane-fueled pipe known as a hash pen or vaporizer, which can slip into a pocket. Smoking the oil or finely ground marijuana at high temperatures is called "vaping."

These days, an increasing number of drug-abusing youths from white, upper-middle-class families are showing up at clinics in affluent communities such as Marin County, California, reporting "weird thought patterns" and that they are flunking out of school. In addition to vaping, young people are using LSD again, which is simply dropped onto the tongue.

It's happening "way more today," Smith said, and it's no longer just in concentrated areas like the Haight. These kids are all over the country, and many are accessing information on the "dark web" of the Internet instead of consulting with clinicians.

With the decline of investigative journalism and the proliferation of "fake news" on social media, anyone can and does spread ideas and misinformation on the Internet. Even someone behind bars can do so, simply by sending word or posting on websites through friends on the outside.

In recent years, a number of mass murders have been committed by single young white men such as white supremacist Dylann Storm Roof, who killed nine black churchgoers, hoping to ignite a race war. More recently in Las Vegas, a sniper injured more than five hundred people, killing fifty-eight, by shooting out of a hotel window. These men are often mentally ill or using drugs, or both, and they seem to feel disenfranchised, disillusioned, and disconnected from reality. They are also drawn to violence, groomed through the dark web of the Internet, video games, and the gore-filled action movies and TV shows that overload our culture.

The racial divide in our nation has become increasingly palpable once again. The 2016 election campaign and its aftermath have also resulted in the widening of our political and socioeconomic divides, resulting in the largest and most violent protests since the 1960s. This proves that angry, scared people can be motivated to take action, to resist whatever forces they feel need to be resisted.

History can repeat itself. Many of the social conditions present in the late 1960s exist today, only more powerfully additive, especially in light of the national opiate epidemic, which has affected all age groups.

This dangerous set of factors could easily coalesce into a perfect storm of conditions that enable another ideologue, cult leader, or domestic terrorist group to take advantage of vulnerable, lost youths with addled minds, lure them into a band of armed citizen soldiers, and instruct them to carry out a drug-enhanced copycat slaying spree in a celebration of Manson's memory.

People who say such a perfect storm could never come again fail to see the signs or recognize the potential for an even more devastating tragedy to sweep our nation, where new technology serves as a delivery system to make ideas go viral within minutes, and vehicles are used as weapons against innocent pedestrians or protesters.

As the Manson case shows, the failure to see parallels and to share information is no way to stop or solve a crime. We must be smarter, more diligent, and more collaborative as we work to identify and overcome the threat at its source—before another Manson or Family decides once again to "shock the world."

ACKNOWLEDGMENTS

Embarking on a writing project as vast as *Hunting Charles Manson* was daunting and could not have been accomplished without the indefatigable spirit of our editor, Webster Younce, who is a star among editors. Also in the shining star category, Todd Shuster and Nate Muscato of Aevitas Creative Management gleamed brilliantly as my agents. They worked tirelessly, in every phase of this project, to see it to fruition. I'd also like to thank the wonderful nonfiction team at Thomas Nelson, whose creativity sparkled in everything from compelling cover designs to creative sales and promotional efforts: Brian Hampton, Kathie Johnson, Kristen Andrews, Belinda Bass, Jeff James, Karen Jackson, Janene MacIvor, and Tiffany Sawyer.

And closest to my heart, I'm grateful to my children, Jacob and Dani, and all my family for their love and support.

LIS WIEHL

I'd like to thank my agent, Peter Rubie of FinePrint Literary Management, for his help shepherding this project to its glorious conclusion. I'm also grateful to my mother and stepfather, Carole and Chris Scott, and my boyfriend, Géza Keller, for all their loving support throughout the process.

CAITLIN ROTHER

SOURCES AND
METHODOLOGY

Our purpose in writing about Charles Manson was, above all, to advance the story. With our experience in newsrooms, both print and broadcast, we felt it was important to bring readers to the present day with as much new information as possible. We also wanted to avoid aggregating previously offered opinions and theories, many of which are laced with conspiracy theories or pro-Manson agendas. Most importantly, we wanted to tell the story afresh, not rehash the prosecution's narrative as relayed by Vincent Bugliosi in *Helter Skelter*.

One of our ground rules, then, was to use *Helter Skelter* solely as one point of reference among others—mostly for cross-referencing, fact-checking, and identifying primary source material. We wanted to form our own view of the facts and evidence in order to provide readers with a new understanding of Charles Manson and his Family. We also wanted to see what *we* could discover about the motives behind the killings. We therefore approached the research with fresh eyes, as if we were conducting a cold case investigation, reviewing all the original forensic evidence and source materials while also gathering new details that came out long after the procession of trials was over.

Seeking out as many original source materials as possible to take a closer, more contemporary look at the forensic evidence investigators collected may sound relatively simple, but it was not. Researching a fifty-year-old case, with social histories of defendants that go back an additional twenty or more years, posed formidable challenges. Calls and public records requests to the LAPD and LASD resulted in curt refusals, as both agencies declined to release any investigative reports, crime scene photos, or information related to the case, even though one sheriff's official indicated some *thirty* boxes of materials are housed in a warehouse. Nor would either agency help us locate retired detectives to interview. Because this case occurred so long ago, many of the key players are dead, so we can only speculate why LASD officials (and parole officials) failed or chose not to act on Manson's multiple arrests, probation violations, and other crimes—ranging from rape to auto theft, weapons and drug possession, trespassing, and assault—before the murders.

By the same token, our letters to Charles Manson, Tex Watson, Leslie Van Houten, and Patricia Krenwinkel went unanswered. We even tried sending letters separately, on different occasions, asking to hear Manson's story in person, but he never responded. With Manson's limited reading skills, his friend John Michael Jones says that the infamous prisoner could not possibly get through all the mail he received—an estimated ten thousand–plus letters every three months. Bruce Davis and Bobby Beausoleil were the only ones to respond to our letters, but given that they were still trying to obtain parole, both politely declined our interview requests. Repeated requests to interview Manson's close confidantes, Star Manson (Afton Elaine Burton) and Gray Wolf (Craig Hammond), were made and declined through numerous sources who know them. Same with Sandra Good, one of the original Family members.

Through a public records request, the National Archives provided us with reams of Manson's federal court, sentencing, and probation/parole records, from 1955 to 1969. But how to get at the actual trial record?

Thanks to a source who for years ran a research blog on this case, we learned that the Los Angeles County DA's office had possession of court exhibits and trial transcripts. Through a records request, we obtained four CDs containing thousands of pages of transcripts, documents, exhibits, and crime scene and booking photos. Even so, we were still not able to obtain a full historic record of the case. Entire transcripts from more than half of the ten trials were missing, and even in the primary Manson trial, entire days of testimony from key witnesses were not included. Moreover, these thousands of pages of transcripts were not indexed by trial date or witness names, and because they were PDF files with large "LADA" watermarks on every page, they could not be searched with keywords. Large portions of text were also obscured by the watermark if the pages were printed out.

That meant we had to be enterprising in how we obtained additional records to fill in gaps in the official record. The Internet—and Facebook in particular—proved to be a tremendous resource for us. An amazing volume of information exists in the public domain, including numerous archival websites and Facebook groups dedicated to studying and discussing this case. We received a lot of help from members of these groups, where news articles, research blogs, photos, and other obscure case-related documents are posted regularly. Many of these groups are secret or closed, but we managed to enter more than a dozen of them. When asked, the members would e-mail or send links so items' legitimacy could be confirmed when necessary. In turn, the members—who include longtime case researchers and some of Manson's longstanding pen- and phone-pals—gave us their own eyewitness observations, detailed their interactions and correspondence with Manson, and helped us connect with people who provided us with little-known information. A few of these folks then helped us get Manson's story when he wouldn't respond to our letters. Using Facebook also helped us reach hard-to-find sources such as Manson's grandson, Jason Freeman, and others who were off the beaten path, who could offer new perspectives and allow us to bring forward a story somewhat different from the one that has been parroted for the past fifty years.

Wherever possible, we authenticated whatever materials we found online or received from unofficial sources by cross-checking them with the official record. These materials included numerous timelines; birth, death, and marriage records; supplemental autopsy reports; evidence collection logs; booking sheets for other crimes over the years; historical photos; maps/diagrams of the Cielo Drive and Waverly Drive properties; court transcript excerpts; police evidence and records; and crime scene photos.

Our methodology was to look at the evidence outlined in historic records—such as police reports and interviews, court testimony, and statements by witnesses and attorneys in the media—and meld it with new information that has come out since. As it turned out, the more recent parole hearing transcripts were not only much more complete and easier to search than the trial transcripts, they were far more relevant and fruitful in providing new and illuminating details. Manson's codefendants, who didn't get to testify at trial because their attorneys prevented them from implicating themselves to protect Manson, are telling a more complete truth now. After finding their consciences and obtaining emotional distance from their former guru and fellow Family members, they are speaking their minds. Many of these transcripts were hundreds of pages long, and we drew details from as many as eight hearings per defendant. Family members, such as Dianne Lake, have also written books and given interviews quite recently, which we reviewed as well.

Of course, memories change over time, and many stories conflicted with one another, so we used only those details that were credible in light of all the evidence we compiled from investigators and other witness testimony, past and present. Interestingly, some of what Manson and his advocates claimed recently about what happened accords with some of the investigators' initial, but later-discarded, theories.

Overall, we wanted to show not just what made Manson tick, but to illustrate the curious dynamic of the Family that he created, because, as he taught his followers, they were him and he was them—they acted as one, so even when he wasn't there, they were his messengers, his proxies. We set out to present the social history of each murder defendant, the set of emotional vulnerabilities each brought to the group that, in turn, helped Manson manipulate them and exert influence over the whole Family.

We then wanted to show the ramifications of those group (i.e., cult) dynamics and how the group policed itself to conform to Manson's erratic and irrational set of beliefs—a tapestry woven from philosophical and religious threads from the Bible, cult leader Krishna Venta, L. Ron Hubbard, Dale Carnegie, Vincent Peale, Robert Heinlein, and even the Beatles.

Many of the people who still believe Manson was wrongly convicted don't seem to understand conspiracy law, that if you are part of a conspiracy that results in a murder, then you are all guilty, even if you weren't at the scene of that specific crime. Manson was clever that way—he not only convinced his Family members that it was *their* idea to carry out his wishes and that they were acting on their own accord, he also had Tex train them how to kill, how to insert and twist a knife to cause as much tissue damage as possible. As a result, some case buffs today place all responsibility on Tex, whom Manson put in charge of the killings. Because Tex gave the orders at the Tate house, we told that scene primarily from his point of view, gathered from statements at his parole hearings, his book, his website, and his psychiatric reports, which detailed the thoughts, intentions, and acts as he described them to a dozen clinicians.

We also felt it was important to show the little-discussed role of mental illness in this story, which, in Manson's case, he likely inherited. Deemed mentally ill by his own mother as well as by doctors who diagnosed him with aspects of schizophrenia, paranoia, and other personality disorders, he remained categorized as a mentally ill inmate in the prison system until his death. This was rarely discussed in earlier coverage of the case. Similarly, few have discussed the drug-induced psychosis caused by the chronic use of hallucinogens by Manson and his codefendants, which resulted in diagnoses of organic brain damage in Tex Watson, personality disorders in Bruce Davis, and aspects of schizophrenia in Steve Grogan. As Dr. David Smith pointed out, these drugs also played a role in helping Manson exert his influence over his followers, who saw him as a Christ-figure and a "guru" with special powers, and viewed his stream-of-consciousness rants as profound "mysticism."

We also wanted to show how this case has affected not only the victims' families but Manson's own children and grandchildren as well, and to underscore the alarming parallels between that period and today—and the possibility of a similar calamity happening again.

This gigantic research project entailed reading a massive amount of material, which involved ten trials, nine defendants, and at least nine victims—and possibly as many as thirty-five. In terms of volume, the paper research files filled multiple storage boxes in addition to thousands of digital computer files containing various court and witness interview transcripts, as well as countless news articles, exhibits, photos, and other important documents. In addition, we conducted a series of targeted personal interviews while surveying the wealth of information found in YouTube video clips, films, and documentaries.

Finding and reviewing the original documents in the Los Angeles Superior Court archives was itself an adventure. In the dark basement on Hill Street, well-meaning and hard-working clerks told Caitlin during numerous trips that an unknown number of boxes appeared to be missing (in addition to individual documents that "walked away" over the years). Even the several boxes the clerks did manage to produce for Caitlin to review and copy with a battery-operated wand scanner seemed to have been thrown up into the air and their contents tossed back into the box in no particular chronological order. No cameras, cell phones, laptops, or copying machines are allowed in the area, where the public can view files only after handing over a driver's license and then standing in a roped-off area under the watch of a security guard and clerks behind glass windows. Some of the older files, such as Rosalie Manson's divorce files, are on microfiche, while other files, such as the Bobby Beausoleil trial records, are on a different computer system and inaccessible to the public.

Only working media—no book authors—are allowed to attend prison parole hearings. Lis worked at FOX News at the time of Tex Watson's hearing in October 2016, so she was able to observe the proceedings as the only media representative in the room. Lis's personal observations helped craft the real-time scene at the hearing, and her presence enabled her to meet the victims' family members face-to-face with the hope of getting interviews with them for the book. But other than Kay Hinman Martley, who talked to us about her cousin Gary, the others chose not to grant interviews for the book, saying they didn't trust the media or were working on their own competing book or movie projects, an unusually common refrain we heard as we conducted our research. Nonetheless, we were committed to fairly representing their continuing efforts to keep the defendants behind bars all these years later.

Rather than convey an exhaustive list of every single document we read, we thought it more useful and helpful to list only the most notable and key items used in writing the story, broken down by category and subject matter.

PEOPLE WHO GRANTED INTERVIEWS; PROVIDED NEW INFORMATION, DOCUMENTS, SOURCES, AND PHOTOS; OR OFFERED OTHER HELP WITH PUTTING THE BOOK TOGETHER:

Roger Smith, interviews

Dr. David E. Smith, interview

Gina Judd, interviews, research, beta reader

Jason Freeman, interviews, recent recorded phone calls with Manson

Shawn (Freeman) Moreland, interview

Bill Freeman, interview

Paul Dostie, interviews, research

Arpad Vass, interview, research

Jack Cook, email interviews, research

Gary Stewart, email interviews, research

John Michael Jones, Manson friend, interviews

Bruce Fox (aka Stoner Van Houten), interviews

Matthew Roberts, interview

Sharmagne Leland-St. John-Sylbert, interviews

Ben Gurecki, Manson friend, interview

Kay Hinman Martley, interviews

Gary Kent, movie production manager at Spahn Ranch, interview

Jeff Rose, IT help

Gilbert Wright, DA's office, four CDs of grand jury and trial transcripts, crime scene photos, exhibits used in the ten trials

Terry Thornton, California Department of Corrections and Rehabilitation (CDCR), inmate bio and general case information, record requests, and photos

Luis Patino, CDCR, Board of Parole Hearings, parole board transcripts and records requests

Arineh Shahverdian, LA County Department of Medical Examiner-
Coroner, autopsy reports

Kermit Hicks, retired LA county courthouse employee, email
interview

David Ogul, interview

Chad Sandifer (George Spahn's grandson), interview

Jim Powers, public library in Ashland, Kentucky, news and
genealogy research

Larry Ramos, LA County Assessor's Office, info on 10050 Cielo
Drive

Campbell County Clerk's Office, Kentucky, Kathleen Manson's first
marriage license

Carole Scott, beta reader

Laurel Corona, beta reader

Bob Koven and Myra Chan, opened their home in LA for research
trips

Géza Keller, studio audio enhancement on DA/police witness
interviews and general support

Joe Rosignolo, studio audio enhancement

Alexandra Badalamenti, news research support

Peter Chiaramonte, donation of his book about Leslie Van Houten

Glenna Schultz, interview, research

Jaxon Van Derbeken, source referrals

PUBLIC RECORDS REQUESTS THAT PRODUCED NOTABLE MATERIALS:

California Board of Parole Hearings: transcripts dating back to 1978,
when Manson and most of his codefendants first became eligible
to request parole (some additional years are posted on cielodrive
.com). Manson's transcripts were obviously the most important,
but because he was not present when the killings occurred, only
the transcripts of his codefendants could describe what happened
at the crime scenes. Bruce Davis leads these defendants with
thirty-one parole hearings since he first became eligible in 1976.

We reviewed hearing transcripts as well as appeals, letters, and statements read aloud or submitted for hearings, and Gov. Brown's statements overturning parole board approvals:

Of Manson's twelve hearings, we reviewed these years: 1978, 1980, 1981, 1986, 1992, 2002, 2007, 2012

Of Krenwinkel's fourteen hearings: 2011, 2016

Of Atkins's thirteen hearings: 2002, 2008, 2009

Of Van Houten's twenty-one hearings: 2010, 2016

Of Beausoleil's eighteen hearings: 1978, 2005, 2008, 2010, 2016

All four of Grogan's: 1978, 1979, 1980, 1981

Of Davis's thirty-one hearings: 2010, 2012, 2014, 2015, 2017

Of Watson's seventeen hearings: 2011, 2016

LA County District Attorney's Office: partial transcripts from grand jury testimony (among the most notable witnesses were Mary Brunner, LASD detectives Charles Guenther and Paul Whiteley, Susan Atkins, Terry Melcher, Gregg Jakobson, and Danny DeCarlo); transcripts from pre-trial motion hearings and witness interviews; trial transcripts and exhibits, the latter of which were reused in multiple trials. Exhibits included items such as news articles, audiotaped witness interviews, crime scene photos, Shorty Shea's pawn tickets, booking sheets, a partial transcript of Stovitz's interview with *Rolling Stone*, and detective interviews with Atkins's cellmates Ronnie Howard and Virginia Graham.

LA Superior Court: archival records for several of the main trials, including the court clerk's minutes describing courtroom drama and other highlights; motions with backup documents and transcripts; witness interview excerpts and other compelling evidence or arguments, some of which didn't make it into the trial.

Federal Bureau of Prisons: Manson's prison timeline

National Archives and Records Administration: Manson's federal court files for charges of violating the Mann and Dyer Acts, stealing US Treasury checks and mail theft, from 1955 to 1969. These provided filings, rulings, handwritten letters from Manson and his mother to judges, arrest warrant authorizations, and probation/parole records, including Manson's reports to his probation officers and their reports to their superiors.

CDCR: basic inmate info, disciplinary records, news releases, and inmate photos

LA County Department of Medical Examiner-Coroner: official autopsy and toxicology reports for all nine victims. Other pages were found online, which may have since been either stolen, misplaced, or made unavailable for release due to privacy or other reasons. (Sharon Tate's, for example, doesn't show she was pregnant.)

State of West Virginia Department of Public Safety: arrest/investigative reports on Kathleen Maddox Manson's 1939 arrest for armed robbery in the Ketchup Bottle caper

NOTABLE RECORDS ACCESSED ONLINE OR THROUGH OTHER SOURCES:

FBI files for Charles Manson, Jay Sebring, Joel Rostau, Eugene "Gino" Massaro, and Vincent Bugliosi, the latter of whom reported extortion attempts against him

Mendocino County probation records for the Family's drug arrest in June 1968: These included a useful social history for Susan Atkins and Mary Brunner, and details on their relationship with Manson and the Family.

Tex Watson's pre-trial medical and psychiatric examination records from his time in LA county jail and at Atascadero State Hospital

William Garretson's polygraph exam transcript

LAPD Sergeant Michael McGann's arrest and incident report for Garretson, which describes events at the Tate murder scene and afterward, in response to Garretson's claim against McGann and the city of Los Angeles

The first two LAPD homicide investigative reports from each of the Tate and LaBianca cases

Paul Grassner's interview/story with former LA sheriff's deputy Preston Guillory, also published in Grassner's 1993 autobiography

LASD investigative reports from the Spahn Ranch raid and witness interviews concerning Family history, and the Shorty Shea and Gary Hinman murder cases, done in Inyo County after the raids at Barker and Myers Ranches

LASD search warrant affidavit for the Spahn Ranch raid

Numerous witness interviews by law enforcement officials from the DA's office, LASD, LAPD, and Inyo County Sheriff's Office, including Leslie Van Houten, Paul Watkins, Brooks Poston, Danny DeCarlo, and Stephanie Schram

Appellate court briefs and rulings for Manson et al. (Tate-LaBianca case) 1976; Manson (Hinman case) 1977; Watson 1970, 1976, 1977; Van Houten 1980; and Brunner 1973

California Office of the Attorney General: founding and annual filings for the ATWA non-profit, tax-exempt organization (2011–2016)

Historic photos helped us flesh out many descriptions, such as the Family's life at Spahn Ranch, the raids, and dumpster diving; Susan Atkins's stage revue as a topless vampire; Manson's immolation incident at Vacaville; Family members' courthouse dress and demeanor; the house at 10050 Cielo Drive, which was demolished in 1994; Sharon Tate and Roman Polanski's wedding, etc.

Alcohol, Tobacco and Firearms: report for the Barker Ranch fire in 2009

Forsher v. Bugliosi, Supreme Court of California ruling and appeal of dismissal of libel and invasion of privacy case re: *Helter Skelter*, both in 1980

Inyo County Office of the Sheriff, news release re: Barker Ranch "dig," 2008

Letters to US Sen. Dianne Feinstein, Office of the Inspector General, and others from retired Mammoth Lakes Police Sergeant Paul Dostie

Tuscarawas County, Ohio, Juvenile Court filing in 1986 proving that Charles Jay White aka Charles Milles Manson Jr. was Jason Freeman's father

Colorado death certificate for Charles "Jay" White, aka Charles Milles Manson Jr., by "self-inflicted gunshot to head" on Interstate 70 in June 1993

"Eye of the Beholder, The Wrongful Conviction of Charles Manson,"
by Carrie Leonetti, *Southwestern Law Review*, 2016
"The Group Marriage Commune: A Case Study," by Dr. David E.
Smith and Alan J. Rose, *Journal of Psychedelic Drugs*, 1970
Obituaries for Rosalie Handley (2009) and Colonel Scott (1954), also
Scott's death certificate
Leona Rae Manson's divorce decree in Denver, Colorado, 1964

TV MOVIES AND SHOWS, FEATURE FILMS, DOCUMENTARIES, VIDEO:

Helter Skelter, 1976
Charles Manson Superstar, 2002
Six Degrees of Helter Skelter, 2009
Aquarius, 2015–16
Diane Sawyer TV interviews, 1993
The Manson Women, now on Biography.com
Truth and Lies: The Family Manson, ABC documentary, 2017
Dateline: The Summer of Manson, 2017
Good Morning America, interview with Dianne Lake, 2017
YouTube archives containing countless video clips of interviews or
statements on this case over the years, including those featuring
Manson and Family members; witnesses such as Phil Kaufman,
who had dealings with Manson and the Family; investigators
involved in the raids such as CHP Officer James Pursell, who
arrested Manson at Barker Ranch, and LASD Sergeant Gleason,
who helped find Shorty Shea's remains in 1977; Bruce Davis and
Lynette Fromme speaking to media or protesting; a BBC video
of Bruce Davis prison interview; a TV interview with author Ed
Sanders and Debra Tate; and news clips.

WEBSITES:

Some of the most helpful Facebook groups included Helter Skelter
Alternate Theories; In Memory of the Parent, Tate, LaBianca
Murders of 1969; Manson Family Myth 1967–present, and others

that were formed, renamed, or disappeared after running their course.

Cielodrive.com

Mansonsbackporch.com

Murdersofaugust69.com

Mansondirect.com

Mansonblog.com, with original ATWA site archived at accessmanson.mansonblog.com

ATWAearth.com, ATWA's Facebook and Instagram pages, atwaatwar.wordpress.com, atwaatwar.com

tlbradio.com, TLB radio podcasts of interviews with all types of people involved in the case or parties to it from yesterday and today

lsb3.com, Tate-LaBianca Homicide Research Blog

releasemansonnow.com

cdcr.ca.gov

cdcrtoday.blogspot.com

University of Missouri-Kansas City School of Law, http://law2.umkc .edu/faculty/projects/ftrials/manson/mansonchrono.html

Aboundinglove.org, website for Watson's Abounding Love Ministries

bobbybeausoleil.com

leslievanhouten.com

biography.com, including "The Manson Women" show

jasonfreebirdfreeman.wordpress.com

criminal-justice.iresearchnet.com

findagrave.com

NOTABLE BOOKS:

Manson: The Life and Times of Charles Manson, by Jeff Guinn

Helter Skelter, by Vincent Bugliosi with Curt Gentry

Manson in His Own Words, as told to Norm Emmons

Will You Die For Me? The Man Who Killed for Charles Manson Tells His Own Story, by Tex Watson as told to Chaplain Ray

The Killing of Sharon Tate, by Lawrence Schiller and Susan Atkins

Child of Satan, Child of God: Her Own Story, by Susan Atkins with
   Bob Slosser
The Myth of Helter Skelter, by Susan Atkins-Whitehouse
The Family, by Ed Sanders
If Republicans Had Any Hearts, They'd Be Democrats, by Jon Fisher
Restless Souls, by Alisa Statman with Brie Tate

PRIMARY AND NOTABLE NEWS OUTLETS, MAGAZINES, WIRE SERVICES, AND ARCHIVES:

Los Angeles Times
New York Times
Rolling Stone
Los Angeles magazine
Washington Post
California Digital Newspaper Collection: mostly AP and UPI
Ashland Daily Independent
Charleston Daily Mail
People
Variety
New York Daily News
New York Post
Riverside Press Enterprise
Long Beach Press-Telegram
Time
Newsweek
Sacramento Bee
CNN
San Francisco Chronicle, sfgate.com
Bakersfield Californian
The Guardian, theguardian.com
TMZ
Daily Mail, dailymail.co.uk
Bloomberg.com

CAST OF CHARACTERS

MANSON FAMILY MEMBERS AND ASSOCIATES

Charles "Charlie" Milles Manson, leader of Manson Family

Patricia Krenwinkel, aka Katie, Marnie and Mary Ann Scott, helped kill Tate/LaBianca victims

Susan Atkins, aka Sadie Mae Glutz, helped kill Gary Hinman/Tate victims

Charles "Tex" Watson, aka Charles Montgomery, self-described "Manson's right-hand man," led Tate-LaBianca killings

Leslie Van Houten, aka Leslie Sanskton, helped in LaBianca murders

Robert "Bobby" Beausoleil, aka Cupid and Jason Lee Daniels, killed Hinman

Bruce Davis, aka Jack McMillan, helped kill Hinman/Donald "Shorty" Shea

Steve Grogan, aka Clem Tufts, and Scramblehead, helped kill Shea

Linda Kasabian, Family member, prosecution's primary witness

Mary Brunner, first Family member, mother of Charlie's third son and reluctant prosecution witness

Catherine Share, aka Gypsy, Family member

Lynette Fromme, aka Squeaky and Red, second Family member, attempted to assassinate President Gerald Ford

Sandra "Sandy" Good, aka Sandy Collins Pugh and Blue, loyal Family member, threatened to kill 171 corporate leaders

Ruth Ann Moorehouse Heuvelhurst, aka Ouisch, early Family member

Catherine Gillies, aka Cappy, Family member

Nancy Pitman, aka Brenda McCann, Family member

Katherine "Kitty" Lutesinger, Bobby's girlfriend

Barbara Hoyt, Family member, prosecution witness

Dianne Lake, aka Dianne Bluestein, Family member, prosecution witness

Stephanie Schram, Family member, prosecution witness

Brooks Poston, former Family member, prosecution witness

Paul Watkins, Family member, prosecution witness

Danny DeCarlo, aka Richard Allen Smith, Straight Satans biker, reluctant prosecution witness

John Philip Haught, aka Zero/Christopher Jesus, allegedly committed suicide by Russian roulette

MURDER VICTIMS, DATE KILLED

Gary Hinman, musician and friend of Family members, July 27, 1969

Bernard Crowe, aka Lotsapoppa and Poppa (attempted murder by Manson), August 1

Sharon Tate Polanski, wife of director Roman Polanski, August 9

Jay Sebring, aka Thomas Kummer, "Hairdresser to the stars," August 9

Abigail "Gibby" Folger, heir to Folgers coffee fortune, August 9

Wojciech "Voytek" Frykowski, August 9

Steven Parent, August 9

Leno LaBianca, supermarket owner, August 10

Rosemary LaBianca, dress shop owner, August 10

Donald "Shorty" Shea, ranch hand at Spahn Ranch, late August

LAW ENFORCEMENT OFFICERS, MURDER CASE, AGENCY

Sergeant Michael McGann, lead detective on Tate team, Los Angeles Police Department (LAPD)

Sergeant Jess Buckles, lead detective on Tate team, LAPD

Sergeant Danny Galindo, Tate/LaBianca, LAPD

Sergeant Frank Patchett, LaBianca team, LAPD

Sergeant Paul Whiteley, Hinman/Shea, Los Angeles County Sheriff's
Department (LASD)
Deputy Charles Guenther, Hinman/Shea, LASD
Deputy Bill Gleason, Spahn Ranch auto theft ring/Shea, LASD
Officer James Pursell, raids at Barker and Myers Ranches, California
Highway Patrol in Inyo County (CHP)
Ranger Dick Powell, Barker/Myers raids, US Park Service in Inyo
County
Deputy Don Ward, Inyo County Sheriff's Office (ICSO)

ATTORNEYS/JUDGES

Vincent Bugliosi, lead prosecutor for Tate-LaBianca trials
Aaron Stovitz, prosecuting co-counsel for Tate-LaBianca
Burton Katz, prosecutor for Hinman trial
Judge William Keene
Judge Charles Older
Judge Malcolm Lucas
Evelle Younger, LA County District Attorney
Irving Kanarek, defense attorney for Manson
Paul Fitzgerald, defense attorney for Manson, then Krenwinkel
Richard Caballero and Daye Shinn, defense attorneys for Atkins
Ronald Hughes, defense attorney for Manson, then Van Houten
Maxwell Keith, defense attorney for Van Houten

WITNESSES OR OTHER CHARACTERS

William Garrettson, caretaker for Cielo Drive property
Winifred "Winnie" Chapman, Polanskis' housekeeper
Dennis Wilson, Beach Boys drummer and unwitting Manson
Family benefactor
Rudi Altobelli, talent manager and owner of Cielo Drive property
Terry Melcher, music producer and son of Doris Day
Gregg Jakobson, talent scout, friend of Dennis and Terry
Juan Flynn, ranch hand at Spahn
Rosina Kroner, Tex's dealer girlfriend

Paul Crockett, gold prospector in Death Valley

Alan Springer, Straight Satans biker

Ronnie Howard, Susan Atkins's cellmate

Virginia Graham, Susan Atkins's cellmate

George Spahn, owner of Spahn Ranch

Ruby Pearl, forewoman at Spahn

Gary Kent, film production manager at Spahn

Roger Smith, Manson's parole officer

Dr. Roger Smith, founder of Haight-Ashbury Free Clinic, addiction specialist

Sgt. Paul Dostie, retired from Mammoth Lakes Police Department, cadaver dog handler

Arpad Vass, scientist/expert in identifying human remains in soil

John Michael Jones, contemporary Manson confidante

Sharmagne Leland-St. John-Sylbert, one of Jay Sebring's girlfriends

Rosalie Willis, Manson's first wife

Leona Rae "Candy" Stevens, aka Leona Rae Musser, Manson's second wife

Charles Milles Manson Jr. or Jay White, Manson's son with Rosalie

Jason Freeman, Charlie and Rosalie's grandson

Shawn Freeman Mooreland, Jason's mother

Afton Elaine Burton, aka Star Manson, Manson's former fiancée

VICTIMS' FAMILY MEMBERS

Doris Tate, Sharon Tate's mother

Debra Tate, Sharon's sister

Anthony DiMaria, Jay Sebring's nephew

Kay Martley, Gary Hinman's cousin

Lou Smaldino, Leno's nephew, son of Leno's older sister

Tony LaMontagne, Leno's grandson

Frankie Struthers and Suzan Struthers LaBerge, Rosemary LaBianca's children

INDEX

A

Abounding Love Ministries website, 251
Access Manson (ATWA), 232
Altobelli, Rudi, 36–41, 46, 83, 120, 138, 278
American culture, change in, ix
Anger, Kenneth, 14
Aquarius (TV), 277
Atascadero State Hospital, 218
Atkins, Susan "Sadie," xii, 1, 15–20, 34–35, 58, 61, 75, 114–116, 223
    alternative version of murder, 31
    arrest, 158
    at Cielo Drive, 37–40
    cooperation with prosecution, 188–189
    in court, 195–196, 204
    death penalty, 215
    fact vs. fantasy, 193–194
    before grand jury, 174, 175
    grand jury indictment, 178
    parole hearing, 253–254
    and pregnant woman, 40
    psychiatric assessment, 254
    statement to lawyers, 173–174
    talking in prison, 163–165
    on witness stand, 206
ATWA (Air Trees Water Animals; All The Way Alive), xiii, 232, 270
Atwaearth.com website, 270
auto theft, 96–97, 98, 103, 157
autopsies, on LaBianca bodies, 74

B

Bailey, Ella Jo, 118
    immunity offer, 189
Ball, Joseph, 187–188
Barker Ranch, 132, 153, 275

battered woman syndrome (BWS), 279
Beach Boys, Charlie's songs, 123
Beatles, 134
    Helter Skelter, 257–258
    "Piggies," 65
Beausoleil, Bobby, 6, 13–14, 18–20, 128, 158
    arrest, 29–30
    charges, 91
    efforts to contact, 292
    on Family motive for killing, 249
    guilty of first-degree murder, 185–186
    jury impasse, 170
    jury selection, 169
    Manson on Hinman murder, 236
    Mary's testimony and, 222
    parole hearing, 255
    trial, 169
    trial continued, 183
Benedict Canyon, 34
Bergen, Candice, 46, 50
bikers
    at ranch, 89
    Straight Satans, 170
Black Panthers, 19, 30, 87
    efforts to blame murders on, 66
black people, 10
books, 277
Box Canyon, 129
Boyd, Roland, 172
Brown, Jerry, 256
Brown, Roger, 175
Brunner, Mary, 1, 14–19, 107, 108, 112, 175–177, 180, 217, 223
    arrest, 127
    arrest for stolen credit cards, 31

childbirth, 126
court testimony, 184
guilty of LSD possession, 127
immunity offer, 222
pregnancy, 109–110
release from prison, 223
testimony, 222
testimony refusal, 185–186
Brunner, Michael, 224, 283
Buckles, Jess, 54
Buddhist monasteries, Clem and, 125–126
Bugliosi, Vincent, x, 165, 171, 184, 194, 198, 211
closing argument, 209–210
on compassionate release of Atkins, 253
contempt, 201
on Family murders, 274
Helter Skelter, 277
Wilson to, 123
Burton, Afton Elaine, 269
letters to Manson, xi
visits to Manson, xii
Butler, Dale, 86

C

Caballero, Richard, 173
California Highway Patrol (CHP), 29–30
California Institution for Women (CIW), 215
California, laws on parole, 257
California Men's Colony (CMC) in San Luis Obispo, 256
Call, Joseph, 216
Canoga Park, "Yellow Submarine," 133
Carnegie, Dale, *How to Win Friends and Influence People*, 104
"Cease to Exist," 123–124
Chandler, Cecil, 226–227
Channels, Michael, claim of will, 283
Chapman, Winnie, 50–51
Charlene, 111
children
in foster care, 90–91
Manson and, 61, 112
Chillicothe, Ohio, federal reformatory, 97
Christian tradition, x
Cielo Drive, 278
Chapman arrival, 50–51
LaBianca murders viewed as unrelated, 77
murder investigation, 81–82
murders, 36–41
neighbors, 48–49
public reaction to murder, 59
survivor, 44–49

Clem, 182
communal lifestyle, 4
Como, Kenneth, 220, 223
Cook, Jack, 281
Cooper, Priscilla, 274–275
copycat influences, 257–258
Corcoran State Prison, xi
Protective Housing Unit, 239
Costello, Frank, 104
Crabstreet, Darren, 29
"creepy crawlers," 33, 60
criminal education, in prison, 104
Crockett, Paul, 132, 150, 155–156, 162
Crowe, Bernard "Lotsapoppa," 22–24, 213–214, 243
shooting by Manson, 25–26

D

Dale Carnegie leadership-building course, 101
Davis, Bruce, 6, 14–17, 136, 140–141, 165, 208–209
charges against, 180
efforts to contact, 292
life sentence, 225
parole hearing, 255–257
separate trial, 216
on Shorty's murder, 147–149
death, Manson perception of, 9–10
death penalty, 215
as unconstitutional, 225
Death Valley, Manson planned move to, 152–160
DeCarlo, Danny, 34–35, 42–43, 88, 143, 150–151, 170
Dell, George, 222
DeRonde, Glen, 235
detectives, information sharing, 84
Deuel Vocational Institution, 226
Dickson, Jim, 120
diet pills, 111
DiMaria, Anthony, 252–253, 257
Division of Alcohol, Tobacco and Firearms (ATF), arrest warrant for Charlie, 136
Dorgan, Joe, 247
Dostie, Paul, 275, 276
drugs, 285–286
"awareness drugs," 35
Bruce and, 140
Charlie and, 234
Clem's use, 42–43, 126
distribution, 127
Grogan recovery from damage, 228

hallucinogens, 295
hash, 113
Hinman murder and, 255
and homicide theories, 78–79
Leslie and, 129, 196
LSD, 7, 8, 113, 164, 286
marijuana, 285
suppliers, 244
Voytek and, 79
Watson and, 123
dune buggies, 140
theft, 134

E

Elder, Lauren, 207, 208
elderly offender program, 257
Ellis, Diane, 231
environmental activism, xiii
chemical products, 270
Manson and, 6
Star and, 269

F

Family of Infinite Soul, Inc., 191
Farr, William, Graham interview release
to, 205
Father Flanagan's Boys Town, 96
fear-deprogramming exercises, 9
fear, Manson on, 9–10
Federal Correctional Institution, Terminal
Island, 100
fetus, legal status, 200
Fisher, Jon, 130
Fitzgerald, Paul, 187, 193, 204, 205, 211–212
Flynn, Juan, 3, 35, 68, 273
Folger, Abigail "Gibby," 46, 53, 56, 80, 108, 243
"folie à deux," 218
Folsom prison, 233
Forsher, James, 207, 274
Fountain of the World (cult), 67, 129
Fox, Bruce, 242
Frank, Ira, 218–219
Freeman, Jason, 263–264, 277
contact with grandfather, 266–268, 281
efforts to control grandfather's remains,
283–284
Knocking Out the Devil, 266
knowledge of grandfather, 263
as martial arts fighter, 265–266
and Star, 272
Fromme, Lynette "Squeaky," xii, 1, 85, 108–109,
112, 118, 119, 163, 182, 184, 229

arrest, 158, 275
death threats to Hoyt, 181
Ford assassination attempt, 230
in prison, 231–232
protests during trial, 195
threatening calls to Grogan, 226
Frykowski, Wojciech "Voytek," 46, 56, 243
and drugs, 79, 244–245
Fury, Magdalene Velda, 145, 147

G

gag order, 183, 193
violation, 201, 203, 204
Galindo, Danny, 71–74
Gallo, Vincent, 272–273
Gardner, John, 239
Garretson, William, 44–49
arrest, 53, 57
police and, 52
Garrido, Phillip, 239
Gibault School for Boys, 96
Gillies, Catherine "Cappy," 132, 192
girls, relationship with Manson, xiv–xv
Gleason, William, 177–178
search warrant creation, 88
Spahn Ranch investigation, 86
Glutz, Sadie Mae, 115, 161, 254
conviction of weapons charge, 115
Good, Sandy, 192, 220, 229
arrest, 158
arrest for stolen credit cards, 31
conspiracy to mail death threats, 230–231
death threats to Hoyt, 181
environmental activism, 232
in prison, 231
protests during trial, 195
threatening calls to Grogan, 226
Graham, Virginia, 163, 179, 205
Gray Wolf, 269, 270–271, 272
efforts to contact, 292
Grillo, Nick, 120
Grogan, Steve, 125, 180–181. *See also* Tufts,
Clem "Scramblehead"
mental competence, 226
parole, 226, 228–229
parole hearing, 227
recovery from drug damage, 228
second trial, 220–221
separate trial, 216
Guenther, Charles, 30, 161, 175–177
discovery of Hinman body, 27–28
Tate/Hinman murder connection, 55

Guinn, Jeff, *Manson: The Life and Times of Charles Manson*, 248
guitar, 105, 273
guitar lessons, 104
gun grip, 82
Gurecki, Ben, 272, 281–282
    claim of will, 283
Gypsy. *See* Share, Catherine "Gypsy"

H

Haight-Ashbury, 106
hallucinogens, 295
Hammond, Craig, 292. *See also* Gray Wolf
Handley, Rosalie. *See also* Willis, Rosalie "Rosie" Jean
    obituary, 265
Hart, William S., 2
Hatami, Shahrokh, 137
Haught, John Philip "Zero," shooting, 165
"HEALTER SKELTER," 77–78
Heinlein, Robert, *Stranger in a Strange Land*, 104, 107
Helter Skelter, 10, 65, 134, 140, 167, 198–199, 200, 233, 248
    Beatles song, 257–258
    Lone Star Saloon as, 135
Hinman, Gary
    discovery of body, 27–28
    LAPD notice of murder, 55
    Lutesinger on murder, 161
    Manson trial for murder of, 221
    murder, 13–21
Hitler, Adolf, 199
Hollopeter, Charles, 192
Holmstrom, Jan, 237–238
Howard, Ronnie, 163, 166, 179
Hoyt, Barbara, 4, 10, 58, 146, 254
    escape, 154
    statements to prosecution team, 181–182
Hubbard, L. Ron, 104, 140
Hughes, Ronald, 193, 196, 200–201, 274
    absence from court, 207
    body discovered, 214–215
humiliation, 8

I

Indiana School for Boys, 96–97
"Infinite Soul," Charlie as, 4
International People's Court of Retribution, 230
Internet, misinformation, 287
intimate partner battery, 279
Inyo County Sheriff's Office, 157

J

Jakobson, Gregg, 120, 123, 135, 138–139
Jesus Christ, Manson seen as, 9, 36, 130, 191
Jones, John Michael, 242–244, 246, 272, 282, 283, 292
justice, x

K

Kanarek, Irving, 196, 197, 200–201, 210
    juror dismissal efforts, 213
    objections, 199
Karpis, Alvin "Creepy," 104
Kasabian, Linda, 32, 39, 88, 243
    arrest, 171
    arrest surrender, 172–173
    court testimony, 200–201
    grand jury indictment, 178
    immunity offer, 189, 202
    LSD use, 197
    pregnancy, 66
Katie. *See* Krenwinkel, Patricia "Katie"
Katz, Burton, 180, 184, 216
Kaufman, Phil, 105, 118, 278
Kay, Stephen, 203, 214, 234
Keene, William, 179, 187
    affidavit of prejudice, 196
    gag order, 183, 193
    on Manson self-representation, 191–192
Keith, Maxwell, 209, 225
The Killing of Sharon Tate, 179
knives, 41, 167–168
Kolts, James, 220, 226
Kosinski, Jerzy, 80
Kott, Mr. and Mrs. Seymour, 48–49
Krenwinkel, Patricia "Katie," 1, 8, 12, 63, 110–114, 118, 162–163, 193
    arrest, 157, 171, 172
    on Cielo Drive, 37–38, 39
    compliance with Charlie, 113–114
    at courthouse, 195–196, 204
    death penalty, 215
    dune buggy theft, 134
    efforts to contact, 292
    freedom from Family, 223
    grand jury indictment, 178
    on Manson, 9
    parole hearing, 279–280
    reaction to Cielo murders, 41
    return to ranch, 67
Krishna Venta's cult, 129
Kroner, Rosina, 22
Kummer, Thomas John, 79. *See also* Sebring, Jay

L

LaBerge, Suzan, 247
LaBianca home, LAPD at, 71–74
LaBianca, Leno, 59, 92
   Cielo murders viewed as unrelated, 77
   Manson on, 236
LaBianca, Rosemary, 59–60
Lake, Dianne, 5, 67
LaMontagne, Tony, 252
Lansbury, Angela, 4
law enforcement, blind spots and poor
   coordination, 91
Lebowitz, Donna, 250
Lee, Bruce, 46
Lee's Trading Post, 3
Leland-St. John-Sylbert, Sharmagne, 120–121
Lone Star Saloon, as Helter Skelter, 135
Los Angeles County Sheriff's Department
   (LASD), 27–28, 85
   information sharing, 163
   raid on Spahn Ranch, 143
Los Angeles, fear and panic, 75
Los Angeles federal probation office, 131
   Charlie's lies to, 135
Los Angeles Magazine, 256
Los Angeles Police Department (LAPD)
   arrival at Cielo Drive, 15, 51–52
   fingerprint on file, 171
   information sharing, 163
   investigation mishandling, 167
   at LaBianca home, 71–74
   on murders, 77
Los Angeles Superior Court archives, 295
Los Angeles Times, 92, 201, 211
Los Feliz, 61–64, 76
love, 11
Love, Mike, 121
LSD, 7, 8, 113, 164, 286
Lucas, Malcolm, 189, 190
   change of venue denial, 194
Lucifer Rising, 14
Lutesinger, Kathryn "Kitty," 158, 161

M

MacBride, Judge, 231
Maddox, Kathleen (mother), 94, 95, 211
Maddox, Nancy, 93
Mafia mobsters, and LaBianca homicides, 247
Manson, Charles III, 265–266
Manson, Charles Luther, 104
Manson, Charles Milles
   alternative versions of murders, 242–249
   appearance, xii
   arraignment, 179
   arrest, 101–102, 143, 159–160
   birthday, 93
   on blacks, 133–134
   burglary charges, 91
   change of venue request, 189–190
   claims to estate, 283–284
   death, 282–283
   death certificate, 283
   death penalty, 215
   discussion with parole officer, 107–108
   disrespect in court, 195, 197
   education, 97
   efforts to contact, 292
   ER for gastrointestinal issues, 280
   at Federal Correctional Institution,
    Terminal Island, 100
   guitar lessons, 95
   heart problems, 271
   interest in Melcher, 137
   killing spree plans, 32
   legacy, 268
   legal representation, 187, 191–192, 196, 212
   lies about income, 133
   mail, xi
   marriage, 98
   mental competence, 98–99, 102
   and mixed race marriage, 145
   murder count, 273–276
   murder instructions, 34
   music, 278
   "not guilty" plea, 188
   parole hearing, 233–241
   parole officer and, 1
   parole violation, 99
   perception of death, 9–10
   on probation, 105
   psychiatric assessment, 233–234
   release from prison, 106
   supporters, xiv–xv, xv
   sympathy for, 7
   talks with Tex, 35
   travel, 6
   trial for Shea and Hinman murders, 221
   Vacaville inmate attempt to burn, 237–238
   vision for second wave, 60–66
   as ward of state, 96
   on weapons, 87
   and women, 1
Manson, Charles Milles Jr., 260–268
   birth, 100

Manson Family, xiv–xv, 107
  children, 7
  color nicknames, 229
  connections in prison, 258
  food sources, 6
  indoctrination and programming, 8
  intimidation within, 150
  men, 7, 139–140
  move to Spahn Ranch, 125, 134
  preparation for revolution, 133
  request to contribute, 5
  rules governing life, 6
  at Spahn ranch, 5
  women's relationship with Manson, xiv
Manson Family trial
  case to jury, 211
  closing argument, 209–210
  defense motion for mistrial, 200
  defense witness, 205
  Kasabian testimony, 200–201
  Manson acting out, 203–204
  Manson statement, 206
  opening statements, 198–200
  Sadie on witness stand, 206
Manson, Marilyn, 278
Manson, Star, xii, 269, 272. *See also* Burton,
  Afton Elaine
  as Charlie's wife, xiii
  efforts to contact, 292
  view of Charlie, xiii
  wedding plans, 271–272
Manson, William, 89, 94
mansondirect.com website, 270
Manson's Right-Hand Man Speaks Out, 251
marijuana, 285
Martin, Frank, 94–95
Martley, Kay Hinman, 29, 252, 255
mass murders, 287
Massaro, Gino, 245–246
Mathes, William, 102, 103, 104
  Manson letter to, 105
McCaffrey, Karlene Ann, 245
McCann, Brenda, 146, 184
  arrest, 158
McEachen, Angus, 102–103, 132–133, 136, 159
McGann, Michael J., 54, 55, 166
  report, 78
McMillan, Jack, 136. *See also* Davis, Bruce
McNeil Island Penitentiary, 104
McNiel, Edwin, 99
  psychiatric assessment by, 102
meditation, Clem and, 125–126

Melcher, Terry, 34, 46, 54, 120, 127, 137–143, 243
men, in Manson Family, 7, 139–140
mental illness, 295
Methylene Dioxy Amphetamine. (MDA), 79
monkey wrenching, 154
Montgomery, Charles, 68. *See also* Watson,
  Charles "Tex"
Moorehouse, Dean, 110, 121–122
Moorehouse, Ruth Ann "Ouisch," 110, 119,
  181–182
  arrest, 158
Moreland, Shawn, 261, 262–263
motorcycles, at ranch, 91
Moundsville State Prison, 95
Mule Creek State Prison, 250
Murphy, Susan, 229
  conviction of sending death threats, 231
Musich, Donald, 203
Musser, Leona Rae. *See* Stevens, Leona Rae
  "Candy"
Myers Ranch, 132, 275

N

National Inquirer, 272
National Training School for Boys, 97
Natural Bridge Honor Camp, 97
"Never Learn Not to Love," 124
news media, 75–76, 194
  gag order, 183, 193, 201
  on murder parallels, 77
Nixon, Richard, 201–202

O

Older, Charles H., 196–197, 204, 212
Olmstead, Samuel, 87
Order of the Rainbow, 229

P

Pacific Palisades, 118
Pacoima, 66
Parent, Steve, 44, 47
parole. *See also under individual names*
  opposition to, 250–259
Pasadena, church, 61
Patchett, Frank, 166
  interview of Manson, 168
Peale, Norman Vincent, *The Power of Positive
  Thinking*, 104
Pearl, Ruby, 3, 145
Peck, John, 251
Petersburg, Virginia, federal reformatory, 97
Phillips, John, 46

Philo, house rental, 127
Pitman, Nancy, 184, 274–275. *See also* McCann,
    Brenda
Polanski, Roman, 46, 54
    learning of Tate's death, 82
    and Voytek, 80
"POLITICAL PIGGY," 28
Poston, Brooks, 132, 134, 155, 162
Powell, Dick, 155, 159
presidential election of 2016, 268
probation, 103
Pursell, James, 155, 159

Q

Quant, Dawn, 181

R

racial divide, 287
rape, 97
Record Mirror, 117
reincarnation, 130
Release Charles Manson Now blog, 270
reporters, 54
Retz, Frank, 85
Revelation (Bible), 134
revolution, 133
    Manson on, 10
Reznor, Trent, 278
Roberts, Matthew, 283
Rolling Stone, 202–203
Roof, Dylann Storm, 287
Rose, Axl, 278
Ross, Mark, 192
Rostau, Joel, 245
Rother, Caitlin, x

S

San Quentin State Prison, 95, 187, 215, 221, 233,
    238–239
Sanders, Ed, *The Family*, 243–244
Savior (seed gun), 270
Sawyer, Diane, xv
Schiller, Lawrence, 178
Schram, Stephanie, 31, 152–153, 158, 178
Schwarzenegger, Arnold, 256
Scott, Colonel Walker, 93
Scott, Darwin, 94, 274
Sebring, Jay, 46, 56, 243
    drugs, 244–245
Security Housing Unit (SHU), xiii
self-worth, 12
Share, Catherine "Gypsy," 5, 119, 128, 182, 192,

197, 217, 223
    arrest, 157
    release from prison, 223
Sharmagne, 46
Shaw, Deirdre, 4
Shea, Donald "Shorty," 85, 91
    Manson trial for murder of, 221
    mistrial for Grogan, 216
    murder, 144–151
    murder witnesses, 162
    remains found, 227
    rumors of murder, 178
Shea, Magdalene, 180
Shinn, Daye, 202
Siddons, Bill, 108
Sirhan, Sirhan, 239
Smaldino, Lou, 252, 280
Smith, David, 117, 248, 285, 286
    free clinic, 108
Smith, Roger, 107, 117, 131
    foster care of Mary's son, 127
Smith, Valentine Michael, 126
sodium amytal, 219
sodium pentothal, 219
Spahn, George, 2, 91
    living conditions, 3
Spahn Movie Ranch, 2
    bikers, 89
    move to, 125, 134
    probation officer check, 132
    search warrant, 92
    security, 26
    sheriff's deputies at, 89–91
Spahn Movie Ranch raid, 84–92
    neighbor complaints, 84
Spence, Gerry, 246
Springer, Alan, 88, 170
stabbing, 64
    instructions on, 153–154
Stevens, Leona Rae "Candy," 101, 103–104
    divorce, 105
Stimson, George, 232
Stovitz, Aaron, 165, 184, 190, 198
    gag order violation, 203
    pretrial interview, 202–203
Straight Satans bikers, 170
Struthers, Frankie, 59–60
    discovery of dead parents, 69–71
Struthers, Suzan, 59–60, 70
Summers, Charles Milles, 87
swastika, xii
Sweeney, Jason, 257–258

Sybil Brand Institute, 31, 163–165

T

Tarantino, Quentin, 277
Tate, Debra, 252, 257, 279–280
Tate-LaBianca case. *See also* LaBianca, Leno
  grand jury indictments, 178
  profit from, 277–278
Tate, Sharon, 44, 47, 243
  homicide team theories, 78–79
  murder, 40, 53, 56–57
  news of murder, 54
  and Polanski, 80–81
  public reaction to murder, 59
Tennant, William, 54
Tex. *See* Watson, Charles "Tex"
Tex tapes, 258
THC (tetrahydrocannabinol), 285
Thornton, Terry, 240
Topanga Canyon, 13
travel, 108
truth serums, 219
Tufts, Clem "Scramblehead," 42–43, 58, 125–126
  arrest, 157
  on Shorty's murder, 147–149
Twenty Pimlico, Inc., 178

U

US Park Service rangers, 154
University of California, Berkeley, protest, 106

V

Vacaville
  California Medical Facility, 255
  psychiatric facility, 233, 237–238
Van Houten, Leslie, 4, 8, 10, 11–12, 61, 63, 128
  arrest, 157
  at courthouse, 195–196, 204
  death penalty, 215
  "diminished capacity" plea, 212
  efforts to contact, 292
  forced abortion, 129
  freedom from Family, 223
  grand jury indictment, 178
  guilty verdict, 226
  legal representation, 196
  at Manson trial, 221
  mistrial, 225
  parole, 258
  retrial ordered, 225
  return to ranch, 67
  surrender to Charlie, 65

tasks and chores, 135
transfer to Sybil Brand, 171
vaping, 285
Vass, Arpad, 275, 276
vehicles, at ranch, 91
Venta's "Golden Gems," 130
Vietnam War protests, 106
violence of Manson, 113
  toward women, 11

W

Walker, Lenore, *The Battered Woman*, 279
Ward, Don, 157
Watkins, Paul, 7, 9, 162
Watson, Charles "Tex," 5–6, 62, 121–123, 156, 243
  arrest, 142, 171–172
  attorney transcript, 258
  at Cielo Drive, 36–41
  death penalty, 220
  dietary problems, 218
  drug supplier to, 245–246
  drug use, 33
  efforts to contact, 292
  extradition, 217
  grand jury indictment, 178
  guilt phase of trial, 219
  insanity plea, 212
  Manson's talks with, 35
  mental state, 218–219
  mother and, 67–68
  parole hearing, ix, 250–253
  plan for drug burn and steal, 22–24
  return to ranch, 67
  "sanity" phase of trial, 219
  sex with Linda, 32
Wattley, Keith, 279
weapons, 10, 14
  bayonet, 55
  Buntline revolver, 25, 34
  knives, 41, 167–168
  Leno's cache, 73
  Manson on, 87
  mishandling of gun evidence, 167
  purchases by community, 76
  rifles at ranch, 88–89
Weiss, Steven, and gun, 167
Western films, 2
Western Surplus Store, robbery, 217
Westover, Harry, 98, 99
Wheeling Downs racetrack, 98
White, Jack, 100, 260–268

White, Jay, 260. *See also* Manson, Charles
   Milles Jr.
     suicide, 264–265
Whitehouse, James, 253
Whiteley, Paul, 30, 161, 175–177, 180, 188–189
     discovery of Hinman body, 27–28
     Tate/Hinman murder connection, 55
Wiehl, Lis, 250
Willis, Rosalie "Rosie" Jean, 98
     break with Charlie, 100–101
     death from cancer, 265

Wilson, Dennis, 118, 121
     handouts for Charlie, 123
     property damage by Manson Family, 124
Wise, Marc, 275
women, submissive, 7

Y

Young, Neil, 120
youthful offender measure, 257

ABOUT THE AUTHOR

Lis Wiehl is one of the nation's most prominent trial lawyers and highly regarded legal commentators. The former legal analyst for Fox News and the *O'Reilly Factor*, she has appeared regularly on *Your World with Neil Cavuto, Lou Dobbs Tonight*, and the Imus morning shows, and was the host of the *Wiehl of Justice* podcast. She is also a professor at New York Law School and a host on the *Law & Crime* live trial network. A former legal analyst and reporter for NBC News and NPR's *All Things Considered*, she also served as a federal prosecutor in the United States Attorney's office and was a tenured professor of law at the University of Washington. Wiehl earned her JD from Harvard Law School and her master of arts in literature from the University of Queensland. She lives near New York City.